Donated
by

The Author

Iowa Girl

The President Wears a Skirt

Dr. Frances Bartlett Kinne

Published by
Bailey Publishing & Communications, Inc.
10 North Newnan Street
Jacksonville, Florida 32202

First printing 2000.

ISBN 0-9701049-0-1

Iowa Girl
The President Wears a Skirt

Dr. Frances Bartlett Kinne

All
Proceeds
from the
sale of
"Iowa Girl:
The President Wears a Skirt"
will go to
charity.

Dedication...

To each wonderful person who
helped weave
"The Golden Thread,"
but especially to
my parents and brother —
and to the thousands
of students who have touched
my life throughout many years.

Special gratitude...

Special gratitude is due Barry Benson. Barry patiently edited, changing the index dozens of times as I wrote and rewrote my story. He accepted graciously my caveat, "I am writing this. It must be mine." Since he is a gifted writer, I am confident this called for unusual understanding on his part.

Thanks to all my friends, to my graduate Frank Pace for the title to my book, as well as Betty Hadden, my faithful administrative assistant for so many years, who patiently puts up with my high energy level.

And thanks to publisher Jim Bailey, Jill Hartman-Nettles and John Terry for their professional expertise. They made it a "fun" project. And to Kevin Cadora for his great proof-reading.

To Winston S. Churchill — my gratitude and fond affection for his fine writing and friendship.

To Charlton Heston — my devotion and admiration for the greatest of actors.

To Bob Hope — my dear friend and loyal supporter these many years. What more can I say to the legendary hero than "Thanks for the memories."

Acknowledgments...

**TO MANY WHO WERE INVOLVED IN
THE WEAVING OF THE "GOLDEN THREAD":**

It was my parents, Charlie and Bertha Bartlett, who imbued my brother and me with the "Wow" in life — the search for excellence, as well as the need to justify each day the space we take up on this planet.

Since I am the last surviving member of my immediate family, my cousins have become particularly dear to me. It is important the Olsons remember their fine Scandinavian heritage, and the Bartletts have a motivation to recall the noble and patriotic life of the Signer of the Declaration of Independence, Josiah Bartlett.

Of course, I couldn't have managed most of my career without the loving support of two Army Colonel husbands — not at the same time! In fact, Harry Kinne often said laughingly, "I have to keep my Francie healthy and well-educated so I can enjoy my hobbies when I retire."

My "Midwestern Work Ethic" was inherent in hometown Story City, Iowa, where a concerned citizenry could well have been the model for Norman Rockwell. The educational experiences I received at the University of Northern Iowa and Drake University prepared me well for my European doctorate. And among the most rewarding has been my continued association with Drake University as a member of the Board of Governors, and with Jacksonville University as a member of the Board of Trustees.

My 37 years at Jacksonville University changed my life. The students, faculty, administration, staff and thousands of graduates gave me reason to be proud, and the outstanding Board of Trustees and J.U. Council made it possible for us to build and/or restore seven buildings during my ten year presidency. And with their incredible support we founded a College of Business (as Dean I had founded a College of Fine Arts in 1961), a Nursing School, a College of Weekend Studies, both the MBA and Executive MBA programs, one of the three International Students of English programs in the U.S., the dual-degree Engineering programs, etc.

Thanks to Mayo Clinic for keeping me vertical! I am grateful to be an Honorary Staff Member, and I appreciate the persistence of the doctors in encouraging me to put my philosophy on paper.

Table of Contents...

Iowa Girl: The President Wears a Skirt

Addendum: By Charles M. Bartlett

Pictures & Illustrations...

Foreword...

Bob Hope

When you're around Fran Kinne — things happen. I don't know what it is — her energy, charisma, or karma — but it works. Everybody not only respects her — they love her. And that includes me. The fact that she laughs at all my jokes has nothing to do with it.

It has been a pleasure just being in her company...whether at Jacksonville University, visits overseas, at home or on the telephone. And she is responsible for one of the most pleasant afternoons in my life — sharing honorary degrees with Jack Benny at commencement exercises at the university.

Now, Dr. Fran has penned her memoirs which she is calling a "fun" book. Well, it sounds like a "tell-all" book to me. So before she shares any secrets, I want to make a confession. Fran is the first, and only, university president I have ever kissed. What's more, I enjoyed it.

—Bob Hope
18 October, 1999

Charlton Heston

I was pleased to hear from Dr. Frances Kinne that she had decided to write a book about her life. I have known her for a number of years and found her to be an exuberant and enthusiastic educator, a tireless fund-raiser, a delightful dinner companion, a proud American and a loyal friend. All of these traits make her a most intriguing woman whom I have enjoyed getting to know in her various capacities.

Fran's book will entertain you with her adventures. It was my pleasure to be even a small part of them.

—Charlton "Chuck" Heston
18 October, 1999

Winston S. Churchhill

Anyone who has had the privilege of meeting Fran Kinne in person will know what a wonderful, dynamic and special person she is. I have had the privilege of getting to know her in the course of visits to Jacksonville University of which she is Chancellor Emeritus, over the past twenty years.

In the book she writes of her childhood, her love of music and of her love for an older man, an Army Colonel, who swept her off to China as a young bride. There she was caught up in the Communist take-over and describes her narrow escape from Hankow which was surrounded by Communist forces.

She writes of her later experiences in Japan and of General MacArthur and of her time at the University of Frankfurt, where she was the only American, before moving on to Jacksonville University where she had thirty-seven years of exciting experiences.

Fran Kinne's impact on Jacksonville University was quite remarkable. Inspiring it with her dynamic go-getting attitude, she helped transform it into the vibrant, successful and much sought after University that it has now become. I suspect that the secret of her success is the fun and enthusiasm that she brings to everything she tackles — something I am sure the reader will share in the enjoyment of this book.

—Winston S. Churchill
18 October, 1999

Chapter One:
Borne by
Charlie and Bertha's Bromides — and Music

October 2, 1948 — Harry at the dock as we landed in Shanghai. Picture shot from the deck of the ship.

Bertha (Olson) Bartlett

The setting was San Francisco Bay, and Fran was an enthusiastic and excited bride standing on the deck of the ship, the General Blackford. What bride wouldn't be anticipating a reunion with her handsome bridegroom, an Army Colonel?

Charles M. Bartlett "Charlie"

We sailed under the Golden Gate Bridge, and I felt a flutter in my throat, an increased pulse, facing the prospect of a great adventure. As I turned to witness the receding skyline of San Francisco and my country I experienced ambivalent emotions. Certainly there was joy, but three years away from family, friends and the United States confronted me.

My parents had always taught me to be independent, and I had a general optimism about my own capacity to live unhampered by doubt, hesitation or fear. But for a slight moment I thought to myself, "What am I doing here!" And then that moment turned to 26 days of mixed emotions on my trip to China. I thought about my parents. I thought about my brother. I thought about my country, and I couldn't wait to see my husband.

It is always nostalgic to draw reflections of childhood, and one of my earliest memories is of waiting for my father to come in the door. I would grasp his ankle, sit on his foot, straddle my small legs around his ankle. As he took long strides I would explain to anyone who would listen, "We're sailing to China."

It was natural that I soon found a cozy nook behind his favorite rocking chair, pretending I was on a ship "sailing to China." And there I was, in the middle of the Pacific Ocean, doing just that.

As a child I was fortunate to have parents who were intellectual, loving, tolerant and active in the arts. My father, Charles M. Bartlett (Charlie), was a scholar who knew Latin and Greek, was an avid reader of the Classics, and was an accomplished writer — as well as a tournament contract player in bridge, and excellent in the game of pool as well.

But Dad saved his Sunday afternoons for walking with us in the woods that bordered the Skunk River which flows through Story City. His forceful visual representation titillated our imagination. We anticipated a bear lurking behind every tree, as Dad would describe the wonders of the great outdoors. Of course, we never met up with the bear. But we learned to appreciate a sparkling drop of dew on a maple leaf, and the patches of clouds with their flickering sunlight.

There was an elegance about his

language. Even as a child I recognized my father was quite an extraordinary man.

One of my great joys several years ago was to visit the excellent Historical Society Museum in Maxwell, Iowa (my father's hometown) and discover photos of his graduation in 1892. And an unexpected reward came from reading his Valedictorian address. It is ironic the subject was on the evils of tobacco, for it was carcinoma that took my father's life, after

Fran's father (left) and his brother, Frank Bartlett.

years of smoking cigars and pipes.

At the same excellent museum I discovered facts and photos of my father's siblings: Ansel Bartlett, my father's older brother (later a Judge in Oklahoma); the sister, Mary Bartlett (John); and the younger brother, Frank Bartlett, who moved to Santa Barbara, California. From the latter's marriage came two daughters, Mary and Frances. That meant there were two Frances Bartletts in our family.

Dad was proud of his heritage, the Bartletts having come to America in the 1600s. Josiah Bartlett always was the pride of the family: first Governor of New Hampshire and a Signer of the Declaration of Independence. Dana Anderson (grandson of Frank Bartlett) and I traced Josiah

Bartlett's steps and visited his home in Kingston, New Hampshire. I never forgot my Dad's caveat to be circumspect in my youthful exuberance, for "there may be some horse thieves along the way."

Mother was 15 years younger than my father, but they were a perfect match. They met at the office of The Story City Herald where they discovered they had a great deal in common. Mother was a second grade teacher, young and pretty, working at the newspaper office after school was dismissed, as well as on the weekends. In the summers she attended the Iowa State Normal School (now the University of Northern Iowa).

Prior to my father's purchase of the newspaper, just after the turn of the century, he had been in Des Moines studying to be a physician. His congenital eye problem made it necessary for him to change course, however, and writing was his great gift.

Father loved the newspaper business, but because his eye disease was getting progressively worse, he felt he could no longer perform

his duties in a professional manner. So in the early part of the century Dad sold The Story City Herald (of which he was owner, publisher and editor) to Paul A. ("Uncle P.A.") Olson, my mother's brother. After selling The Herald, he continued to work at the paper on free days, but his time was occupied with representing The Riebs Co. in Milwaukee, buying and selling grain for them.

Having been graduated at the age of 16, Mother immediately started her teaching career in rural schools near Story City. As if it were Homer describing the adventures of Helen of Troy, Mother often related her stories to me in an amusing and masterful manner. One school was five miles from town, and it was fortunate her high energy made it possible for her to walk that distance and

Josiah Bartlett (top) and his house.

Mother in her early teaching career.

teach all day. She had never ridden a bicycle, but after saving for months she purchased one, and in a blinding rain storm rode the muddy road to the country school.

Disaster struck. Mother found herself in the ditch on the very first day, ruining her carefully ironed dress and the bicycle as well. She walked the rest of the way, never again to attempt to bicycle. When the winds and snow of the Iowa winter set in, however, she found it necessary to stay at a farmer's home adjacent to the school.

Disaster struck again. In the middle of the very first night, she was awakened from a sound sleep as her bedroom door was opened. There was the farmer at her bedside, leering at her in the moonlit room. Mother fought him off, and he retreated to his own bedroom and sleeping wife. I must admit that my mother took the opportunity to retell this story on numerous occasions, with the sole purpose of enlightening me on the facts of life about the birds and bees, and the opposite sex.

That was my mom —Bertha [Olson] Bartlett, born June 14, 1888 in Story City, Iowa. That date is Flag Day, but when my brother and I were small we were convinced the flags were flying high celebrating Mother's birthday. Many years later my Harry Kinne would tease me and laughingly say, "My wife isn't very bright. She was 12 years old before she figured out the flags weren't up for her mother's birthday."

Mother was a trail-blazer, and because of her record I only considered it natural for women to compete in the professional arena. Years later, Dr. Franklyn Johnson appointed me Dean of the new College of Music and Fine Arts, the first woman in such a position in the U.S. and very likely in the world. I did not consider myself a pioneer, as Mother was there before me, paving the way for me to follow. After all, she was a librarian for 43 years, first woman to serve on the Board of Education, first woman to be President of the Board, first

Republican Committee Woman — and the list of "firsts" goes on and on.

When discussing issues which today might be categorized as glass ceiling resistance to efforts of achievement and accomplishment, Mother would quote a Norwegian proverb: "Speak to the king in the man, and the king will come forth." Of course, Mother meant that each of us has that spark, and if challenged it will come forth.

Mother's great talent was her voice, an operatic coloratura. At a youthful 15 years of age, while waiting in a train station in Fort Dodge for a delayed train, she was persuaded to sing. A voice teacher heard her and offered to give her free lessons if she could travel to Fort Dodge. Unfortunately, limited resources made it impossible to accept the offer; she continued to sing, however, in that exquisite voice.

One of my earliest memories of her public performances was her interpretation of Schubert's "The Erl-King." Dramatic and poignant as the story is, the words became more meaningful to me as an adult. On many occasions I enjoyed the fine trio of Mother, Alvina Holm and Jeanette Henderson. They often appeared locally and on WOI, the first public radio station in the United States, located at Iowa State University in Ames, which is very near Story City. While they were broadcasting I was placed on a chair and sat quietly in the studio, promising myself that some day I would be that performer.

Bertha Bartlett at the age of 100.

As I was growing up I always referred to my parents as my great levelers — just as gun powder had been for the foot soldiers during the Middle Ages. No longer did the horse soldier dominate the scene, for with firearms the playing field was leveled — taking care of social inequities. In my speeches I frequently make this reference about my parents.

Because of this story, I was called (in a Jacksonville, Florida news story) the "gunpowder equalizer" during my "vibrant decade of power" at Jacksonville University. But I was only following my parents' advice — "Charlie and Bertha's bromides."

When I married Lt. Col. Harry Kinne he was much older and certainly wiser than his bride. This prompted my father to give me some sage advice. "The Colonel's Lady an' Judy O'Grady are sisters under the skin." Father's last words to me were, "Please don't ever forget that, Franny." And unfortunately those were the last words I ever heard from his lips. We were at the train station in Ames and the train was many hours late, but my parents sat with me until it arrived at 2:00 a.m. Dad put his arms around me and whispered Kipling's words in my ear as we said farewell. Years later Mother said, "I thought you were going to the end of the world when we said goodbye." Of course, I was.

The Colonel's Lady advice (quoted from the last lines of Kipling's "The Ladies") relates to the custom in our largely Norwegian town to shake hands with everyone, whether coming or going, to treat everyone with respect, no matter what station in life. Mother conscientiously spoke to me about this when we left for our second overseas tour, and I assured her of my commitment to be courteous to others and to treat everyone with respect.

Mother and cousin Olive visited us in Frankfurt, and the occasion presented itself on the first day of their visit. The German Hausmeister (janitor) came to check to see if any maintenance was needed in the house. I shook hands with him when he arrived and when he departed. And on his return 15 minutes later I did the same. When he finally left, Mother put her arms around me and said, "I am so proud of you."

Charles Bartlett

I am convinced "Charlie and Bertha's Bromides" greatly assisted me in the amazing adventures of my life.

And as we moved from country to country it was fascinating to recognize the many proverbs, maxims, sayings, adages, epigrams and epigraphs that came to light in different languages. I was so surprised to find my parents' bromides in these far-off lands.

But sometimes I would discover myself drawing on the immediate, foreign environment for a philosophical reference. For example, in Japan I visited a pearl farm where pearls were cultured in a controlled environment. Farmers nurtured baby oysters for three years and took the oysters from the water and inserted a small bead made of clamshell. The bead had the same composition as the secretion of the mollusk, and the pearl developed from the production of the nacre.

The idea of placing an irritant in an oyster to develop a pearl fascinated me, and I was astounded to learn that the Chinese had developed this before the thirteenth century. I was so impressed that I often thought of this when I would face my Humanities students. Each one of them would become a wonderful pearl if I could just inspire them in the right way.

Columnist Robert Hullihan wrote in <u>The Des Moines Sunday Register</u> (May 4, 1980, p. 1): "Kinne simply has the instinct of an oyster encountering a scratch of sand. When she comes upon a negative she immediately begins to build a pearl around it. People respond well to this and, sometimes, even submit to being turned into pearls."

For years my friends have encouraged me to write about my adventures and include my philosophy of life. In the early years it was Harry Kinne who said, "Write about what makes you tick." The same plea was continued by my second husband, and then the Mayo Clinic doctors picked up the appeal. Dr. Henry Randle was the first of the physicians (and the most persistent); we had developed a fine friendship and often discussed philosophy. Then Dr. Elliott Richelson and the late Dr. Richard Fleming took up the theme, imploring me to "get at it." When I did the Eulogy at Dick Fleming's funeral I felt a sense of guilt for my delay. And my former Humanities student Lynn NeSmith, English teacher par excellence, presented me with a box full of blank notebooks "for your book." And when Dr. Paul Pettit performed my hysterectomy, and Dr. Mark Broderson my arthroscopic knee surgery the Mayo persuasion continued.

The main idea the doctors encouraged me to explore in my writing was why everything is such a miracle to me, and I continue to return to Charlie and Bertha's Bromides. Einstein said it well: "There are only two ways to live. One is as though nothing is a miracle. The other is as if everything is a miracle." My parents taught me that everything is a miracle, and so it has been in my life.

Iowa Girl

It is natural for me to describe and reflect on the environment that influenced and affected me so much. Much of this was indirect — intangible forces that shaped my life. The Middle West and specifically Iowa were right for me. Memories of my childhood are happy ones. I was a Depression child, and in Story City no one had material wealth. But it was a time of loving family and friends, filled with music, music, music.

During the entire time my mother was pregnant with me she sang and played the piano. Mother was an early advocate of prenatal reading and music, and at the time of the pregnancy my parents must have had an instinctive feeling for the vital value of music in child development — a fact we now know scientifically. I am convinced that during the ten years I played piano and led singing for Senior Citizens as a volunteer, their requests often were those songs I must have heard in my mother's womb and as a baby.

The family gathered around Mother at the piano to sing the popular songs and operettas of the day. Cousin Art Olson, with his lovely tenor voice, was a daily visitor and would harmonize with Mother. And Cousin Paul Olson would often sit quietly enjoying our performances, while brother Chuck sang or played the trumpet. Uncle P.A. Olson was musical, so it was not surprising the two sons appreciated music. His daughter, Olive was a gifted musician and continued to play organ and piano in her church until shortly before her death. In fact, Olive was my 4th grade teacher and taught me some piano along the way. So all of those melodies always stayed with me. This is how I learned every popular song, as well as many of the old favorites. As I sat on the piano bench I found harmonizing was fun.

My father was also musical and possessed a nice tenor voice. As a small child I recall standing beside him at the Grace Evangelical United Brethren Church. I remember listening to him sing, and sometimes I would pull at his coat as I said in an embarrassed whisper, "Not so loud, Daddy." He was always patient with me. How I wish I could hear that voice today.

Every Sunday my dad would listen to scholarly sermons broadcast on the radio, from different denominations world-wide, and certainly it was all in an ecumenical spirit. Respect for others for me was learned by example.

I started playing the piano when I was two years old, standing at the keyboard. First I picked up melodies I had heard, and I translated them to the keyboard with one hand. Soon after that, Mother taught me to use my left hand to accompany the right hand. In fact, I played music before I learned to read. I didn't realize I had a musical gift, and thought everyone could play by ear, and I certainly thought everyone should love music.

I remember vividly the many art masterwork reproductions Mother framed and arranged near the piano and throughout our home. Although there was little money for "extras," art museums in those days offered classical and contemporary artwork reproductions at a very reasonable cost. Mother ordered ours from the Metropolitan Museum of Art for twenty-five cents apiece, and the copies of masters were all around me.

My closest playmates were all at least a year older, so it was natural I wanted to start school when they were all enrolled. There was no kindergarten in Story City, so I was in first grade a few months after my fifth birthday. School was always fun for me, and I was ready for first grade.

Soon after my fifth birthday I was playing my piano at the annual Fourth of July celebration in the North Park. A Band Stand in the park was the scene for this Story City tradition of entertainment all day and evening with

*Anna Jacobson
Fran's piano teacher*

*Fran's Steinway
made for her*

(above) Operetta: "The Golden Whistle" - all school operetta. Frances Bartlett in the lead—center.

(left) Budding actress.

people sitting on blankets, folding chairs, or on the grass near the small creek meandering through the park. What I played could not have been very entertaining, but perhaps my age made it more interesting.

Later, members of the audience would request popular songs, and I would play them by ear — probably not very well.

I started to compete in state-wide piano competitions when I was in fifth grade, and the climax came when I was 15 years old and won first place in the Iowa state-wide competition. Anna Jacobson was my superb teacher and had

emboldened and encouraged me. I knew I was competing against older students who had an abundance of talent, but Anna's confidence in me was heartening.

Uncle P.A. drove us to the state competition, and I wore my favorite red, chiffon dress which had gone through a magical transformation several days previous. Of course it was white, but Mother had dyed it red for the competition Psychologists enjoy associating the color red with power, but I know why my closet is filled with red. That white dress was my Confirmation dress in the St. Petri Lutheran Church. I guess the dress was blessed!

My selection to play for the judges was Mendelssohn's "Rondo Capriciosso," and, much to my distress I discovered three of the 18 pianists were performing the same number. I was the last of the 18 to play, and one of those miracles happened — I won. As Mother told me later, Anna Jacobson was imitating every note with her hands playing an imaginary keyboard on

her lap. Uncle P.A. took us to lunch at Bishop's Cafeteria, a photographer appeared out of nowhere, and my photo was on the front page of The Des Moines Register. My classmates made a lot over it, but my great levelers went to work and I was inspired to seek another challenge.

I also remember competing in the state declamatory speech contest each year. In seventh grade my dramatic interpretation selection was "The Sign of the Cross" — about the Christians sacrificed in the Roman Coliseum: "It was the Festival Day in Rome. / Nero had decreed it..." My brother Chuck competed in the same state speech contest with an oratorical selection. We practiced our selections for one another — a test of memory as each required pages of memorized text. The one challenge was trying to "keep a straight face" as we practiced our oratory.

Also that seventh grade year, I vividly remember attending the Chicago World's Fair — as a first place prize in the contest to sell the most subscriptions for the town's weekly newspaper, The Story City Herald! I still have vivid memories of the Adler Planetarium, the Shedd Aquarium, and the amazing Field Museum. It was at the latter I saw for the first time an Egyptian mummy. My parents were amused when, as an 11 year old, I later described my experience in an excited tone at the dinner table: "I saw a real live mummy!"

Mother and Uncle P.A. also took me to visit Marshall Fields Department Store on that visit to Chicago, with lunch in The Oak Room. Since that trip so many years ago, I have often returned for a few moments of pleasant nostalgia.

Story City and Iowa have always

been tops in the U.S. in academic achievements, ranking first or second in S.A.T. scores. Likewise, music education has always been a priority. Because I have perfect pitch I was started on the cello, but it wasn't for me.

The fact Chuck was already playing the trumpet influenced me, and I gave up the cello for trumpet and baritone euphonium. But there was only one trumpet, and Chuck was much better than I. So I learned the baritone and oom-pahed my way through the Sousa marches. Actually, the baritone was almost as big as I was, but there usually were eager young classmates (male) offering to carry the instrument for me.

We all looked forward to Saturday evenings. Summer Saturday evenings in Story City meant shopping, movies and the band concert on the town square. Chuck and I played in both the high school and town bands, but it was the latter that gave the wonderful flavor of small town America — the Band Shell on the town square, and a mixture of adults and adolescents on that platform must have presented a Saturday Evening Post cover picture. It was a Norman Rockwell scene.

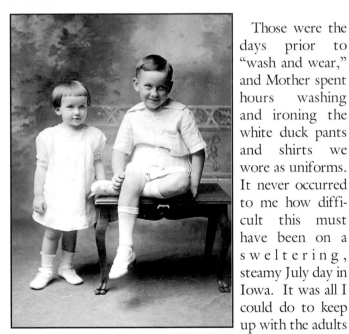

Those were the days prior to "wash and wear," and Mother spent hours washing and ironing the white duck pants and shirts we wore as uniforms. It never occurred to me how difficult this must have been on a s w e l t e r i n g, steamy July day in Iowa. It was all I could do to keep up with the adults in the band as we marched in snappy rhythm to the "Washington Post March."

Brother Chuck at five, and Fran at the age of two.

My brother's performing ability on the trumpet was matched by his athletic prowess. He was a star in baseball, basketball, football, track and (outside of school) in golf. He amazed everyone by hitting his first hole-in-one at the age of 12 at Lake Comar, the recreation grounds three miles south of Story City. The three adults in the foursome included our family doctor, (former U.S. Army doctor) A.A. Rose, who was also my father's best friend. Years later Chuck was to repeat his feat on a California course, testifying to the suggestions of sports enthusiasts that he should have "gone pro." Students have often asked me about my brother, and I have always responded, "Chuck was a four-letter man in school when 'four letter' had a much different meaning than it does today."

When Chuck was the quarterback on the high school football team he would sit down at the piano and play prior to each game. It was an outlet for pre-game nerves, and his heavy foot on the pedal resulted in my learning how to repair broken pedals.

After being a Professor of Humanities for many years, my study of the qualities of the Renaissance man has convinced me that both my father and brother displayed characteristics at an early age of being just that. These qualities were priceless to Chuck as he served as Personnel Director at the Naval Air Station in San Diego where he received many awards for his ability to serve society. It is unfortunate his premature death in 1962 deprived the world of a very talented man. It is fortunate his life prior to his demise was filled with a loving family — his wife, Thelma, and her two children, Richard and Helen (Ginger) — of whom he was very proud.

From the time I was a child, performing became natural for me, and I always entertained ideas about going on the stage. The Schaffner Players (possibly best known for their "Toby" shows) were scheduled each year in our Story Theatre/Opera House, as well as annual appearances at Lake Comar, and they often needed a child in their plays. I was it! But the all-school operettas presented each year were the most fun for me. In second grade I had the lead in the all-school production of "The Golden Whistle," playing a little, old woman (!) who is under a spell and is released to become a fairy princess. I can't imagine any make-up artist handling that one, but parents and friends must have been understanding. Both the Junior and Senior class plays also provided the opportunity for me to play a lead role in each.

I'm sure some of my interest in the theatre came as a very small child. Mother played the piano in the Story Theatre/Opera House as movies were becoming talkies, and I would sit in the front row, behind her, mesmerized by the music and the screen. The films were family-oriented. Imagine this happening today!

Summers were filled with fun and frolic. My friends and I walked every day to swim and actively participate in the social activities and adventures at Lake Comar — a magnet for the children and adolescents (as well as adults) from Story City and a wide area of central Iowa. I remember what fun we had working in the food stand — serving ice cream and hamburgers to the customers while we were still dressed in our wet bathing suits. We didn't think it unusual at all at the time! I probably was the recipient of a few harmless pinches that would very likely be considered sexual harassment today.

It was at Lake Comar where I earned my junior and senior lifesaving certificates. Grandmother Jorstead (on the Olson side of the family), however, was horrified when she beheld my sun-tanned skin turned from white to berry brown.

We were fortunate to have such amazing recreational facilities — a swimming lake, an adjacent boating lake, golf course, picnic and camping grounds, horseback-riding, baseball field, roller-skating rink, merry-go-round, concession stands, dance pavilion, and a stage for plays, variety shows, etc. Crowds of over 10,000 visited the resort — quite a statistic, since at that time my home town boasted a total population of 2000 inhabitants.

Commencement

Those twelve years in the Story City Public Schools were filled with the challenges of a superb education, as well as the joys of the development of close friendships. And if I were to indicate what was the ultimate experience I would be compelled to answer as Frank Lloyd Wright. Asked at the age of 83 which of his works was his greatest masterpiece, he responded, "My next one."

Our Commencement speaker that hot summer night I was graduated was the ultimate motivator in encouraging us to have hope for the future. I have presented hundreds of commencement addresses throughout the years, but I doubt any of mine was as inspirational as that of The Reverend F.J. Wertz, the pastor of a large Lutheran church in Des Moines. (Later his son, the famous Roger Williams, and I shared the same piano teacher at Drake University, Paul Stoye).

Rev. Wertz electrified me with his message, "You can do anything if you are willing to work." It was a familiar theme in the Bartlett household, but now the message was communicated by a dynamic stranger. As he spoke I felt he fastened his penetrating brown eyes on me and challenged me to produce.

I played a piano solo, a Chopin Ballade, and the performance went well for a 16 year old I was told. And who conferred the diplomas? Who was the first woman President of the Story City School Board? Yes, it was my mom.

There were opportunities for scholarships at various colleges, but the height of the Depression made it necessary for me to attend Iowa State Teachers College in Cedar Falls (now the University of Northern Iowa). I knew I could manage two years to earn a teaching certificate.

My dorm at that time was the largest women's dorm in the U.S.

Charles Bartlett in 1948 at home.

and was called Bartlett Hall. I would have liked to claim the person for whom it was named, but no such luck. The name, however, may have opened a few doors for me.

Since my mother was a librarian it was natural for me to work in the college library, and my joy was being assigned to the Fine Arts area. To this day I recall the beauty of the copies of the Medici Prints, and the interest this aroused in me concerning the Italian family that dominated Florence and Tuscany during the Renaissance. The experience proved very valuable to me when I lived in Europe and visited the major galleries.

I didn't want to be a financial burden on my parents, so I had to figure out a way to have an additional source of funds. Open Sesame! I ate at the Commons. It had excellent food, but no music background at dinner. In fact, no piano! I had become acquainted with the janitor in the Music Building and he informed me they were disposing of an aged piano. But first I had to convince the Commons manager he needed some mood music at dinner. When he agreed, I marshaled some of my classmates, borrowed a truck, and voila — I had it made. Of course, popular music was too expensive to buy, so I played by ear. The requests poured in, as the students gathered around the piano, and the campus radio station decided to broadcast our efforts several times a week. As for me, I had my dinner paid for and fun as an aspiring pianist and singer, and I didn't have to eat any more peanut butter sandwiches. I had lived on them for three weeks prior to my piano playing in the Commons.

In the summer between those two years the head of the piano department at Iowa State

University called me and offered to teach me at no cost. I felt very much at home at Iowa State, since I had grown up attending concerts on the campus. There had been Galli-Curci, Rubinstein, Lily Pons, Lawrence Tibbett, and my hero, Walter Gieseking, as well as many others — amazing opportunities for a small child.

While working on my Ph.D. in Frankfurt so many years later I met Gieseking at a Master Class. I told him I had been an ardent admirer of his since I was a small child. And he was touched when I told him I applauded in such an enthusiastic manner, my tiny wrists were sprained, requiring a visit to Dr. Rose the following day.

I enjoyed my lessons that summer at Iowa State with Professor Ira Schroeder, and I practiced six hours a day. Since our home was on Main Street, my parents' closest friends (Ben and Margrit Larson) suggested I practice at their home. They both worked and didn't have to listen to me. If I had practiced at home, the store-keepers would have been in rebellion! I had no intention of remaining at Iowa State, for I was determined to study piano with Professor Paul Stoye at Drake University. And the following summer my dream came true, and at the same time I signed a contract (at age 18) to teach music at Kelley, a consolidated school.

It was at that point I was forced with making a choice that would challenge every fiber of my being. A friend of my family, Arnie Olson, played string bass in the Freddie Martin Orchestra at the Coconut Grove in Hollywood, from where they had a nation-wide radio broadcast each evening.

Arnie had heard me sing and play, and the offer came (via

telegram from Hollywood) to this 18 year old who had just signed a contract to teach. I sought advice and parental guidance, and they wisely responded, "You must make this choice, for you will have to live with it." Since I had been raised with a heritage of ethical principles, I knew what I had to do.

A sleepless night brought forth a decision I have never regretted. I had made a commitment when I signed the contract. But it was one of the most difficult decisions of my life. I still have the telegram.

My friend, Ash Verlander good-naturedly reminds me fairly often, "If you had decided to go the California route, we'd be listening to your records now instead of Doris Day."

Life's fabric is a complex, yet exquisite combination of patterns, woven into a myriad of colors. The lovely, single, golden thread seems to find its magical way from conception to one's fading, last breath. That decision I made at age 18 became an important addition to that golden thread.

The vocalist Peggy Lee looked at it all cynically in her recording of "Is That All There Is?" But it was never that way for me.

Quite the contrary, life's richness allows for a daily adventure. Perhaps that is why I selected an appropriate Shakespeare quotation for my inaugural theme on two occasions — when I was inaugurated as President and ten years later as Chancellor of Jacksonville University: "The day will not be up so soon as I to try the fair adventure of tomorrow." (And these are just two of the many times I have credited William Shakespeare!)

Fran as Parade Marshall for Scandinavian Days—Story City

Brother Chuck at 21 & Fran at 18

Glenn Davis (All American) & Fran aboard the General Blackford

"General Blackford" sailing to China

Chapter Two:
Iowa Girl Chooses Teaching

So instead of singing and playing with a dance band I became a music and English teacher at Kelley, Iowa. That was only the beginning, for I was assigned homeroom duties with 3rd and 4th graders. And in my spare time I taught piano lessons and directed the Lutheran church choir.

I was filled with enthusiasm — idealistic and eighteen, and I hoped all of that would make up for lack of experience. I settled on a project for my 3rd and 4th graders based on my own family newspaper background.

"What about a newspaper to be published by my 3rd and 4th grade home room?" And my Superintendent bought in to the idea.

The editor of the <u>Ames Tribune</u> was a close friend of Uncle P.A.'s. This provided an invitation for me to pile 40 little "eager beavers" into a school bus and visit the newspaper office and news room in Ames for a day. The youngsters excitedly deluged the editor and his staff with an incessant stream of questions, and the results of the trip were quite amazing.

The children voted on which youngster would be Editor-in-Chief, as well as sports editor, arts editor, and even a Business Manager - whose task it was to get advertising.

When the paper was published we sent a copy to Mr. Rupe, the kind gentleman at the <u>Ames Tribune</u> who made it all possible. And he very graciously wrote an article about us in which he said, "This teacher, Frances Bartlett, has a divine spark."

It was generous of him to make this reference to me, but my great levelers had already taught me that everyone has a divine spark. It is never "I"; it is always "we" or "us."

I was promoted the next year to the School Music Supervisor position at Boxholm, a consolidated school in a Swedish community approximately 30 miles from Story City. I had already been working on my B.M.E. (Bachelor of Music Education) at Drake with Saturday classes and summer work, so I felt better qualified to direct chorus, band, orchestra, small groups and

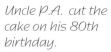

Uncle P.A. cut the cake on his 80th birthday.

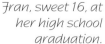

Fran, sweet 16, at her high school graduation.

all the music from first through twelfth grade. Oh, yes, there was also the Lutheran Church Choir I directed, and the Christmas Cantata.

Most teachers in Boxholm lived in "the teacherage" — with men and women in the two different buildings, although we did come together for meals and entertainment. The men taught us to play poker. Instead of a regular card table we had a portable table top (with no legs) which we balanced on each others' knees as we dealt the cards.

One hot evening while playing poker we had drawn all the curtains as usual, because one of the many rules for teachers was "No card-playing." Suddenly there was a tapping at our door. And in walked the Methodist minister. Shock caused us immediately to jump to our feet. Cards and poker chips flew everywhere!

Those three years at Boxholm were wonderful years of learning for me. And my music organizations were highly successful in music competition. As I reflect on that strenuous schedule I wonder how I ever had time to sleep. I was in all the classrooms each day for music, and what fun were those little first graders. No matter what I wore, some little child would say, "Miss Bartlett, you've got such a 'purty' dress."

When I told the first grade teacher how cute her students were she replied, "That's only because you see them for 15 minutes."

While I was teaching at Boxholm I attended Saturday classes at Drake University. I conducted the band at the basketball games on Friday night (and the sports writers kept writing about that "girl band-leader"), and then I always had a date after that.

The alarm rudely awakened me at 4:00 a.m., and at 5:00 a.m. three Superintendents from various county schools picked me up for our trip to Des Moines and our 8:00 a.m. classes at Drake.

It is amazing what motivation can do for a 19 year old, and I had been inculcated with a strong desire to complete my education. Simple, the parents told me. Hard work, excellence, hard work and excellence.

Then the great opportunity presented itself. I had met the Supervisor of Music from Des Moines when I attended his workshop at Drake, and he offered me a position in the "big city."

The opportunity to teach in Des Moines was an outstanding promotion for me, and Supervisor of Music Lorraine Watters requested that I not reveal my age. I discovered I was the youngest (by more than several years) of all the Des Moines teachers.

I was ecstatic about teaching music. I continued my studies at

Fran as a teacher in Boxholm

Drake, and my life truly was an adventure. While I was at Kelley and Boxholm I had learned a great deal, and my intensive teaching load made it necessary to plan and organize every minute.

My parents had prepared me well for making independent decisions, with the understanding that I live with whatever were the consequences. And it is fortunate, part of the lesson was to make the most of any mistakes. If I made an unfortunate decision, it was important for me (my parents constantly stressed) to realize it was my fault, not that of someone else.

The next step was to learn from it, so it wouldn't happen again.

And the final action was to find something good about it and put that to use. In every obstacle there is an opportunity. And most importantly — place the action in perspective and even find a humorous lesson in it when appropriate.

When World War II broke out I was still the youngest teacher in the Des Moines Public School System. My life was teaching music, and each day was a new adventure. I did notice how handsome some of those senior boys were, but looking at them was a "No-No."

In later years The Des Moines Register published an article about me: "What Ever Happened to Franny?" — and the circulation of that story brought letters from many former students.

One wrote in a poignant tone, "You won't remember me, but I was a senior in your chorus. I fell madly in love with you. I can remember the colors you wore, particularly that blue dress that matched your eyes. I am happily married now, but I have never forgotten you."

It isn't unusual for students to have a crush on a teacher, but such situations require sensitive understanding on the part of the teacher, no matter the age. Years of teaching at Jacksonville University brought proposals from young men who weren't discouraged by my statement, "I'm happily married." My strategy with them was largely successful. "Why don't you invite a friend and join my husband and me for dinner?"

My own first crush on a teacher came as a 13 year old freshman in high school. The handsome basketball coach was also the algebra teacher. All of the freshmen girls were mesmerized by him, and we were prone to giggle at anything he said, as we crossed our legs so that he would notice us. We must have provided a rich amount of material for his evening dinner conversations with his wife.

Fran's father at their home in Story City, Iowa.

Chapter Three:
Seeing the World With New Eyes

My father endured years of minimal vision, but a trip to California in 1942 brought about dramatic change. Chuck took him to an eye surgeon, and Dad called the results "a miracle." He described "the halo around" his vision immediately after the bandages were removed, and his ecstatic surprise at the vivid colors and distinct shapes he could now discern — comparing his story to the relevant tale from Lewis Carroll's <u>Through the Looking Glass</u>.

His were both congenital and senile cataracts, and the diagnosis of my own problem was identical. My own surgery in 1962 by the leading eye surgeon in the world, Dr. Charles Schepens, brought the same miracle to me.

Dad's writings reflect the Latinate influence — his use of such vocabulary as "effulgent" — obviously indicative of his background in Latin. Father rarely began a paragraph with "I" - almost as if he considered it a self-conscious violation of propriety. This resulted in his use of the passive voice — definitely part of his elegant style of writing. If one examines General Douglas MacArthur's articulation, both spoken and written word, there is a similarity. Also, I observed this in the writing of my "Vater Doktor," Professor Dr. Helmut Viebrock, and in the eloquence of Charlton (Chuck) Heston.

I recalled my father's change of life after his eye surgery when I underwent my own, and I was more fortunate that I didn't have to live a lifetime with the problem as he did. Because of this I am providing readers (in Addendum following the index) with the narrative he wrote after his surgery.

This is my memorial to my father's character, as well as his fine abilities as a writer. It seems particularly appropriate to include it.

Charlton "Chuck" Heston during Fran's trip back to California in 1998.

(Top-left) Norwegian plates in the Iowa Room of Fran's home.
(Middle-left) Quilt Fran's Grandmother made.
(Bottom-left) Mother's quilt in the Yellow Room at Fran's home.
(Right) Fran's Mother's quilt which she made (on bed) and a tapestry of the
Story City Antique Carousel hangs on the wall above
the bed in Fran's home.

Chapter Four:
Everyone Wanted to Sit with Grandmother, Because She Always Had Stories to Tell

There must be a time when each of us faces our mortality — and a time when we must face the fact we're not Olympian gods destined to be remembered in centuries to come. I am not sure when I first had that uneasy feeling, but certainly it was present for me as a young 15 year old. My grandmother passed away when I was a junior in high school, and it presented a sad loss. Death suddenly became very personal.

I adored my grandmother, and many happy moments were spent at her knee. My mother had always told me how sad it was my grandmother never was able to return to Norway to see her mother, and as a sympathetic child I felt an empathy for her.

After she died my Uncle P. A. visited Norway, attending a Sunday School Convention, and his wonderful and descriptive book written as a travelogue inspired greater understanding of the bravery of both my grandparents.

My grandfather was born near Gudbrandsdalen in Norway. The early years of the 19th century provided scant opportunity for a young man to make a living, so he decided to make his way to a better life — very likely walking to Lillehammer, taking a boat to Eidsvoll, walking on to Oslo, and then by boat again to Drammen.

There he married his first wife who bore five children. But life was difficult in Fredrikstad where they lived, and he lost his wife and three of his children. When he finally remarried, it was to my grandmother, a woman many years younger than he, a bundle of energy and personality.

In 1871 my grandfather decided to move to America, since there was a demand for construction contractors in the Chicago area, where he also had relatives who were in the contracting business. So one early winter day he and his two sons sailed for the United States, and in the spring of 1872 my grandmother came to America with their first child. It was here that the first baby died and left his name for the next baby, my Uncle P.A.

Baby had more sense than any of the rest of the family

On my father's side history had been initiated for me when the Bartletts arrived in this country in the 1600s. On my mother's side, however, history started for me in the fall of 1873, for it was then my grandparents decided to move to Iowa. On a beautiful winter day, the three of them took the train from Chicago to Nevada, Iowa, and from there to Story City they rode a sleigh. Uncle P.A.(then a baby) later wrote in his book that he cried all the way. His father (my grandfather) was challenged when he saw the snow-covered, trackless prairie, with so few settlers along the way, and suggested that the baby had more sense than any of the rest of the family.

But Story City was to be their home, and they were determined to make a success of it. And it was my grandfather who was the main contractor in Story City, where he built many of the homes for the early settlers, some of those early structures still remaining today.

The family grew with many happy voices around the dinner table. However, Grandfather passed away, leaving a large family for my grandmother to raise. And this spirited woman found ways to support the family.

Ask your friend Mary Yane to bring her Payamas

She learned to speak English, even though it was with a Norwegian accent. She believed it was very important for each of the children to learn the most beautiful of languages, and she spent those precious moments before sleep in reading whatever literature she could find, with the dim light of the kerosene lamp casting shadows on the pages of her book.

She must have been weary from hours of labor, washing clothes for her family. She must have been discouraged as she faced the challenges of the new country, a strange land.

It was not surprising she eventually found comfort in a soulmate, and he carried a share of the burden. He was the only grandfather I ever knew, and I was fascinated by his artistic ability and gentle nature. His recreation was drawing, and his pencil artistry displayed a gift I now recognize as unusual.

Both of my grandparents would welcome my friends and me to the cozy home so filled with memories of Norway. With her delightful mixture of English and Norwegian, my grandmother would extend the invitation, "Ask your friend, Mary Yane [Jane] to bring her payamas [pajamas], and you girls can spend the night."

Everyone Wanted to Sit with Grandmother Because She Had Amusing Stories to Tell

Since I was a musician, my grandmother enjoyed singing Norwegian ballads to me. Stanza after stanza of tear-jerking stories, always with a tragic ending, kept me mesmerized. It did something else for me, however. I became interested in performing folk songs and ballads, and the climax to this was my doctoral thesis published in Germany — A Comparative Study of British Traditional and American Indigenous Ballads. This allowed me to study the rich tradition of the folklore from other countries, and it was fascinating to discover the "floaters" that moved from country to country.

The greatest memories of Grandmother's holidays were the festivities of Christmas Eve, the Scandinavian custom allowing us to open our gifts on that blessed evening.

All of Grandmother's children and grandchildren gathered around a bounteous table, but not until it had been preceded by a ceremonial sip of wine. Grandmother's specialties were wines she made — dandelion and grape. As children we were allowed one thimble full, only adding anticipation to our ravenous appetites, soon to be delighted by the Norwegian foods before us.

Of course, we always had the traditional beef roast, fluffy mashed potatoes and the divine gravy stirred with care on the top of the coal range. But it was the Norwegian food that brought us kumla, kringla, potato cakes, lefse, krum kakke, and such creations I shall never forget.

The door to the living room always remained closed until after dinner, but that did not stop our wishful and curious glances toward that sanctuary. We knew there was a green, fragrant Christmas tree my grandfather had brought from the woods. We knew there was popcorn strung on every limb, and we knew those hand-made ornaments would be glistening in the shadows of the lighted candles. And there would be a present for each one of us.

With great ceremony we entered the room, children giggling in nervous excitement, finding our places hovering next to the tree or the elaborate pump-organ.

This was a sacred time for all of us. Mother or cousin Olive played Christmas carols, and our family joined voices in the celebration of this special evening. Everyone was musical, and the voices brought forth angel music in perfect harmony.

Snow drifts outside and howling winds only

A display of the badges Fran collected in World War II.

(Left) Grandmother at 40 years of age.
Mrs Alette Olson-Jorstead
Born March 26, 1852
Died March 28, 1933

(Right) Thank you card
sent to attendees of
Fran's Grandmother's funeral.

We Extend to You Our Heartfelt Thanks and Appreciation for Sympathy and Kindness Shown During Death and Burial of OUR MOTHER Her Children.

(The accompanying picture was taken when mother was 40 years old.)

accentuated the warmth and love of this Norwegian-American Christmas. There was no Norwegian spoken, and each Christmas Carol was sung in English, all of which made my father very happy. He was proud of his English heritage, but he was equally respectful of the heritage of my mother.

Thursday was always a special day for me. Since the family published The Story City Herald on that day each week, my grandmother would invite the men and me to enjoy a hot meal at noon.

She would always serve kumla, my very favorite dish to this day — a potato dumpling cooked in a soup-broth with either ham or salt pork as a base. With generous portions of butter served on the dumpling, my challenge as a child was to eat as many dumplings as my adult cousins — Harry Butcher, Paul and Art Olson — and brother Chuck.

What a delightful surprise it was to me to find variations of this food in other countries where my husband Harry Kinne and I lived while he was serving in the Army. And the German equivalent was the closest to the Norwegian. As we sat in a restaurant in Frankfurt our first evening, my eyes recognized potato dumplings on the plate the waiter was serving to a customer at an adjacent table. The dish was Kartofel Klose, and I was to enjoy it during our three and 1/2 years in Frankfurt.

It is no wonder my grandmother was so popular, bubbling with personality, sense of humor radiating from twinkling eyes. As she moved around the house she would intermittently sing and hum, but never whistle, "Whistling girls and cackling hens are sure to come to

some sad end." In the meantime, the ever-present coffee pot wafted enticing aromas, luring every guest to the source — the kitchen. In fact, her coffee made in the granite pot became famous in our little town. Of course, she was drafted to make coffee for the St. Petri Ladies Aid Society, which met every Thursday afternoon.

There were usually quilts to be quilted. Everyone wanted to sit with my grandmother, because she always had amusing stories to tell. Bent over the quilt, my grandmother deftly made her tiny stitches a part of the patterned fabric, as she related humorous stories to those around her.

I treasure the precious cocklebur quilt she quilted for me when I was 11. After hundreds of launderings and its use in China, Japan and Germany, I display her quilt proudly on the wall of my master bedroom.

The pangs of loss were poignant when I lost my grandmother, and I resolved that grief by playing special passages of my concert piano pieces for her. In fact, a lovely, melodic phrase in Mendelssohn's "Rondo Capriccioso" was always played for her. And this was the selection I performed successfully in the Iowa music competition. Music has always been that meaningful to me!

Grandmother lived on in my mother, as she had the same wonderful disposition, the caring spirit and loving nature. Certainly she lived on in her other remaining living children — Uncle P.A., Aunt Mary, twin Aunts Josie and Lina, Aunt Petra and Aunt Lillie. Those who followed in the ensuing generations have a rich heritage to emulate.

Fran in her Army Hostess uniform. (Inset) Color Badge worn by the U.S. Army hostesses.

Chapter Five:
Uncle Sam Wants You: From Camp Crowder to the Veterans Administration to a World of Languages and Cultures

*Service Club #1,
Camp Crowder, Missouri.*

*Fran (highlighted) and the Service
Club Hostesses at Camp Crowder.*

World War II was well under way, and I had the patriotic urge to do something. As a small child I would say, "Some day I will entertain soldiers." This very likely stemmed from the Memorial Day parades, where veterans of World War I would march carrying the American flag.

I was too young to qualify as a U.S. Army Hostess, but Uncle

P.A. called our Representative, Paul Cunningham in Washington, and he maneuvered the labyrinth of the bureaucracy. He waved the magic wand, and I was sent to Camp Crowder, Missouri (one of the largest camps in the country) and a training camp for soldiers in the Signal Corps.

My responsibility as a Hostess was to direct one of the three Service Clubs on post. The uniform was an attractive suit in air blue, with a rainbow patch on the shoulder and the jaunty cap. The hostesses had the equivalent rank of a 2nd Lieutenant.

I never realized what the experience would do for me in my later positions of leadership, for the responsibilities included scheduling all recreation activities and operating a cafeteria and snack bar. This meant keeping the books and supervising all of the employees.

The sing-alongs were favorites of the GIs, and I played the piano, led the singing and sang "He's My Guy" hundreds of times.

One evening as I was playing a request, a young man who looked familiar leaned on the piano, looking at me with dreamy, home-sick eyes. He said wistfully, "I wonder what they're doing at Sevold's Cafe tonight." (Sevold's was the popular hangout for teenagers in Story City.) The young man was from Story City.

I must have posed for hundreds of photos, as I became a mascot for the 164th Signal Photo Co. At the same time, the members of the Band Training Section (stationed at Camp Crowder) became regular participants in our recreational activities. These were GIs who were professional musicians, all of whom had played in name bands.

Since I had completed all of my Master's degree work at Drake, I explored doing a thesis while at Camp Crowder. I had for my research the finest of musicians, and my thesis developed into a study of music programs in the U.S. Army, with a specific study of

Fran in one of hundreds of photos as a model for Signal Photo Company.

the program at Camp Crowder. And so I was able to be hooded with my graduate degree.

I moved on as Senior Hostess at Service Club 1, where I was able to introduce a variety of exciting entertainment. The Special Services Officer, Maj. Vincent Howe, was highly supportive and cooperative when I suggested we schedule Joe Lewis and Sugar Ray Robinson, the heavyweight and lightweight boxing champions, to give exhibition bouts in the Service Club.

It meant we had to set up a boxing ring in the center of the ballroom, but it was worth all the red tape we encountered. The night was a magnificent success, and it was standing room only. The same response was afforded Cary Grant and Kathryn Grayson on separate programs. I played the piano for both of them, and each offered me a position should I wish to leave. I

(Left) GIs in a service club program, waiting for Fran to entertain.

(Pictured at Right) Everyone enjoys a dance at Service Club #1, Camp Crowder.

explained to them I had the same commitment as they, and I was there for the duration. I will admit Cary Grant was a "charmer" in the eyes of this young Army Hostess.

Of the GIs I particularly enjoyed, several stand out in my memory — Richard (Dick) Crenna and Lon McCallister. Dick is a superb actor and even after all these years plays major roles. Lon was at that time one of the top young actors at 20th Century Fox, and later joined the "Stage Door Canteen" cast.

As a baseball enthusiast, Major Vincent Howe arranged for all the baseball pros stationed at Crowder to visit the Service Club. Detroit Tigers pitcher Tommy Bridges was my favorite. We became good friends, and when my father visited, Tommy and Dad spoke "baseball" into the wee hours of the night. Treasured memories are of the Cardinals-

Browns World Series, when Tommy arranged box seats for Dad and me.

War took a toll among my friends in my age group in Story City. There were few families left untouched. Our own family was fortunate, for cousins Arvin (Alaska), Andy (Europe), Betty (W.A.C.), and Bob Hermanson (3rd Armored) — all came home physically unscathed at the close of the war. Later we lost Harry and Thelma Butcher's son, Bud, in a plane crash in Utah.

However, my two brothers-in-law suffered at the hands of the enemy. Warren ("Bud") Kinne was shot down in the raid over Ploesti, bombing the ore fields of Rumania, and was taken a Prisoner of War; Beale Bordley was severely injured in the Korean War. My second husband (Col. Worthington Bordley, Jr.) was wounded in the Solomon Islands and

received the Purple Heart. The sacrifice made by those in combat is largely an unwritten page in our history. It is gratifying Dick and Kay Munsen (Dick was shot down) wrote a descriptive and valuable book, Bail Out Over the Balkans, about Dick's experiences.

At the end of the war I was assigned to close the three Service Clubs, and with a skeleton force we accomplished this until one of the largest Forts in the U.S. became a ghost town. In 3½ years I had listened to the stories of thousands of homesick GIs. Each of them took a bit of me with them, and each left a bit for me to remember.

Crossroads

Life tosses us challenges whether we want them or not, and I wonder if it is to require us to titillate our untapped resources, our energy and abilities. Another crossroads faced me at

Camp Crowder— (l-r) Tommy Bridges , Major Howe and Neil O'Donnell.

the end of the War.

Drury College in Springfield, Missouri offered me a contract as Dean of Women, and the Veterans Administration put pressure on me to become Recreation Director at the large facility near Leavenworth, Kansas. On my visit to the campus of Drury, however, I had a haunting feeling my work in Special Services was not completed. Many returning veterans were hospitalized, some with major health problems, and the Veterans Administration was recruiting me.

My parents confirmed what I had felt. "You're too young to be a Dean of Women. And do you still feel a commitment to your country?" That was the only occasion on which they entered into a major decision, and they were right. Explaining my feelings to the President of Drury wasn't easy. However, there was someone in the wings who wanted the position, and that decision changed my life and added another segment to that "Golden Thread."

Veterans Administration

Wadsworth V.A. Center had four separate structures with a General Medical and Surgical Hospital, a separate area for T.B. patients, a mental hospital, and a domiciliary for homeless veterans. Every bed was occupied in each facility, and I found there was never enough time to take care of everyone. I did have four assistants who were equally dedicated, all older than I but highly cooperative.

It was a thought-provoking time for me. I had watched the GI's leaving for overseas combat, and now the agony and aftermath of war brought suffer-

Fran and Harry's DeSoto convertible.

ing. It all inspired me to work night and day to provide recreation and morale-building programs.

While working with the Veterans Administration and Service Clubs around the world, I have been proud of some of the innovative programs I introduced which were successful and are part of the V.A. programs still in effect today. For the blind I started golf and bowling with great success; for the mental patients music was the most helpful; for the others a multitude of programs, including sound systems and bedside access to cultural programs, music, books, poetry, plays/drama, concerts, and personal bedside visits to speak with all the patients. Since I had met many celebrities at Camp Crowder and elsewhere, I used my networking to schedule entertainers who were well-known.

Marriage

While this was all transpiring I couldn't worry about my own recreation, but then fate stepped in. One of the doctors told me about an Army Lt. Col. who was in the Command and General Staff College at Fort Leavenworth — "Older," he said, "but handsome, charming," and he wanted to meet me. The blind date was arranged, he appeared at the Nurses' Quarters (where I lived) and I wasn't there. It was a comedy of errors. I worked late, tried to contact him, left a message, but he was already on his way to meet me. I couldn't blame him for being furious.

Harry when Fran first met him.

The next day I called him. "How does one apologize to a Colonel?"

His response was curt: "The same way you apologize to anyone. Is this an apology?" And so the story begins. Harry had a nifty DeSoto convertible and he convinced me to save Saturday nights for the Officers Club's Hops — always formal with long white gloves and a gardenia corsage.

But I guess the door of success swings on the hinges of obstacles, for he called me later and this time I was there.

While I was Director of Recreation and Entertainment for the Veterans Administration I scheduled many celebrities, one of whom was the great pianist, Jose Iturbi. He was performing in concert the next evening in Kansas City, and he agreed to play for the hospitalized veterans if I would arrange transportation. Harry offered to transport Iturbi in the new DeSoto convertible.

The day arrived, and it was the coldest day of the winter, wind howling, and snow blowing into every vulnerable spot of that convertible. Harry and I arrived at the Muehlbach Hotel, and in minutes we had Iturbi seated beside Harry in the front seat. I climbed into the narrow back, where snow had already soaked the leather seat.

In 45 minutes the pianist was at the keyboard of my piano, and his talents and charm elicited a warm response from the appreciative veterans. Iturbi had recently appeared in movies the GIs had seen, and they recognized star quality.

On the return to Kansas City, Iturbi started to sneeze, and I became apprehensive. That was a well-founded feeling.

The following day the Kansas City paper headlined, "Jose Iturbi Hospitalized with Pneumonia — All Concerts Canceled."

As time went on, all the obstacles I had foreseen melted away after that blind date with Harry, and nine months later we were married.

Harry and Fran.

Mr. and Mrs. Charles M. Bartlett entertained 200 guests at a reception, Friday evening at Community Hall honoring Lt. Col. and Mrs. Harry L. Kinne who are leaving next month for Taiwan/ Formosa, where Col. Kinne will be assigned to the U.S. Army military mission. Mrs. Kinne is the former Frances Bartlett, daughter of Mr. and Mrs. Bartlett. Colonel and Mrs. Kinne were married June 24 at Fort Leavenworth, Kansas.

Prof. Stanford Hulshizer of the Fine Arts college, Drake University, Des Moines, and former teacher of the bride when she attended Drake University, sang "Myself When Young," "Persian Garden," "To You," and "Because," He was accompanied by Mrs. Hulshizer, Miss Helen Melass, student at Drake University, Fine Arts department, and a former pupil of Mrs. Kinne when she taught music in Des Moines public schools, played "Prelude in C Minor," "Black Key Etude" and "Whims." The Misses Marilyn Bergeson and Connie Severaid of Story City sang a vocal duo, "Yours is My Heart Alone." They were accompanied by Laurel Peterson.

Talks were given by Paul A. Olson, Story City, uncle of the bride, and Maj. Gen. Sinju Pu Hsiao of Nanking, China. Maj. Gen. Hsiao and Mrs. Hsiao, Army friends of Col. and Mrs. Kinne, have resided the past year at Fort Leavenworth, where Maj. Gen. Hsiao attended the Command and General Staff college. Previously, Maj. Gen. Hsiao was with the Chinese Embassy at Washington, D.C. They also are on their way to China, where Maj. Gen. Hsiao reports for duty with the Chinese government as Military Aide to Generalissimo Chiang Kai-shek.

The reception hall was decorated with white gladioli and white tapers. Mrs. Luther Henderson was reception hostess. Presiding at the tea table was Mrs. A. B. Rosenberger of Estherville, cousin of the bride. Miss Ruth Baumgartner of Des Moines, a former fellow teacher of Mrs. Kinne, presided at the punch. Miss Harriet Higgins, former army hostess and acquaintance of the bride at Camp Crowder, was in charge of the guest book. Mrs. Robert Hermanson, cousin of the bride, played piano selections while the guests assembled, and Mrs. Arthur E. Olson, Story City, presided at the program ceremonies.

— The Story City Herald, July 29, 1948

(top, l-r) Cary Grant at Service Club; Another photo of Fran as a mascot for Signal Photo Company.

(Center) Tom Bridges, who signs the photo on May 10, 1946, "To Frances — a true friend & a real pal."

(Bottom) Lon McAllister with his grandmother and mother.

(Top, Clockwise) Sugar Ray Robinson, Joe Louis and Major Howe; Lon McAllister; Uncle P.A. & Sinju; Fran's mother.

Chapter Six:
A Lifetime on a Path of Education and Travel for the Colonel's Lady — Serving with General MacAuthur

The following letter printed in The Story City Herald was written while being evacuated from the interior of China. I had kept copious notes of those few months in China, and the letter tells a story of adventure:

THE STORY CITY HERALD — Thursday, December 2, 1948

"China Letter From Recent Bride — Mrs. Frances Bartlett-Kinne Writes Interestingly of New Experiences"

Enroute Hankow to Shanghai by C-47,
Alt. 16,000 ft.

The garden at the famous Imperial Hotel in Toyko, Japan.

Dear Uncle Anton:
"Round the world in 4 months." At present, that is what it appears to be for me. I have kept you posted at intermittent intervals, but, until now, no opportunity has arisen to write at length concerning the activities of one Army Colonel and his bride. The past few months have been filled with hectic happenings which have now reached a definite crisis, and, as a result, we are now on an evacuation plane on our way to Shanghai. With the political situation as it is, all dependents are being evacuated, and I shall probably be home by Christmas.

My voyage to China on the General Blackford was delightful — all twenty-two days of it. I was one of the fortunate few to escape seasickness, so I was in a position to enjoy my trip to the fullest extent, and enjoy it I did. The main lounge on the ship boasted a piano, and many of the ship's passengers enjoyed singing; so, in the many days at sea, they kept me busy at the piano, which I enjoyed, of course. Lt. Glenn Davis, the All-American football player from the West Point Academy, was aboard, and on his way to Korea. I found him an appreciative listener and an ardent music-lover, as well as a genuinely nice fellow.

Direct to Yokohama
Our journey followed the 35th parallel pretty closely; therefore, we sailed directly from San Francisco to Yokohama where we put in for two days. A friend of Harry's met me at Yokohama and took me to Tokyo on a "blitz tour" of the city, and lunch at the famous Imperial Hotel.

I was impressed with the evidence everywhere of the excellent work of the Occupation troops. In arriving in Tokyo Bay I had observed the hundreds of smokestacks which dotted the skyline of Yokohama. In my trip around the city it was interesting to note that these smokestacks were the only remnants left of the factories. The factories themselves had been flattened in the bombings. All about in their ruins were mushrooming tiny crude shelters which the Japanese were using to ease the housing problem.

I was amazed, too, with the results of the pin-point bombing in Tokyo. The beautiful Diet building, which houses the Japanese legislative assembly, was left intact, whereas, immediately across the street, Tojo's headquarters proved to be a mass of ruins.

Our voyage from Yokohama to Jinsen, Korea provided much more of interest than our earlier weeks at sea. We skirted the southern coast of Japan, through the strait, into the East China Sea, and north through the Yellow Sea.

We arrived in the harbor at Jinsen at dusk, and never during the entire trip had I witnessed a prettier sight. The water was unusually calm, and the blue-green color provided an artist's background for the dozens of sam-pans with their red sails. In vivid recollection, I recalled the lyrics to "Red Sails in the Sunset" and the song held new meaning to me.

We spent two days in

Harry in uniform.

Korea and then made our way diagonally through the Yellow Sea to Shanghai and my new home in China. We wound our way first up the Yangtze River and then the Whangpoo River with its narrow but deep channel. It took us four hours to dock and when we arrived Harry, Sinju and Chen Meng Hsiao were there to welcome me.

One of Sinju's first queries was: "How is everyone in Story City — your folks and Uncle P. A.? We surely must pay another visit in that remarkable town."

An Amazing City

Shanghai is as fantastic and amazing a city as I had always imagined it to be, though in my mind's eye I had never pictured as many people in such a small area. We spent nine days in the city, and during that visit I began to realize just what an amazing paradox is China — such an incongruous combination of charm and culture as well as filth and poverty. We were besieged by beggars who wanted "Cumshaw" — hundreds of them, all sizes and all ages.

One evening as we were leaving the lovely Park Hotel, a tiny Chinese miss implored me in her most wistful fashion, "Missy, please Cumshaw. Me got no mommy; me got no poppy; me got no flight pay; no orders!" I definitely decided that the Air Corps had been there before me.

The dinner at the Park was given for us, incidentally, by the Hsiaos and in true Chinese fashion. There were eleven courses and we ate them all with chop sticks. I enjoyed, particularly, the dessert, which was a sauce made of Lotus blossom seeds.

On one of our shopping excursions around the city we visited a shoe store which had some shoes I wished to purchase. As we tried to enter the front door, our way was blocked by the broad shoulders of a very bedraggled beggar. Harry tapped him on the arm and he reluctantly moved aside to let me enter. As we did so, we realized he was waving a long snake in the air and asking the shopkeeper for "Cumshaw." He threatened to free the snake in the store if the shopkeeper refused. When the beggar received his money he moved on to the next store.

On my arrival in Shanghai, we were planning to go to Taiwan for temporary duty; however, in the meantime, our orders were changed to the inland city of Hankow, located about a thousand miles west on the Yangtze River.

We flew first to Nanking in a C-47, a la parachute and bucket seats. It was interesting to see the irregularly patterned rice fields in various stages of growth and harvest, and it seemed as though the waters of the Yangtze were everywhere, flooding the greater part of the countryside.

Our visit in Nanking was for a brief two days. Sinju was waiting to see President Chiang when he returned from Manchuria so he had time to entertain us royally, and we enjoyed a delightful Chinese dinner at the home of a Chinese General. Harry taught the hostess his favorite trick of magic as we sipped jasmine tea in their lovely home.

On our flight into Nanking, Harry had pointed out from the air the tomb of Dr. Sun Yat Sen, as well as the tombs of the emperors of the Ming Dynasty. Sinju took us to visit these places as well as an ancient Chinese Buddhist temple, and we were impressed with the architectural beauty of these interesting and historic places.

Airplane Over the Yangtze

The flight from Nanking to Hankow took us over a hundred mile chain of mountains and continued to follow the Yangtze River. Upon our arrival at the Hankow field, we were welcomed warmly by a group of Chinese and American officers who escorted us to our new home.

We discovered our quarters were on the second floor of a large downtown building, and strangely enough, the first floor was occupied by the Norwegian Consulate. It was a surprise to see the Norwegian flag flying from our door. The apartment was to be temporary housing until a large house was made available for us. However, the apartment served us nicely and I was lost in its huge rooms. Fifteen bouquets of flowers were distributed throughout the quarters which added considerably to our welcome.

My first discovery was that we had four servants — two supplied by the Chinese government and two whom we

paid. (Incidentally, the two cost us a total of $6.50 a month.) In addition we had a guard at our door who was employed by the Norwegian consul. Harry humorously referred to them all as my "platoon": Ching, my Number One boy, a Number Two boy, an amah and a cook. Ching made himself invaluable in the month we were in Hankow. He spoke some English, and with the few Chinese expressions I knew, we managed to carry on quite a conversation.

I was particularly interested in his comment to me the day after the U.S. election, which the Chinese people had watched with intense interest. He queried, "Number One man in America no change. Is that bad for China?" Harry and I had not discussed the political situation in the presence of the servants, so his question amazed us.

Gazed at by the Natives

I spent my first few days in Hankow exploring the city. Since I could not travel about by myself, Ching accompanied me on my excursions. There are few Americans in the city so I was a matter of curiosity. Small children gathered about me, pointing at my clothes, and older people stared unabashed at me. This was a bit disconcerting to me until I found out that basically most of them were quite friendly, and I had but to smile and they would answer with a smile or a friendly gesture. On my visits outdoors on days of inclement weather I took a ricksha and observed the life of the city from under a leaky canvas cover.

The missions are very active in Hankow and have done excellent work. I paid a visit to the Lutheran Home and Mission and enjoyed a long talk with Mr. Hanson, the director.

I was amazed to see the destruction as left by the bombing during the last war. The Japanese occupied the city in 1935 and stayed until our airmen destroyed forty per cent of the city.

Incidentally, the Japanese stripped Hankow of all its radiators, elevators and all iron grill work. Just before we left, radiators had been installed in our quarters, and we had the first steam heat in the city. It was fortunate for us as the fireplace did not provide adequate heat. With these evidences of war all around us, it was disturbing to know that the city will have to stand another onslaught. Before we left, trenches had been dug around the city and pillboxes were placed at strategic intervals. Communist guerilla bands were active on the outskirts

of the city and during the last few days our apartment was watched constantly, and our activities seemed to be under close surveillance.

Because of the danger involved, the U. S. Army found it necessary to evacuate us. In Shanghai we shall be under martial law, and it will be much safer.

They Really Stand

Harry enjoyed his work as Senior Officer so much. His work was primarily with Chinese officers. Last week he was called upon to give a short speech before a thousand Chinese troops and ten Chinese Generals, the main address being presented by a visiting Chinese dignitary. Harry stood on the stage, and I mean "stood," for during the two hour program, no chairs were provided, and even the audience had to stand at attention during the entire time.

Four Heralds arrived this last week, and I can't tell you how much I enjoyed reading them. I am hoping there will be a few more awaiting my arrival in Shanghai.

The best of everything to you and the family,

Love, Frances

Harry & Fran in Hankow (November 8, 1948) as they were being evacuated — Fran was wearing her "compulsory slacks."

Updated Version

Many years later I was able to speak more openly about my experience in Hankow.

We had been informed the spacious home we were to occupy in Hankow was not available until the flood waters of the Yangtze River had receded. Our temporary billet was a large and comfortable apartment in the Consular section of Hankow, and I was filled with anticipation at the thought of our very first home a thousand miles up the Yangtze River.

The young Lieutenant who met us explained there were only 30 American officers and enlisted men assigned as advisors to the Chinese Nationalist Army in Hankow. He also exploded my dream of lecturing and attending classes at the University across the river from Hankow. He explained it was not safe for me to go anywhere without a male companion. I discovered this was to be our No. 1 boy, who soon learned he had quite a challenge to keep up with me.

As we arrived at our destination, the Norwegian flag I saw flying in front of our quarters triggered thoughts of my Norwegian grandmother and what she would have said: "Oh, yah, Franny, this is a good sign." And there below the colors of the Norwegian flag stood a handsome Sikh guard, his white turban wrapped neatly around his head. Arms folded and shoulders back, he was in total command of the situation. I found it amusing, however, that he was standing guard in front of an apartment with little or no furniture.

I was aware our household goods had been delayed and were tied up in a strike on the San Francisco docks. (Memories of that farewell glance of San Francisco will remain with me forever) This included our DeSoto convertible, furniture, wedding gifts, and most important to me, my piano. (Harry knew I wouldn't go anywhere without a piano, and we spent the day after our wedding shopping every music store in Kansas City to find the right instrument.) Somehow or other all of these material things seemed very unimportant as we entered the door to our first home.

As we passed the Sikh guard, I remembered the parting advice my parents gave me. I stepped back and extended my hand, saying, "How do you do." I couldn't help but notice the surprised expression on his face, which was quickly replaced by a broad smile, eyes crinkling at the corners. And in a perfect English accent, white teeth glittering against his dark skin, "Welcome to Hankow, Madam. You and the Colonel will be very happy here" — all of this with a snappy salute.

I thought to myself, of course we would be happy. I had been taught one has two choices arising each morning — one may be happy or sad. (At that age I thought that was over-simplified. It was only after I received a Ph.D. that I

SAN FRANCISCO—*Memories of a great city.*

found my parents were wise beyond my comprehension.)

Harry had intended to carry me over the threshold, but four servants and a Sikh standing at attention certainly altered his plans. The No. 1 Boy bowed low, and then said, "My name is Ching." Then he introduced the cook, whose chef's cap seemed to envelop his tiny body, all four feet 11 inches of him. Next in line was the No. 2 Boy, and Ching explained, "He makes fires." Last in line was the Wash Amah, whose eyes immediately reflected humble submission.

As I surveyed the large rooms it was very apparent four servants would have trouble finding enough to do. I knew, however, I could depend on the cook to rescue me from my inability to be effective in the kitchen. I well recall my ninth grade home economics teacher who suggested it might be better for me to learn how to cook instead of how to play the piano. She made this observation when I returned from a music competition at which I had placed first — at age 13. I am happy I did not take her advice!

Our furniture turned out to be a bed with a very tired mattress, two chairs and a card table. And it was difficult to find enough tasks for the four servants. It was no problem, however, for the Sikh guard at the front door, as he just stood there. Harry checked the doors to see if each room could be locked for privacy purposes. This was a natural reaction, since the Wash Amah had previously followed him into the bathroom.

Ching explained the Amah wanted to take Harry's clothes to be washed. That started what I called my "giggle-sessions."

One of the most amusing incidents happened the very first evening. Harry asked Ching to bring the cook into the living room, and in moments the tiny figure was standing in front of us. In spite of his short stature he presented an imposing figure with his ever-present butcher knife in hand. In broken English, the cook said, "What wants Colonel?" Harry asked him if he knew how to make hors d'oeuvres, and the cook answered with delight, "Me make good hors d'oeuvres. You wait!"

And so as Harry mixed a Martini for him and a Manhattan for me, we waited expectantly for the hors d'oeuvres to arrive. We waited and waited and waited. Finally the cook made a grand entrance from the kitchen, and on a silver tray were a dozen hot doughnuts. The triumphant look on the cook's face wouldn't allow either of us even to show surprise.

Harry and I had a first experience of eating doughnuts as hors d'oeuvres with our cocktails, a first and last!

The next day I decided to explore Hankow. Ching was instructed to accompany me and not let me out of his sight. It was an exciting new adventure for me, but I was not comfortable having Ching several steps behind me. I suggested to him I would be happy if he would walk beside me, but he shook his head vehemently from side to side to side and answered, "No, no, no, Madame. Not good."

I realized that would have been a breach of etiquette for him, and my lesson in democracy met its first challenge.

Another interesting shopping trip took me to a book store. I was looking for any Western music I could find, whether classical or popular. And what should I stumble upon but a Frank Sinatra record! How that ever wound up in a shop in Hankow would make an interesting story in itself.

Witness to Suffering

Living in Hankow was exciting but of brief duration. With hundreds of Chinese starving, it was difficult for me to eat. All around me I saw suffering, and as a young bride my reaction was a feeling of helplessness. I became anemic, and there were no American doctors in Hankow. It was determined I should fly to Nanking where I would be able to be treated by an American doctor.

How safe was it? The Communists had already surrounded the city, but it was safe to fly. And so it was I found myself in the city of Nanking, the capital of China. The physician gave me vitamin shots and instructed me to eat properly.

I explained to him this was a challenge, since I was sensitive to the many Chinese unable to find food. In addition, Hankow was the "end of the line" to receive authorized American food. And we were not allowed to eat "on the economy."

Eating "on the economy" meant buying meals at restaurants, or purchasing the ingredients to cook meals directly from the local markets and shops and food dealers. This was against orders in Occupied countries. The reason for this was the threat of poisoning, different standards of sanitation, as well as the uncertainty of the quality of the water, food and other ingredients used in the preparation of the food. Americans also lacked resistance to certain strains of bacteria and other manifestations of the local food for which local residents had developed immunities.

In Nanking

It was my trip to Nanking that started another new adventure for me.

Late that day I received the shocking news that all Americans would be evacuated from China. It had only been days before the State Department had assured us that we would remain in China. Not so.

With my bridegroom in Hankow I was not about to be sent anywhere else, and I insisted I would fly back into the interior to Hankow. The only way I could do this was to take the matter in my own hands.

That is precisely what I did, and I called a pilot friend I knew was stationed in Nanking. I explained in a spirit of desperation my problem. His response: "Fran, I am flying to the interior of China tomorrow to evacuate Americans. I will be flying over Hankow, but if you can be at the airport at 5 a.m. tomorrow you may fly with me."

I quickly packed my suitcase, but the main question remained. With chaos everywhere, how was I to get to the airport? Buses, trains and planes were booked with frantic men and women of all nationalities, and certainly no taxis were available.

A young Chinese jeep driver had assisted me during the day, and I decided to try something I had learned from my husband. I took a ten dollar bill from my billfold, quickly tearing the bill into two parts. I handed one-half to the driver, promising him I would give him the other half if he picked me up in time to get to the airport at 5 a.m. He gladly accepted and promised to return at 4 a.m.

I never closed my eyes that evening, as I was fearful of not awakening. Fortunately the driver appeared at the designated hour, and I found myself on the wildest ride of my life.

The Communists had already surrounded the city of Nanking, and the driver found his way around pedicabs, rickshaws and thousands of Chinese Nationalists trying to escape.

We arrived at the airport to find that my pilot friend was already warming up the engine with props moving restlessly.

In moments we were in the air, the C-47 climbing into the clouds. Of course, my friend could not understand why I was returning to Hankow, since undoubtedly we would be evacuated within a short time. However, he very graciously allowed me my romantic notions about returning to my husband. He radioed Harry to meet us at the airport, and as our plane landed I could see my husband waving a welcome.

After his embrace, his first warning was the dangers we were facing. In fact, he gently chided me for endangering my own life in returning to Hankow. He announced we would be evacuated at dawn the following day.

Since our furniture had not arrived, little time was needed for packing. There was no electricity, and our evening was spent in candlelight. There were no candles, so the No. 1 boy had improvised with a rice bowl of oil and a wick made from a scrap of fabric he scrounged from somewhere.

Harry and I had been aware of the fact that we were being watched for several weeks prior to the evacuation notice, and that particular evening we observed with some trepidation the shadowy figure we saw lurking in the darkness behind our apartment — especially in the "Chinese Godowns" (the alleys or "life in the raw" in this large city).

Perhaps to make me feel more at ease,

Harry suggested we review all of the unusual and ludicrous things that had happened to us since our arrival in Hankow. And so it was we took turns describing in detail each event, interrupting one another only to laugh.

Certainly the prize story involved our first night in our apartment. We had just retired in the large bedroom which housed one bed — Harry in his new silk pajamas, and I in my sheer black night gown (one of the "necessities" I had included in the two suitcases I was allowed to take to China) — when we heard the door open. In the dim light we recognized the figure silhouetted against the shaded window. It was the No. 2 boy quietly moving toward the fireplace, his arms filled with firewood. In moments he had a blazing fire started, and simultaneously dozens of bats flew out of the fireplace.

In occupying Hankow the Japanese had stuffed all of the chimneys — their last gesture of defiance. I screamed, pulling the sheet high over my head, while Harry bounded out of bed and reached for the first thing he could find to combat the flying bats, while I remained under the sheets in gales of laughter. And that something he waved so dangerously as he stood on the sagging mattress was his tennis racket.

He had earlier teased me about my black nightgown, and I had responded with a playful mockery of his "so vital" tennis racket. I don't know about the value of the black nightie, but thank goodness for the tennis racket.

Fran (left) with Army friends Col. Jay Dasche and Mary in Shanghai.

Chapter Seven:
Toyko, the Japanese Occupation, Repatriation

The following letter follows the saga of those turbulent times, another appendage to the life story - another thread entwined and interlaced in the golden thread of life.

THE STORY CITY HERALD — Thursday, June 9, 1949

"A Letter From Far-Off Tokio"

"Frances Bartlett-Kinne Writes Interestingly of Life in Japan"

Imperial Hotel
Tokyo, Japan
May 29, 1949

Dear Uncle P.A.:

Almost six months have passed since my letter which I wrote while flying from Hankow to Shanghai. Those were hectic days and we didn't know one moment where we might find ourselves the next moment, but fate was kind to us and we have a splendid assignment here in Tokyo. Harry is assigned to G2 (Intelligence) in General MacArthur's Headquarters and is happy over his good fortune.

I stayed in Shanghai until the last ship carrying out military dependents. We had several weeks in the city, and I spent the greatest share of the time doing last minute shopping. We didn't want to make too many purchases for we weren't sure just what percentage of our luggage and household effects would ever get safely out of China. Since the anti-foreign feeling had already begun to infiltrate into Shanghai, it wasn't advisable to shop alone, so small groups of us would visit the shops and make our purchases. Even so, it was not uncommon to be shoved in the street or to be spat upon, a bit difficult to accept and even more difficult to understand.

Shanghai, even at that time was breathless over its fate. The City Fathers were doing every-thing in their power to raise the morale of the people and encourage the shopkeepers to stay; however, many merchants had already packed their wares and had left the city. The thousands of beggars on the street were the "men of the moment" and looting was their only business.

I spoke to General Sinju Pu Hsiao just before I left. He was greatly concerned over the plight of his country, but even in this deep concern he asked to be remembered to all his friends in Story City.

Sailing from Shanghai

Harry helped me board the "Republic," an old converted hospital ship, docked in the harbors of the Whangpoo, that early day in December. The ship was crowded with missionaries, Chinese Nationals, and those of us who were Army Dependents. We traveled "troop class" but none seemed to mind the inconveniences — just happy to get out of China; that is, they were — I wasn't, for I had left Harry on the docks the day we sailed, not having any idea where I was going, or when he would join me. We had been told we would be off-loaded in Japan if our husbands were to be assigned

GENERAL MacAUTHUR—
MacAuthur (center-foreground) makes review of his troops in Toyko, Japan.

accordingly.

So it was, that as the large ship steamed out of the Whang-poo, into the Yangtze, China Sea, and then the blue Pacific, I mused over the exciting events of the previous months in China, and the unknown future ahead of me. Perhaps it was this chaos I left behind which made me more appreciative of what I was to find in Japan.

The "Republic" docked in Yokohama, Japan, on December 5, and from the moment we disembarked to this very moment, I have said to myself, "This is too good to be true — there just can't be this much difference between China and Japan." Such organization! As I stepped off the gangplank, Japanese boys carried my luggage and directed me to a waiting train. There an American Lieutenant welcomed us and explained that everything would be done for our comfort. We rode to the edge of Tokyo to a large warehouse where our processing was to be completed. There, four white-helmeted and gloved American MP's took me and my luggage through ten minutes of processing, then led me to a bus which would take me to the Park hotel, where a number of us were to be billeted.

They didn't tell us then, but later I learned that a number of Civil Service employees had given up their rooms to provide temporary housing for us. I was deeply impressed with everything. I could begin to understand the adoration of the Japanese for MacArthur.

Those first three weeks in Japan were eased a great deal by the hospitality and friendliness evidenced by the members of the Occupation. Our names had been printed in the <u>Stars and Stripes</u> and invitations poured in from a number of Harry's friends sta-

(top-left)
General Douglas MacArthur.

(above)
Japanese POW's awaiting processing on their return to Japan.

(left)
Japanese POW's loading on the train on their return to Japan.

tioned in Tokyo. The Occupation arranged for us to speak with our husbands by short wave several times.

One day I answered the telephone to receive the following interesting bit of information: "Mrs. Kinne? This is the United Press. We have a message from Seoul, Korea, that General MacArthur's plane, "Bataan" is there and will arrive in Tokyo tomorrow. The Bataan went to Shanghai to pick up Paul Hoffman, ECA administrator."

This was all very interesting, but I was just beginning to wonder how it concerned me when the voice on the other end of the wire said, "And we feel you will be interested in knowing that Colonel Kinne is aboard the plane." Well, I certainly was!

United with husband

Harry was assigned in G2 (Intelligence) in General MacArthur's Headquarters immediately, and so we decided to live at the world famous Imperial Hotel, which is but a few blocks away. We have every convenience in these lovely quarters - excellent dining rooms, theatre, lounges, ballrooms, etc.

The most amazing revelation to me was to be able to walk about on the streets in Tokyo with every freedom, no guards, etc. It was stranger still, not to be accosted by beggars on every side. The Japanese people were obviously better dressed and clothed and the streets much cleaner, than over in China. I walked a great deal just to appreciate the opportunity of walking by myself and with no protection.

I was intrigued by the GINZA, Tokyo's main street. It boasts a large number of department stores, but the fascination for me was in the thousands of tiny shops lining the curbs, displaying wares of every size, kind and description — everything from Leika cameras to buttons.

These shops are constructed and taken down each day, and if one walks along the Ginza early in the morning the Japanese may be seen nailing and fitting boards together for the small shops. I shall never forget the first day I was walking in downtown Tokyo, I heard music which seemed to come from all sides. It was "Tales from the Vienna Woods," Strauss, and as I walked the entire block the music continued, retaining its volume. It was then that I realized that there were large music boxes on each street corner. Not having heard any Western music for several months it was a welcome sound. It suddenly seemed very incongruous to me — a busy street in downtown Tokyo and Strauss Music — "the universal language of mankind."

Teaching English

I have found a great deal to keep me busy. I am teaching English and Music in a Public Girls' school and at Tsuda College here in Tokyo. This teaching is on a volunteer basis, of course, with no remuneration. Of all my classes, the one I enjoy most is a class of Japanese policemen. I have 50 policemen who have come to Tokyo from all over the country for the purpose of learning English. With them I find it necessary to use elementary

Harry leaving MacArthur's plane on arrival in Tokyo.

Fran (at the piano) teaching at the Girls' School.

doctor's degree now, and I plan to write it on "The Place of Western Music in the Stabilization of Japan." It should be very interesting.

Getting to be a "Flag Waver"

It seems I can't write a letter to anyone without repeating over and over how blessed is America, and how fortunate we are to be Americans. I am not so sure but what the term "flag-waver" would apply to me now. I have always had a deep sense of patriotism, but that same patriotism found new depth and meaning this past year, and I learned truly what it is to be an American. I saw it in the eyes of those Chinese, Koreans, and now the Japanese — their utter amazement at our possessions, our clothes — their admiration for anything American.

And why not? Imagine being able to drink spigot water or to stop along the street and drink water from a fountain with no danger of disease — to visit a restaurant and eat food free from con-

expressions, for they speak very little English. Most of them have never spoken to an American before, and I found them a bit shy, but eager to learn. I have one class in graduate English which is quite advanced — both men and women, and of all ages.

My work at the Girls' School is with sixteen to eighteen year olds primarily.

They all have trouble with the "L" and "R" sounds and sometimes with some amusing results. I gave them some tongue twisters which they enjoy practicing — "Peter Piper picked a peck of pickled peppers" turned out to be "Petel Pipel picked a peck of picred peppels." Bing Crosby wouldn't recognize his name for they call him "Bling Closby." All in all they are intelligent and conscientious students.

I have some college people who spend as much time as ten hours each day commuting — five hours each way. That is pursuit of learning, in my estimation. Incidentally, the Japanese schools have no heat, so during the winter months I taught my classes with my winter coat, mittens, and ear muffs.

I am initiating work on my

Fran and two of her students.

(above) Fran and some of her Japanese students.

(right)
Some of Fran's students
(Japanese policemen)

tamination, or to drive along the highway which has oil stations every few miles for the convenience of motorists — just a few of the million reasons why I am "Sold American."

We are enjoying having our automobile here. The left hand driving was a bit confusing at first, but now it seems quite natural. A convertible is quite a matter of curiosity to the Japanese, and when we press the button for the top to go up or down, we always draw a crowd of interested on-lookers.

The Heralds are making excellent time from the States to Japan and I certainly enjoy reading them. I pass them on to my Japanese students when I finish them.

Our very best to you and the family. Couldn't talk you into a trip to Tokyo, could we?

Lovingly,
Frances Bartlett Kinne
c-o Col. Harry L. Kinne, Jr.
ATIS-GHQ-FEC
APO 500, c-o Postmaster
San Francisco, Calif.

A Very Private Public Call

The telephone call from Harry in Shanghai announcing his planned arrival in Tokyo was not described in detail in my letter to Uncle Anton (P.A.). I knew he would publish the letter, and it was too personal for me as a bride. Harry told the story many times throughout the years, however, and I have often used it in speeches.

His voice sounded so different, not at all the way I thought my bridegroom should sound.

FRAN: "Are you OK?"
HARRY: "Sure, I'm OK."
FRAN: "You sound so cold."
HARRY: "What do you mean?"
FRAN: (almost in tears)
                "Don't you love me anymore?"
HARRY: "Yes."

It wasn't until he arrived that I discovered he was in an auditorium with several hundred American officers and GIs who were the last American men leaving China, and my voice was coming over a public address system.

New Assignments

Also, I didn't include my Christmas tree story in my letter — but here it is:

Because Harry was arriving in Tokyo the week before Christmas, our first away from the States, I decided to welcome him with a decorated room.

General MacArthur's senior staff stayed at the Imperial Hotel, and, even though Harry was a Lt. Col., he was the junior among the officers. That meant we had the one room without a bathroom. When I wrote that to my parents, Mother's response by return mail was, "Don't Lt. Colonels have to take baths?"

The room had a double bed, one dresser and two chairs. But I was undaunted. I walked to the Ginza, found a Christmas tree almost as tall as I, and carried it block by block back to our room. But I discovered there was not room enough for it — a dilemma I soon solved. I moved the dresser (with my lingerie still in the drawers) out into the hall, and put the Christmas tree in its place.

When Harry arrived and saw the dresser in the hall he was gracious in his remark: "I knew you'd be creative,

but this is a surprise - a nice surprise to have a decorated tree."

I found out later he had quietly informed the manager of my action, but no one made me move the dresser back in the room - and we celebrated our own Christmas.

Imperial Hotel — Tokyo

The Imperial Hotel had been built In 1923 — a Frank Lloyd Wright design — as an earthquake proof building. Not long after it opened on September 1, 1923 (about five minutes actually), a severe earthquake hit Tokyo; and, indeed, the building did structurally survive the devastating earthquake, thanks to the "floating base."

The Imperial Hotel had been built on swampland. The foundation was constructed after the hard crust of earth was removed so the earth foundation was mushy — but formed on a "concrete mat." So the hotel was purposely built on these cushions so it would be flexible when earthquakes came.

It worked. The Imperial Hotel survived the worst earthquake in Tokyo's history — on the day the hotel was completed!

I'll never forget the beautiful Peacock Room and Ballroom in the Imperial Hotel — where I was later to meet Bob Hope. I'll remember as well the small but elegant banquet room, so beautifully panelled in kiri wood — "Kiri no ma" — just big enough for 16 guests.

Fran pictured on top of the Imperial Hotel in a return to uniform as part of General MacArthur's Staff.

Repatriation, Japan

Some advice I heard often around the dining room table in Story City: "Life is a journey, not a guided tour." When some friends and I decided to assist the Japanese in re-establishing their schools, we had no blueprint to follow. The journey proved to be one adventure after the other. Likewise, as Harry commanded the Allied Translator Service in General MacArthur's Headquarters, there was no precedent for what he was to encounter in the repatriation of the Japanese Prisoners of War.

My own volunteer teaching at Tsuda College, the girls' school, and working with the few women in the Japanese Diet certainly presented me with a superb opportunity to emphasize Western culture and the English language. But I also took every opportunity to speak about the magic of democracy. The Japanese Ministry of Education prepared a pamphlet on "Democratic Government and Non-Democratic Government" — specifically to orient Japanese repatriates returning from Soviet-held territories. Later, Harry and his staff distributed these pamphlets to each returning Japanese POW for study. It was fortunate I was able to glean a wealth of information to utilize in my own classes. Most importantly, I recognized that my own actions must be the prime example in support of democracy.

One of the most exciting and challenging subjects was to present our Republic's high regard for the individual, and, in turn, that all men are created equal, and the ultimate authority belongs to the people in a democratic nation. One day in class an eager graduate student at Tsuda College queried,

The scenes of Japanese Repatriates returning from prison in Siberia.

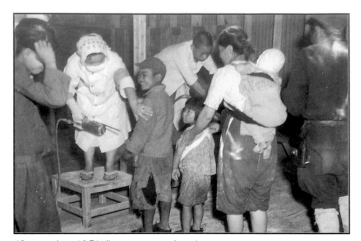

Returning POW's are examined.

"Does that mean my wife has the same rights as I do?" How fortunate for me I had parents and two husbands who would answer that question with a resounding "Yes."

One evening we were invited to a cocktail party on the roof of the Imperial Hotel where we lived. The Occupation was still in place, so the number of Japanese guests was limited. However, it was an evening to remember, with Japanese lanterns caressing the twilight hour and a soft breeze gently teasing my fresh hair-do. I had selected a conservative cocktail dress in deference to the occasion, historic as it was, with both American and Japanese officers in attendance. After all, only recently we were arch enemies. I had not previously seen such a gathering of top brass, most of them General MacArthur's staff. One of the Japanese officers was Lt. Gen. Seizo Arisue, the Japanese officer who had first welcomed the conquering Americans.

Japanese POW's belongings are sprayed for the return to Japan.

In making conversation Harry explained to Gen. Arisue as he introduced him to me, "This is my wife. She is teaching English as a volunteer at Tsuda College, and also to the few women in the Diet." Gen. Arisue bowed graciously to me and responded, "Very good of you." Then he turned to Harry and said with a smile, "But after you Americans go home, no women in the Diet. He laughed. But he had yet to learn of the magic freedom can inspire, and today there are many women in their legislative body.

It was persistent demands of the U.S. which finally brought most of the Japanese POW's back to Japan. Harry and the other officials were stunned when they welcomed thousands of Japanese, now indoctrinated Communists who had transferred their

Repatriates waiting for the health examination.

political beliefs to Marxism. The Japanese Communists who lived in Japan shoved police and military officials to the side to provide an enthusiastic welcome. They pressured the POWs to declare loyalty to the Communist party before recognizing their families, some of whom hadn't seen them in ten years.

The first POWs arrived at the dock at Maizuru on an ex-hospital ship, the TAKASAGO MARU. The first thing they did after exiting the boat (and also from later boats and trains) — they locked arms, marching down the streets of the port city singing the Russian "Internationale" and "The Red Flag." Most of them had been brainwashed to the extent of losing all ability for independent thought.

When one reads <u>The Manchurian Candidate</u> or sees the Sixties film, the power of brain-washing is recognized and is frightening. The Korean and Viet Nam

Japanese POWs on board an ex-hospital ship preparing to arrive in Japan.

Wars provided added testimony to the battle for the mind. And these conflicts with their no-win philosophy certainly gave the needed time to brainwash our own Americans — to confuse, terrify and demoralize prisoners.

For years the Japanese POW's had labored in the forests of Siberia. If they cooperated and accepted Marxism the rations were better. If not, many starved or froze, and thousands never returned home. In December of 1949 the U.S. led the discussion of Reparation in Tokyo at the Allied Council for Japan meetings, and the Soviets walked out in anger. While we were punishing the Japanese for the horrible acts of torture they had inflicted on our own military and civilians, the Russians refused to take responsibility for their acts of depravity. The English speaking <u>Nippon Times</u> in Tokyo in 1949 and 1950, however, pursued their story and wrote of the unspeakable horrors in the Siberian camps, revealing the facts to the world.

Often I have heard peace-loving civilians accuse the military of being war mongers. From my two husbands, and the hundreds of military men and women with whom I became friends, I learned a very different story.

As Harry worked diligently to provide a Homecoming for tens of thousands of repatriates returning to their homeland and families, I spent five days each week attempting to develop greater understanding between the peoples of two very different cultures. It wasn't a "guided tour" for either of us, but it was an exciting and educational journey.

(left) Japanese POWs receiving instructions on arrival in Tokyo.
(above) Japanese women who were field laborers.

THE STORY CITY HERALD —
Sunday, February 16, 1950

Correspondent from Japan

"Mrs. Frances Bartlett-Kinne Writes Interesting Letter from Japan"

Dear Uncle P. A."

Happy New Year to all our relatives and friends — a bit late for a stateside greeting, but strictly legitimate here, for the Japanese celebrate the advent of the New Year throughout the entire month of January.

In spite of the fact we are in a foreign land, and a non-Christian one at that, there were evidences of Christmas all about us during the holidays. In the few years the Occupation forces have been here the Japanese have had the opportunity of seeing a "transplanted" American Christmas with all the trimmings: the Christmas parades tableaus depicting the religious significance of Christmas, decorations, Christmas trees and lights, and pictures of Santa Claus everywhere. A year ago when we had just been evacuated from China there were some indications of the above, but nothing to compare with the extent to which this year's holiday was observed.

The Japanese were quick to realize the commercial value of the aspects of Christmas, and with their imitative ability, commercialization seemed a natural recourse. Large department stores were decorated much like American stores, and the little stalls along the Ginza (Tokyo's main street) sold tinsel, colored lights and decorations. Yet with all this observance of Christmas by the Japanese, it was easy to see that little of it stemmed from an actual understanding of the meaning of Christmas, and my husband and I experienced a nostalgia for our own land, where Christmas is something besides a superfluous imitation of shining tinsel.

A Personal Challenge

I felt gratitude, however, toward many of the Japanese people for they made sincere attempts to "keep Christmas" for me. As I have told you previously, I teach on a voluntary basis in both a Japanese college and a girls' high school. At the college I have a class of Japanese policemen. As a surprise for me they learned "Silent Night" and sang it for me. I was deeply moved for none of them had even heard the song before.

On the morning of the 24th of December I taught Christmas carols to the students of the girls' high school — a thousand of them. As a surprise for me they had trimmed a tree, and as several lovely Japanese gifts were presented to me, they sang "Jingle Bells."

The students are trying to understand and practice democracy, and they imitate everything I do in their attempt.

I find myself scrutinizing my personal habits and speech constantly.

That really is quite a challenge. An amusing incident occurred during Christmas which demonstrates clearly how careful one must be in teaching everything to these students and the necessity for leaving nothing unsaid. I had been teaching the Japanese students Western etiquette — methods of introduction, et cetera, explaining that in America the woman always receives the deference, contrary to the age-old custom in Japan. Some of my students accepted this fact a bit too literally, for when some of our Christmas cards arrived from them the cards were addressed to "Mrs. and Col. Kinne."

Japanese Holiday

Many of our friends have queried us concerning the type of holiday celebrations observed by the Japanese people. Just as Christmas is our religious observance, so is the New Year to the Japanese. Their observance extends during most of the month of January. In every Japanese household great and unusual preparations are made. I noticed that many of the business houses suspended work during the entire first week of January. The women and children and many of the men dress in their brightest and newest kimonos. Houses are cleaned thoroughly, and on New Year's Eve all of their brooms are bound tightly with red and white strings. The gods of good luck supposedly visit the house with the advent of the New Year, and if the brooms are bound the Japanese believe the gods will not be startled out of the house.

Custom designates that all debts will be paid on New Year's.

There is no law concerning this, but the Japanese consider it a moral obligation.

Holiday Food

Special food is eaten by all the Japanese people for their holidays. The favorite is a dish called Ozoni, a broth containing ricecakes and vegetables. There are many other foods — carp (raw and cooked), black peas, chestnuts, seaweed, lotus root, and yellow chrysanthemum petals. The menu includes sake, which is Japanese rice wine.

One of the customs of the celebration is for the citizens to pay a visit to the Imperial Palace and sign the Emperor's Register. On the first few days of the New Year the streets are filled with the thousands of families making the "pilgrimage." The Imperial Hotel, where we live is but a few blocks from the palace grounds so we were particularly conscious of this custom observed by the Japanese.

Baseball, Too

One of the interesting events of the past year was the visit to Japan of the San Francisco Seals baseball team. For weeks nothing else was spoken of by the Japanese, and when the auspicious occasion arrived, the entire country was keyed to the pitch of an American city in which a World Series game is to be played. Large cities of the country drew audiences of approximately 70,000 at each appearance. One game was played exclusively for children — with the same number attending.

Of all my impressions, the one that stood out the greatest was the sportsmanship of the American team and spectators. O'Doul and his team helped to make Occupation history with their excellent demonstration of conduct above reproach. Lefty O'Doul is one of the baseball heroes of Japan, having visited here in pre-war years with Babe Ruth, Lou Gehrig, and a host of other baseball immortals. On this trip O'Doul brought Joe DiMaggio, adored by all the spectators. So O'Doul's welcome here this trip was a rousing one — ticker tape, et al.

In pre-war days the Japanese were not allowed to boo the umpire at baseball games, for he was considered the emissary of the Emperor and his decisions were unquestioned. We were conscious of the fact that democratization had really arrived, even in the baseball world, when the Japanese spectators began booing the umpire.

A "Sacred" Mountain

Since our arrival in Japan we have been exposed constantly to Mt. Fuji-yama, or Mt. Fuji as it is more popularly called (Yama means mountain). I recall studying about Japan as a child, and my two most lasting impressions happened to be two pictures in my geography book — Fuji surrounded by blue sky and white clouds, and the other a Japanese woman peeking coyly from behind a Japanese fan. These were wise selections by the author of the book for they are representative pictures of the country.

Mt. Fuji is considered sacred, and for over a thousand years pilgrims have ascended its heights. It may be seen from twenty-two prefectures, so many people enjoy its beauty. The Japan Travel Bureau (which rivals the California Chamber of Commerce) says: "Peerless Fuji-yama defies description." Nothing is missed in publicizing the beauty of the volcanic mountain — its likeness is seen on practically all souvenir items, jewelry, silk patterns, and dozens of other articles sold everywhere.

Japan's hopes are high as there are more and more talks of a peace treaty. I reiterate (and have done so a thousand times), General MacArthur has performed a tremendous task in rebuilding Japan. Can you imagine trying to democratize 75 million people — a population steeped in age-old traditions and strange superstitions? America has given hope and life to this nation in their newly acquired democracy.

Our very best to you, the family, and to all the readers of The Herald. We read the paper from "cover to cover" and enjoy it so much.

As ever,
Frances

Mrs. Frances Bartlett-Kinne
c/o Lt. Col. H. L. Kinne, Jr.
ATIS G2 GHQ FEC
APO 300, c/o Postmaster
San Francisco, Cal.

Imperial Hotel

Living at the Imperial Hotel in Tokyo had many advantages, and I was intrigued with the American Plains style of architecture superimposed on the Tokyo scene. Harry had grown up in a Frank Lloyd Wright house in Oak Park, Illinois and felt very much at home in our new surroundings.

The Arcade on the lower level of the Imperial was just beginning to get reestablished when we arrived. There was a natural constituency for providing shoppers, since General MacArthur's staff lived in the hotel. At one end was a Japanese Post Office, and even though we sent our mail through military channels, I was a frequent visitor. I was fascinated by the colorful stamps, and I showered my stateside father-in-law (a philatelist) with covers from Japan. I became acquainted with the postmaster, one of my first Japanese friends, and he graciously saved many new editions for me. Another of my friends was the elderly and famous Mikimoto who had a shop attracting Americans to the beautiful pearls.

As I made friends with other Japanese, I began to appreciate their aesthetic tastes. As a sensitive young woman who had been saturated with cultural opportunities, it seemed very natural to develop friendships through the arts. This was certainly true in the months I spent in China, as well as Japan and later in Germany. Certainly I began to recognize the many similarities people of various cultures do possess.

Later I would often observe to Harry, "If we could send enough students to foreign countries, and likewise host an equal number of foreign students in our country we would be much less likely to have wars." The arts truly break down barriers, as they provide an international language for us. In fact, one of Mother's favorite bromides was a Confucius quote: "When music and courtesy are better understood and appreciated, there will be no war."

Eager to learn more about the culture of Japan I enrolled in a flower-arranging class at a flower shop in the arcade. I knew little about growing flowers, but arranging flowers has always interested me.

Ike-Bana is a form of flower arranging in Japan, and I wanted to learn the intricacies of this art. But first it was necessary for me to deny my American tendencies to use a profusion of flowers in one vase. This was my first introduction to the understatement I was to discover, not only in flower arranging, but also in the lives and the homes of the Japanese. This was the underlying principle of my class in Ike-Bana.

Every arrangement I attempted must reflect "Heaven, Man, and Earth." The female style allowed me to use three separate twigs, branches or flowers, and the male style usually used a single plant or branch, with the part that looked upward called "Heaven." The branch or twigs which extended to the side symbolized "Man," and the very bottom branch, bent slightly upward, represented "Earth." Actually this is an oversimplification of Ike-Bana, as many instructional books have been written about the art, describing the intricacies and symbolism of the art of flower arranging.

After a series of lessons I presented my final arrangement to the instructor. I had used the female style with cherry blossoms, and I passed the test with "flying colors." I proudly carried my arrangement back to our room in the Imperial Hotel, and I waited for the final judgment from Harry. He walked into the room, gave me a welcome kiss, as I bowed low in anticipation of congratulations and appreciation from him. His eyes widened as he viewed my arrangement and said, "What in the world is that?" Spontaneously we both broke into laughter, and we never spoke of it again.

Of course, since the Imperial Hotel housed primarily military personnel, everything was administered by rank. Even the parking lot where our cars were kept followed this policy. Even though Harry at first was a Lieutenant Colonel, all officers there out-ranked him. As an officer was promoted or transferred, a parking space would often be available for bid.

As Harry was leaving for work one morning, he asked me to stop at the main desk and make a bid for a more desirable parking spot

Later, on the way to my volunteer teaching at Tsuda College, I stopped in the lobby, where several officers were waiting at the main desk. As I approached, the manager courteously asked if he could help me, and I inquired about the parking lot space which had become available. He handed me the papers to complete, and he offered to assist me.

"What is your husband's rank?" Thank goodness I knew the answer to that question. The next question, however, was one I couldn't possibly answer. "What is your husband's date of rank?" With an amazed look in his eyes, he remarked, "You mean that you do not know your husband's date of rank?" I was embarrassed.

The tall, handsome man standing beside me suddenly turned, put his arm around me and laughingly remarked, "I wish my wife did not know my date of rank." I looked up and saw two stars on his shoulder, broad smile on his face. He introduced himself as Major General Almond. It was later I learned he was General MacArthur's Chief of Staff.

When Harry returned late that afternoon we had a good laugh over the incident, and he assured me I did not need to learn his date of rank. And I never did.

Exploring a Tradition

"The best things in life are free and available." That had been one of the "words of wisdom" I learned at my father's knee. I didn't understand fully what he meant until our lives were caught up in different cultures. Since I had written to Uncle P.A. about Japan's "sacred mountain" I wanted to discover its magic.

I had always had a natural love for our own West, a leaning toward the terrain of the mountainous areas of our great country. Mother read aloud to my father from the adventure tales of our pioneers during the many years of Father's failing eyesight, and those often were my bedtime stories. Mother and Father both knew the best of literature, but they also were fascinated with the travails of the pioneers who settled our West. This surely must have piqued my interest as a child.

Harry and I fulfilled our desire to explore very facet of the Occupied country in which we lived, and Mt. Fuji must be one of the first of adventures. Our Japanese friends told us about the beautiful Mt. Fuji Hotel — Fujiyama, and we planned a weekend of discovery.

The weather was a balmy spring day, cherry blossoms in full bloom, as we found our way through the small village. The DeSoto convertible caused a stir as we drove slowly through the narrow streets, never meant for an American vehicle. As we made our way to higher elevation I was astounded at the mass of humanity — people everywhere — a strong contrast to our own West.

When we approached the Fujiyama Hotel the sun was setting, a roseate glow engulfing the mountain and us. We were to enjoy the sight for an entire weekend. Many Japanese make this trip in one day, however, and they were returning from their trip to the top, a sacred pilgrimage for them.

As we entered the driveway of the hotel we were greeted by young men bowing low in welcome. We were escorted to a beautiful suite, from which we had a panoramic view of Mt. Fuji. Wonders were to continue, for the dining room that evening provided a magnificent setting. As one always interested in sculpture, I found it difficult to concentrate on dinner when lovely and intricate wood-carvings were all around us. The waitress, attired in colorful kimono and obi, explained in broken English that, in the works of art, the years, days and hours would be reflected by the signs of the zodiac. These were readily recognizable in the wood carvings

framing the distinctive and elegant setting. This was a history lesson in itself!

On the same visit to the hotel I saw for the first time the giant, colorful gold-fish (carp) in a pond at the entrance. Later, one of my Japanese students explained the importance of the carp as a symbol of strength. He explained how his father would attach large, balloon carp to the roof on a pole, one for each boy in the family. This was done once a year in the celebration of the Boys' Festival. The symbolism reflected strength which was to be instilled in young boys by transferring the dominant spirit of the carp.

Public Baths

Perhaps the highlight of the hotel itself was the opportunity to experience the Japanese baths, similar to the historic Roman baths. We were told to select which room we wished to schedule, and we had the choice of all sizes and varieties. Our choice was a large room with a pool-sized bath, surrounded by foliage and fragrant flowers.

As we stepped into the heated pool, background music was playing softly — suitable music for relaxation. Many times in the stressful times of later years, memory of that exquisite peace has brought security for a brief moment.

It has also brought laughter, because neither Harry nor I would follow the rules of "sans bathing attire." We didn't trust the lock on the door.

Tea Ceremony and Benefit

It was gratifying to become acquainted with both faculty and students during my time at Tsuda College and DaiHachi Girls' School.

Some of my friends in the United States disapproved of my volunteer teaching, for to them Japan was still our enemy. And, of course, we were still in an Occupied country.

But it was difficult to look into the dark eyes of those lovely young girls and see anything evil. To me they were human beings and certainly had no part in or understanding of the atrocities Japan inflicted on our Prisoners of War.

Two of my students invited me to a Tea Ceremony, and I learned a great deal about the importance of the ritual and its religious influence.

With anticipation I met the young ladies, and we drove to the Tea House — similar to the one in "The Tea House of the August Moon."

We entered through a lovely garden and then into a small tea-ceremony house. My memory took me back to my freshman year in college, and a noble effort on the part of the Dean of Women to educate naive young women about the decorum of The Tea. I was to learn a very different and ancient custom that day in Tokyo, however, in the Japanese Tea House — a ceremony indelibly printed on my memory.

I watched carefully as each step was followed, almost as if the exactness of it all were the end in itself. As we sat on the floor on tatami mats, I observed the beauty of the lovely Japanese woman as she mixed the powdered green leaves of tea. I was surprised to find she provided a fresh bowl for each of us for each part of the ceremony, rinsing out the container with fresh water after each use.

During my three years in Japan, I attended other ceremonies much more formal. This, however, was my first exposure to Japanese green tea.

A visit to Kyoto, the summer palace of the Emperor, taught me much more about tea. This area was known for the quality of its tea, and in the eighth century tea was brought from China to this part of Japan. At that time it was used primarily for medicinal purposes.

I find it fascinating that many centuries later we now are beginning to recognize the value of the chemical ingredients of green tea. But no matter where or when I drink any kind of tea, my appreciation is much greater because of my life in the Far East.

(above) General MacArthur and staff at Inchon Landing in the Korean War.

Harry and his DeSoto in Tokyo.

Chapter Eight:
Father's Cancer, Korea and Changes

One of the joys of the military life is the bonding — friendships that develop over a period of years when assignments bring couples together who have served in the same locations.

Col. Jay and Mary Dasche were married at Fort Leavenworth at approximately the same time as we. We were together in China and Japan and again in Germany — living through a hectic time in the history of the world. Even though we were in different cities they provided great support and companionship in the changing pattern of our lives.

Father's Cancer

When I received word Father's cancer was terminal, I wanted to leave Tokyo to be with him. But the military policy at the time was that no dependents could be flown back to the States without Red Cross approval, and the Red Cross didn't approve my request because "There is no point. He would die before you could get there."

This was not acceptable to me or to Harry (who found out the Army Bowling Team had higher "priority" for flights to the U.S. than did dependents).

Gen. MacArthur, fortunately, assured Harry that I would receive the highest priority to return to the states. In fact, his exact words were, "Get Fran whatever she needs to get to her father's side."

I was a passenger on a military flight from Tokyo to Guam to Kwajalein to Johnston Island to San Francisco to Omaha.

There was no flight from Omaha to Des Moines, so I took the train — now into my third day and night without sleep. It was 3 a.m. and I was afraid if I fell asleep I would miss my stop in Des Moines.

A soldier sitting near me, aware of my situation, told me to go to sleep for a couple hours and he would awaken me when the train arrived in Des Moines. I accepted. And he did.

Fran's father in 1950 just before his death

I did get to the hospital in time to be with Father before he died. He couldn't speak. But he was able to smile to show me he recognized I was with him. What a great man he was, and too young at 75 to leave us.

Korean War

Mother accompanied me to San Francisco for my return by ship to Tokyo. While at the port, waiting to board ship, I learned of the announcement of the official beginning of the Korean War, and there were to be "no departures of dependents to the Far East."

I was devastated, and kept asking everyone, "Who is the Port Commander?" I soon found out the Port Commander was General Lester. I made an appointment to see him. At first he was confused and thought I was Col. Kinne's daughter.

I was persistent — perhaps there was a tear in my eye. General Lester told me there was a troop ship, actually a President's Line passenger ship, with 1200-2000 servicemen leaving shortly. But "no dependents" was the policy.

I pointed out to the General that I could play the piano to entertain the troops, and could assist musically with church services. "What about troop morale?" I added.

"We haven't had time to think about morale," General Lester responded.

My persistence paid off — and $800 probably helped secure my passage. "Please let my husband know I'm on my way," were my last words to the General.

And I entertained 2,000 troops for 21 days as we did a zig-zag across the north Pacific in order to avoid submarines. I couldn't wait to get back to Harry and the Imperial Hotel.

That is the "inside" story of what happened. My letter to Uncle P.A. relates in greater detail the pressure of the times.

"Frances Bartlett-Kinne Writes From Tokyo"
Tokyo, Japan — January 29, 1951

Dear Uncle P.A.:

My return to the Orient six months ago plunged me into a cauldron of activity which has really accelerated daily. Correspondence has been sadly neglected — necessarily so.

On arrival in San Francisco from Iowa last July, I was met with the startling announcement that all dependent travel to the Far East had been canceled. Only by a mere stroke of chance was I allowed to purchase a ticket on a President liner, already crowded with troops and ready to sail. The rails of the ship were lined with G.I.s in full battle gear - the majority of them young, fresh troops bantering and chiding one another, but the faces of the men whose uniforms boasted combat ribbons were grim and grave.

Unfortunately, the liner had not had sufficient time to prepare for its unexpected passengers and the recreational equipment aboard the ship was entirely inadequate - a few magazines and a snack bar. The demands of troops going to combat are few, but we know from experience that they must be kept busy. There were several missionaries who conducted religious serices and activities, and a volunteer group of talented and cooperative officers organized variety shows which we presented every evening. (Incidentally, we taught "We're from Ioway" to everyone on the ship.)

I had been back in Tokyo but a few days when Harry was sent to Formosa as a member of General MacArthur's Mission. I spent every afternoon and evening of the next month playing the piano for the wounded men in our Tokyo hospitals. I spoke with hundreds and hundreds of wounded, and I was impressed with the fact that they didn't feel that they had been involved in a "police action," but rather in an honest to goodness war.

The Universal Language

I recall playing the piano one day for American, British, Swedish, Turkish, South African and Philippine troops — all in one ward, and such gibberish of tongues I had never heard. They all seemed to love music, the international language.

About that time I turned all my efforts toward my war-time field, and I returned to Special Services as Director of Music and Assistant Entertainment Director for the Far East Command - Japan, Korea, Guam, Philippine Islands and Okinawa. I am grateful to be able to be of service and to have the opportunity of being back in my blue uniform again.

Back in Service

Since I accepted a position, I have had to give up my volunteer teaching, and I have missed my contacts with the Japanese people. However, they do visit me frequently. One of my former English students, a brilliant, middle-aged, political leader recently returned from America where she had studied American life and custom. She came to see me, starry-eyed over what she had seen. She seemed most impressed with the graciousness and kindness of the American people — all of them, rich and poor. She had been welcomed in Congress, the United Nations, in city and farm homes all over the country. Naturally, the place of women in American society was almost unbelievable to her. She was pleased to note the willingness of the American women to invite the Japanese women to share their homes and offer the use of their automobiles. In Japan the woman does not have the prerogative. She observed, too, that in America such a large proportion of older women are employed, whereas in Japan they must depend on families for support. She was amazed at the cleanliness evidenced everywhere in homes and cities, and, of course it was obvious to me why this should be one of her observations. Her over-all impression was that never had she seen a land or a people blessed with so much.

There have been pleasant reunions for us the past months. Thanksgiving dinner we shared with Dr. Stalnaker from Drake (who has since returned to Des Moines) and John Bartlett, our cousin from Oklahoma, who is stationed near Tokyo. The following week we enjoyed an evening with Lt.Col. Marion Johnson of Story City, a fine person and splendid officer. We are all anticipating the day when our reunions will be on the other side of the Pacific Ocean. May that day come soon.

Belated but blessed wishes for a Happy New Year to our relatives and friends.

Frances Bartlett Kinne
Address: Colonel and Mrs. H. L. Kinne, Jr.
G3—GHQ—FEC
APO 500 c/o Postmaster
San Francisco, California

— <u>The Story City Herald</u>, February 15, 1951

Chapter Nine:
From Walter Reed Hospital
to Ft. Bragg, North Carloina

Our three years in China and Japan had been life-enriching, but they had also brought many changes Stateside. Harry's mother had passed away, and his father had remarried. I had lost my father, and in a sense we had a feeling the world had passed us by for those three years. Troubling was the Chinese fever Harry had very likely picked up in Formosa.

For this reason we spent a month at Walter Reed Hospital where a number of different treatments were attempted. It wasn't at all comforting when the specialist informed us there were over 2000 kinds of Oriental fevers, and the solution was to let this one "just wear off." One treatment resulted in fine hair growing on the top of Harry's shiny head. He suggested

(tongue in cheek) that he and the doctor should collaborate in discovering a cure for baldness. The doctor wasn't amused, but he discharged Harry so that we could proceed to a nine month assignment at the Armed Forces Staff College in Norfolk.

Housing was difficult in Norfolk and at the Naval Base. Priority was given to couples with children, but we were just happy to be in the U.S. and went house-hunting. We finally found a new duplex and rented the second floor.

The faithful piano, now safely arrived from Japan, was squeezed up those stairs, and I composed a song about my well-traveled piano. By this time it was part of our family. If it could have talked it prob-

ably would have said, "That crazy woman keeps hauling me back and forth across oceans, mountains and rivers. How in the world does she expect me to stay in tune? I wish she'd stay in one spot."

And I learned how to cook! Three years of living first with a Chinese chef and then the gourmet dining at the Imperial Hotel inspired me.

The very first evening in our upstairs duplex we had a guest. Harry called me to tell me that Brig.Gen. Stan Malloy had just returned from Korea, was in town for 24 hours, and it was his birthday.

Since we had no furniture except a bed, piano, card table and two

Chuck entertains Fran in San Diego on her return (with Harry) from the Far East.

chairs, this was presenting a challenge. I felt much as I did at the age of five, standing on the edge of the high diving board at Lake Comar, trying to decide if I had nerve enough to try it.

There were no deli's to rescue me, and I decided if I managed that dive at 5, I certainly could cook a meal for a General.

What an adventure developed. Yes, I prepared a beef roast, a potato dish, and I baked a cake "from scratch." I borrowed a chair from the occupants of the first floor, dashed to the market for fresh flowers and candles. Stan Malloy arrived for his birthday dinner and the very first meal I ever prepared.

It was a celebration in another sense, as he escaped from the Communist onslaught in Korea by swimming the Yalu River, and this was his return home.

A year later he visited us at our next assignment in Fort Bragg and said, "You will never know how much it meant to me to arrive to a home-cooked dinner. It was delicious, but this is even more so." He was being very gracious, as I recalled how difficult it was to get everything timed to come out at the same time. It still is!

Upon graduation from the Armed Forces Staff College we were assigned to Fort Bragg, North Carolina, where Harry was a member of the Joint Tactical Air Support Board.

It was while assigned to Fort Bragg that the fateful flights to White Sands "Frenchmen's Flat" in Nevada occurred — where Harry and others (including my second husband) were observers at the test atomic drops, and also where they were exposed to radiation, a later tragic development for each of them.

The three years at Fort Bragg were interesting years for me. We were assigned a large three-story Post house, and we found ourselves entertaining at weekly dinner parties. By this time I had learned how to cook. That was fortunate, since our dining room seated 24 guests, and the many guest rooms were usually occupied.

I saved time to teach my twenty-some piano students, as well as do the programs for the Officers Wives' Club, and direct a choral group.

I planned a celebrity North Carolina year for the Club, scheduling Inglis Fletcher, Pulitzer Prize-winning author of the Carolina Series. Our friendship developed, and she invited Harry and me to visit her at the historic Bandon Plantation at Edenton, N.C.

North Carolina had a superb state magazine, edited by Carl Goerch, and I was determined to schedule this colorful speaker for our program series. His fee was $300 — and we had no funds for speakers. He explained he could fly his own plane from Raleigh to Fort Bragg, but he needed the fee to do so. I continued to call him, and he finally agreed to speak and contribute his services.

The appointed day arrived, and Carl Goerch "wowed" his audience, as I knew he would. A month later he sent me a copy of the magazine with the back cover and an amusing editorial by him:

Mother and Harry at home at Fort Bragg.

Funny Experiences
— by Carl Goerch

I'm looking forward very much to meeting Mrs. Frances Kinney. (Or maybe it's Kenney. Thus far I've only talked to her over the phone.)

Mrs. Kinney wrote me a letter a month or so ago, asking if I could come down to Fort Bragg and speak at a luncheon of officers' wives.

During the last several years I've put my speaking engagements on a sort of commercial basis. I charged a fee, the amount depending on the distance to be traveled. I felt that this was only fair because it's quite a strain to drive a hundred miles or more, especially when the return trip has to be made late at night, and sometimes through rain or fog.

Knowing that the organization to which Mrs. Kinney referred probably didn't have any funds for a purpose of this kind, I wrote her that I was just as sorry as I could be, but I already had so many engagements that it would be impossible to accept her very kind invitation.

That ended that.

Not for long, however.

Two weeks later my secretary told me that Fort Bragg was calling.

"Is that you, Mr. Goerch?"

"Yes it is."

"This is Frances Kinney at Fort Bragg. It's so nice to talk to you, Mr. Goerch."

"Thank you, Mrs. Kinney."

"You have such a wonderful voice. I get a real thrill out of listening to you on the radio."

"That's awfully nice of you, Mrs. Kinney"

"I received your letter and all the ladies are so distressed! You don't know how popular you are down here, Mr. Goerch. So many of our members tell me that they never miss a single one of your Sunday-night programs. You tell us so many interesting things."

"Glad you think so."

"But it's true, Mr. Goerch. When I delivered your message I don't believe I ever have heard so many expressions of regret."

"Well, it's like this, Mrs. Kinney. Most of my talks are made to civic groups or at some big industrial meeting, and I charge a certain fee for taking these trips. I felt that it would be an imposition to charge your group and that was my real reason for declining."

"That's perfectly all right. Of course we'd expect to pay you for coming down here. When I told our members that I was going to call you up they were thrilled to death. Right now I know they're just as excited as they can be, hoping to receive a favorable answer. And Mr. Goerch, they'll be so disappointed if I have to tell them you can't come."

I thought I detected an indication of tears in her voice. Anyway, it trembled just a little.

"Well-" I began.

But she didn't let me finish. "It'll be the happiest day they've known in a long time when I tell them you have accepted our invitation," she stated.

"Well—" I said again. "When would you want me to come? I'm pretty well booked up during December."

"How about in January?"

That gave me a definite out. "That's just too bad," I told her. "You see, beginning with January 5, I expect to have my regular assignment of broadcasting the Doings of the Legislature. This prevents me from making any trips out of town until after the General Assembly has adjourned. I'm just as sorry as I can be, but that's how it is."

"But ours is a luncheon meeting, and you broadcast in the evening."

"That's true, but I have to be up in the capitol all day long in order to gather material for the broadcast." This time I was sure I detected signs of tears. "Oh, Mr. Goerch, I'm so sorry. If you just knew how badly these women wanted to see and hear you. They've been wanting you to come to Fort Bragg and make one of your wonderful talks for the last two years. I just know they'll blame me when I tell them you can't come."

I did some quick thinking. "Wait a minute, Mrs. Kinney. The legislature doesn't meet on Mondays: not until Monday night. If yours is a luncheon meeting, maybe I could fly down to Fort Bragg, attend your meeting and then get back to Raleigh in time to get up my broadcast for that evening."

"W-o-n-d-e-r-f-u-l! Oh, I can't begin to tell you how happy you have made me feel, Mr. Goerch. I think you're the n-i-c-e-s-t man! And I know our members will just scream with delight when I tell them. They'll be so excited! We won't be able to talk about anything else until you get down here to our meeting."

"Glad that we were able to reach an agreement, Mrs. Kinney. I'm looking forward to the occasion very much."

"And so are all of us."

"Just one more thing, Mrs. Kinney: there'll be no fee in connection with this engagement."

"Oooooh: marvelous! You're so sweet!"

I came within an inch of asking her if her organization needed any funds — that I'd be glad to contribute a little something — but she hung up before I had a chance to do so.

What a magazine saleswoman Mrs. Kinney would make!

Of course he spelled my name wrong, but he sent me $300 after he returned home — "for future speakers," he said. Also, he arranged for Gov. Luther Hodges to make Harry and me Honorary Citizens of North Carolina, the ceremony at a special Monday night meeting of the Legislature.

Opportunities for the Hunter

Fort Bragg provided splendid hunting opportunities for Harry, and our two bird-dogs were the ideal pair — a pointer and a setter. They lived in luxury in a duplex house built for them and surrounded by a fence. However, they had the bad habit of howling when the chapel bells (near our home) rang out the hours of the clock and played a little melody as well.

Often I thought I was married to Daniel Boone, for Harry was completely at home in the wilderness and with animals (actually he was equally at home in the Grand Ballroom of the Imperial Hotel). So he had no problem rigging up a crazy contraption to control the howling dogs.

We slept on the large sleeping porch on the second floor with windows encircling the porch. Harry bought a long hose and put a funnel at each end, leaving one end by his pillow. He then strung the hose through the window and down to the dogs' duplex in the yard, hanging the end with the funnel where the dogs would hear their master's voice. It worked.

When Harry brought back his dove and quail after a successful shoot I remarked, "Don't you feel sorry? How could you possibly shoot these little birds?"

Of course, I couldn't shoot anything, but I was eager to accompany him when he hunted the wild turkey, and Harry agreed to take me on the opening day of the season - if I would "be real quiet."

Since we were going to spend a week-end in New York, Harry suggested I go to Abercrombie and Fitch to get outfitted for a hunt. When the salesman asked me what I needed, I felt much as I did at the desk of the Imperial Hotel when the clerk asked for Harry's date of rank. And I wished Harry hadn't slipped off to see his brother, Bud, whose office was in the Empire State Building.

"Never mind," the salesman assured me. The next thing I knew I was wearing jodhpur breeches, boots and a safari hat, and I thought I looked pretty snappy for a girl from Iowa. I decided not to show my outfit to Harry until that Thanksgiving morning we would pursue the beautiful bird. That was a mistake.

The morning arrived and pre-dawn dressing prepared me for the grand entrance at 5:00 a.m. at breakfast.

Indeed, it was an entrance. Harry took one look at me and said, "Where in the world do you think you're going in that outfit?!" Before I could blame the salesman, I was taken by the hand, up the stairs to our room.

Harry brought out a pair of old khaki pants with leather knee caps, a camouflage shirt, jacket and cap. Then he instructed me to leave the pants legs over the boots. "Never tuck them in," he said. "Snakes have a more difficult target."

I looked at myself in the mirror as I held back the tears. My image was so ludicrous (nothing fit), and suddenly we both laughed. Harry, the seasoned hunter, realized his momentary lapse of diplomacy.

It didn't help much when my Cavalry Officer husband added, "Oh, we'll save the outfit for when we go riding." (Ouch! The only time I had ever been on a horse was when at the age of 12 a dear friend of mine lifted me up to sit on his horse, Geso.)

I remained silent, for I knew the new clothes would hang at the back of the closet, never again to see the light of day!

In 1953, Sinju and Chen Meng Hsiao were sent back to Washington, D.C. and we had a memorable visit with them – as recorded in my letter to Uncle P.A.

Fort Bragg, N.C.
March 21, 1953

Dear Uncle P.A.,

Harry and I just returned from several days with Sinju and Chen Meng in Washington, D.C.. It was a splendid reunion for us, as we had not seen them since we were evacuated from China. They expressed sadness over Father's death, and they asked to be remembered to Mother and you.

Sinju is a Major General and is the Military Attache for the Nationalist Army. Of course, you know he has been the Generalissimo's aide in Formosa.

We were invited to the Chinese Embassy by Ambassador and Madame Wellington Koo for a reception for five visiting Generals. One was Chiang Wego, the second son of Chiang Kai Shek, and a good friend of ours. Harry and he had worked together in Formosa when General MacArthur sent his seventeen man mission to map the defense of the island. Harry and Chiang Wego were both Armored officers and spoke a common language.

At the reception, we met the Cabinet leaders as well as many members of Congress, and the Ambassador and his wife were gracious in welcoming Harry and me. I wore a burgundy velvet dress with a matching hat, which brought this comment from Senator Joseph McCarthy, "Wow, that's a stunning outfit."

After the reception Sinju and Chen Meng had a dinner for Chiang Wego and us at the lovely home of the Hsiao's. With big band music as accompaniment Chiang asked me to dance. He spoke wistfully about leaving the mainland of China, and his parting comment to me was, "We shall meet again – the next time on the Mainland." It was never to be.

I have written some details to Mother. You and she might enjoy exchanging letters.

Love and our best,

Danny

Chiang Kai Shek's son,
Chiang Wego.

Heidelberg in the retracing of the path Harry's
781st Tank Battilion took in World War II.

Chapter Ten:
Germany, the Occupation and a Ph.D

Germany developed into a remarkable assignment for both Harry and me: two Commands for him, and my doctorate for me.

After World II the Allies divided Germany for the purpose of restoration and control during the Occupation, and Harry and I had the unusual experience of being a part of our second Occupation — and living in Frankfurt.

Frankfurt am Main is a great city in the heart of Europe, and it was our home at a historic period in our world's history. By the time we arrived in 1955 some restoration had been initiated, and certainly the American sector showed greater progress than those sectors controlled by the Allies.

History teaches us that throughout the ages Germany has often experienced devastation and major destruction. In spite of this it seemed to me at every turn was another castle, a cathedral, rolling countryside and charming villages.

The Headquarters of Harry's 4th Armor Group was at Gibbs Kaserne on the edge of Frankfurt. The six battalions of the Group were located at strategic locations throughout Germany, since the Cold War was at its peak, and the border between East and West Germany was a hot line of controversy. How ironic in our assignment in conquered Germany to have as a major security concern, Russia - supposedly our ally.

Prior to assuming his Command, Harry and I retraced the path he and his 781st Tank Battalion had fought during World War II. He was the only Armored Commander to activate, train, go overseas, command the unit in combat, return to the U.S., and inactivate the Battalion. So when he and I arrived it was in his heart to recapture, even for a brief time, the bravery of his GIs, those who survived, and especially for those who died for freedom.

I knew the history of the 781st Tank Battalion - its remarkable record in combat. Prior to their deployment overseas they spent time at Fort Knox testing tanks and other equipment. Their most significant task was assisting in the development of the General Sherman M4A3 medium tank.

Because they had reviewed the combat reports from North Africa, the Armored experts determined that the Army must have a better medium tank than the General Grant. Day and night Harry's battalion tested the vari-

781st Tank Batillion in village they captured in WWII.

The Colonel in his tank.

A separate battalion in combat was called upon to support different units, and at one time the 781st supported five different divisions — including the famous "Battered Bastards of Bastogne," the 101st Airborne Division. In fact, it was Harry's association with General Anthony McAuliffe that changed Harry from a Reserve officer to Regular Army.

As the 781st fought its way across France and through Germany, they liberated those prisoners still alive in a concentration camp at Landsberg. This was particularly meaningful to Harry since his brother was a Prisoner of War in Rumania - later to be liberated.

The Alps were next, and there were brief stops with little combat in Oberammergau and the beautiful Garmisch-Partenkirchen - where they weathered a five-day blizzard. Then it was on through the Alps and Brenner Pass - the first tanks in the history of war to do so.

While they were winding their circuitous route, scaling narrow roads between perilous peaks, Harry was concerned because the tanks weren't keeping a safe distance from one another. In the cold clear crispness of the night he drove his jeep, weaving along and between the tanks to warn the drivers. As he passed he heard the voice of one G.I. saying, "Was that Hairless Harry that just went by?"

It amused Harry, and he took it as a compliment, for he realized what they might have said!

And so it was in 1955, I joined Harry in following the path he and his 781st Tank Battalion had taken in WWII. He chose to buy a wine glass in each town they had captured — and during Harry's lifetime those glasses were hallowed in our household.

When we reached Heidelberg, Harry told me about the close call he experienced as he and his jeep driver, under heavy machine gun fire, zig-zagged across a very large field. We found the field, but it was obvious the field grew larger each year in Harry's memory. As

ous tanks, and it was determined the General Sherman with the V-type eight cylinder Ford engine was the right one for mass production. And the 781st found it was the correct decision in their assault on the Maginot and Siegfried Lines — even more, in the subsequent race through Germany and into Austria.

(above) Siegfried Line.
(right) Hitler's Bunker.
(far right) Harry's unit
in combat in WWII.

we parked our car to take a photograph, his comment was, "I can't believe how small that field is now!"

I am pleased I could share those experiences with Harry. When we stopped to pay our respects at a location where he had lost men and/or tanks, I had a deeper understanding of the horrors of war. And I certainly had a clearer understanding when Harry would explain to me, "The military man wants peace. After all, he's the one who has the most to lose in war."

Dachau

Harry insisted I visit Dachau, although it was against my wishes. He felt it was vitally important for me to witness first hand evidence of the atrocities against the Jews, so that I, as an educator, would enlighten all the students with whom I came into contact.

The horror of what I saw was devastating.

Earning A Ph.D

I had attempted in China and Japan to initiate my doctoral studies, but circumstances never allowed me to complete my plans. I had contacted Stanford University prior to sailing for China. They were eager to have me utilize this unique opportunity to study the presence of music of the West as opposed to the traditional Chinese music.

Our friend, Sinju Pu Hsiao had made appropriate contacts so that I could lecture and study at the same time. However, the evacuation ended that dream, but undaunted I pursued it again in Japan. My volunteer teaching and the Korean War again placed obstacles in my way.

The Colonel on Armed Forces Network Radio.

Second German Assignment for Harry

When Harry completed his assignment as Commanding Officer of the 4th Armor Group, the Commanding General in Europe was aware of the importance of my studies since I was the only American student in a German university. Harry wanted me to complete my doctorate in Germany. And the various Generals were in complete support — Hart, Van Brunt, Farrell, Adams, Bell and Hodes. I had won a bet from General Hank Hodes at tank maneuvers Harry was running at Belsen-Hohne, scene of one of WWII Concentration Camps. Gen. Hodes bet me a dollar all the tanks wouldn't start. I won.

So Harry was offered and accepted his assignment as Commanding Officer of the Frankfurt Sub Area of the Northern Area Command in Germany — where he literally became the American Mayor of that section of Germany.

Graduation, Frankfurt Nursery School, 1957. Col. Harry Kinne congratulates Robert Porter, Jr., son of Robert W. Porter, Commanding General, 3rd Armored Div., Frankfurt, Germany.

There were never enough hours in the day or night, and between the two of us we tried to cover all bases. Certainly we had an interesting and challenging assignment, and one we both relished.

Harry's duties involved everything from German-American relations to shaking the tiny chocolate-smeared hands of kindergarten youngsters receiving their diplomas.

For me it was speaking, playing the piano for programs, still attending classes, reorganizing German clubs, and cutting the ribbon on the stage of the new Frankfurt Theater. This was the first American stage in Europe, a project of special symbolic interest to English-speaking people. In fact, a silver cigarette lighter was presented to me in appreciation for my efforts. (Obviously they didn't realize this was all second nature for me!)

Third Try is a Charm

Now in Germany was the third doctoral attempt, this time successful. And from this adventure came lasting and very special friendships with three remarkable, internationally recognized professors.

Obviously our initial association was academic in nature, but eventually, these gentlemen and their wives emboldened me to the extent I knew I could accomplish what seemed impossible.

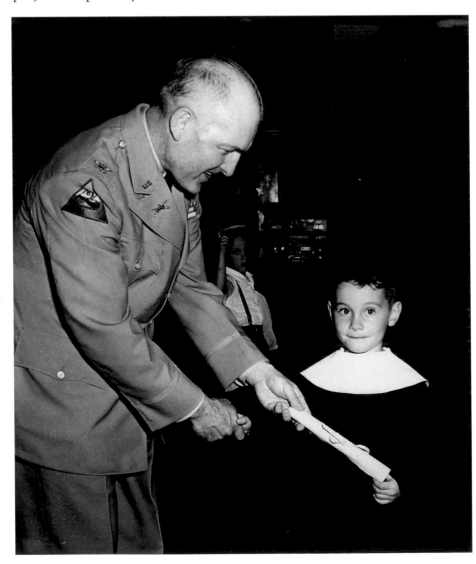

They entered my life at the point when I had been pushed out of line repeatedly when I tried to register. It seemed I encountered one obstacle after the other, since I was the only American. One evening I drove home in tears, and an older, wiser husband met me with understanding. He encircled me in his arms, explaining the fact that every family member in Frankfurt had lost a loved one, and very likely a home in the bombing.

The support Harry provided gave me the courage to return, but the hurdles were to continue. The first barrier was presented when I registered for the classes, and the professor of one course I was required to take told me he didn't want an American in his class. Again Harry came to my rescue after more tears on my part. This time we made an appointment to meet the Rektor (President), and Harry accompanied me.

The Rektor was very sympathetic and suggested I take the course the following year, since the professor was retiring at the close of the current year. And it was the Rektor who arranged for me to meet three gentlemen who were to play a significant role in my life.

One of them was Prof. Dr. Max Horkheimer, who will be remembered as one of the great philosophers and sociologists of the 20th Century. I cherish the time I had studying with him.

In 1931 he had become Director of the Institute for Social Research in Frankfurt. He saw the political problems as they started to develop, and later emigrated to the United States, becoming the Director of the Institute of Social Research at Columbia University. After World War II our govern-

(above) Col. Kinne at parade review.
(left) Fran in a gondola in Venice.
(below) Col. Kinne, now American Mayor of the Frankfurt sector of Occupied Germany, awards Letter of Appreciation to Germans for leading German — American relations. (l-r) Herr Rudi Gramlich, Frau Norgall, Col. Kinne, Mrs. Gramlich, Fran, Countess Zedtwitz and Count Zedtwitz.

ment sent him back to Germany to reestablish the Institute at the University of Frankfurt, while he continued to hold Chairs at both Columbia and the University of Chicago.

This man was the giant of philosophy with whom I had the privilege to study in both the classroom as well as in a one-on-one relationship.

His classes were very popular and it was necessary to arrive at his class at least an hour early or there would be no chairs. On several occasions I found myself seated on the floor or sharing a window sill with other students.

The very first day I wore my usual bright colors, driving my sapphire blue Buick hard-top convertible to the University. I was met by the cry of "Ami ("American"), go home."

From that day on I parked several blocks distant from the bombed out building in which we met, and I wore drab colors matching those of my classmates. The department stores were devoid of colorful merchandise, and in 1955 there was little opportunity for selection of clothes. I should have been more sensitive to this in my first day of classes, and I learned my lesson.

Prof. Horkheimer was internationally recognized for his writings in the periodicals for social research. However, at that early stage in our friendship I recognized his ability as a master teacher of philosophy. Later conversations indicated his support for the democratic process established during the Occupation which was still in effect.

Harry and Fran in Germany at the 4th Armor Group Ball.

The first several months presented a German vocabulary challenge. I had sung German (with what I learned was poor pronunciation); however, my speaking and reading ability was minimal. The only answer was a tutor, and retired Dr. Berthold Cron came to my rescue. He was the original "man who came to dinner." A sensitive, fatherly gentleman, he took me under his wing.

Before Dr. Cron adopted me as his personal project I made some

foolish and amusing errors, probably more than I realize even now. On one occasion I appeared for classes, and there was no one in the building. Bewildered I checked my watch, wandering around the corridor that still showed the effects of the bombs our Air Force dropped on Frankfurt near the close of the conflict.

Relieved, I heard the click of heels in the hallway, and a distinguished appearing gentleman said, "Darf ich sie helfen?" (May I help you?) When I queried where everyone was, he politely covered a smile to inform me that this was a holiday.

I discovered the University observed both Catholic and Protestant holidays, as well as government designated days. And I made the most of those precious days to do my studying and necessary entertaining.

My Vater Doktor (advisor) was Prof. Dr. Helmut Viebrock, a brilliant Shakespeare scholar, who later became Rektor of the University. He had been a young translator and interpreter at the close of WWII, having studied earlier in the United States. Our first communication developed because he enjoyed contemporary, popular music — was a Cole Porter fan. He seemed to be astounded that I knew Shakespeare, and was quite amused when I explained how I was "captured" by the bard.

When I was graduated from Story City High School my parents presented me with a complete set of Shakespeare. It was a brilliant move on their part, hardly appreciated by me at the age of 16. One of my favorite musical works at that romantic time was Tchaikovsky's "Romeo and Juliet," and my father wisely suggested I should read the play and see if I could find a relationship. I was aware that Shakespeare recognized the importance of music, as reflected so often in the dialogues of his characters. In "The Merchant of Venice" two lovers are gazing at the star-studded universe and Lorenzo says:

The man that hath no music in himself,
Nor is not mov'd with concord of sweet sounds,
Is fit for treasons, strategems, and spoils...

When I related this story to Prof. Viebrock I noted a special twinkle in his eye as he responded, "And did you? Find a relationship, I mean?"

Each class with this master professor

was a gem — a polished, exquisite experience. It was quite amazing how my study of Shakespeare seemed to blend with Kant, Descartes, Schopenhauer and all philosophy. How could a writer in the 16th century be so relevant today? And Viebrock brought it all to life.

"The Tempest" fascinated me in man's struggle with life — Ariel representing the blithe spirit, Caliban as evil, and Prospero with reason to provide balance. And "Troilus and Cressida" was an exciting introduction to the many works of literature about these two colorful figures. It was "The Tempest" that entered my life several times years later.

As the months passed, Prof. Viebrock and I had become good friends, and the Horkheimers would often join us for a party of six. Rosi Viebrock was a gifted artist, and Maidon Horkheimer "mothered" all of us.

One evening is indelibly printed in my

Fran at the Palmengarten in Frankfurt.

Occupancy currency.

memory, and I cherish each precious moment of it. Harry and I hosted a dinner party at our home, and after a relaxed meal Prof. Viebrock said, "Let's do Shakespeare. I shall recite, and you will

improvise at your beautiful Steinway grand piano, Frances." (Only he pronounced it "Fraunces.")

The professors knew about my wondrous piano which had been made especially for me.

The Steinways were friends of Harry and his family when they lived near one another in Mountain Lakes, N.J. When we received orders to Germany, Harry contacted Charles Steinway, and arrangements were made for ordering my piano.

We met with the representative in Frankfurt, the ebony wood was selected, and my touch was checked to determine the action of the piano. Nine months later, the exquisite instrument arrived. And now I would be improvising on this very special Steinway.

It seemed so natural then, and I gave no thought to the fact a great philosopher was the audience, and I was accompanying a world-renowned Shakespeare scholar. I credit my parents with giving me that confidence, but I must admit, I was humbled by this experience. And as the years have passed, I recognize my angel was perched on my shoulder, whispering in my ear what I should do. I doubt I would have known otherwise.

Shortly thereafter Prof. Viebrock informed me that many of his students were going to present Thornton Wilder's "Our Town," and Wilder himself would attend and receive an award. Viebrock's request that Harry and I host a reception was quickly affirmed, and excitement mounted as plans developed.

Royal Ancient Clubhouse, St. Andrews. (inset) The Colonel at St. Andrews.

It was difficult in the late Fifties for Germans to buy bourbon, Scotch, etc. They had ample wine and beer, but Viebrock wanted (as he said) "a real cocktail party." Of course, this was no problem for us as Americans, as we had our own sources of food and beverages.

The evening arrived, and at the performance Harry and I sat on one side of Wilder with Viebrock on the other. It didn't seem at all strange to see and hear "Our Town" in German, and Wilder was pleased with the dramatic presentation.

Many years later I recounted this story to Aaron Copland who composed the music for the movie version of "Our Town" and won an Academy Award for it. Copland's laughing response was, "I would have had to do a German polka for that performance."

Both Horkheimer and Viebrock were the epitome of what a genuine teacher should be, and I know they inspired me in the great adventure of learning, much as my parents had done.

In the selection of my doctoral thesis I was determined to explore areas of folk ballads, but I needed to convince the doctoral committee that America actually had indigenous ballads. I had always felt too little emphasis had been placed on the indigenous ballads of the United States. In fact, in many instances they had not been given the dignity of recognition as a field of oral literature.

The study of balladry is a fascinating and sometimes

(above) Arriving in Venice.
(right) Cathedral Milan.

controversial field, and perhaps this is why the doctoral committee finally approved my thesis subject: <u>A Comparative Study of British Traditional Ballads and American Indigenous Ballads</u>. What fun I had tracing the development of characteristic traits from the older field of balladry to the later form in the New World.

And so for three years I was immersed in analyzing (and performing) "Sir Patrick Spens," "Robin Hood," "Johnnie Armstrong," "Lord Randal," and "Tam Lin" from the British ballads. And from the American ballads, "Lovewell's Fight," "Paul Jones," "Jesse James," "John Henry," "Frankie and Albert," and many others.

I wonder what my grandmother would have thought had she realized the spark she kindled in me. It was those Norwegian ballads she sang to me that started it all.

Preparing for my orals came after my thesis was accepted and published in book form. I was informed I was to spend a day with each of my three professors, with a Beizitzer in the room. His presence was to insure fairness for the professor and for me. I was instructed to wear a high-necked black dress and to appear each day at 9:00 a.m. to be questioned in German: the first day it was English Literature, primarily Shakespeare; the second day it was Music History; the third day it was Philosophy. After those grueling days, any future exams would appear simple.

I did feel as if I were carrying the American flag on my shoulders. I dare not fail. And when the news came that I had passed Cum Laude, the first American woman since World War II, I

(left) Mozart's birthplace in Salzburg.
(below) Fran at Leaning Tower of Pisa.

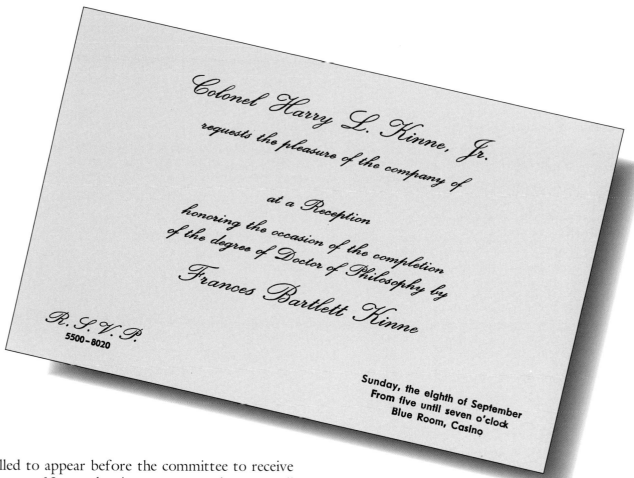

Colonel Harry L. Kinne, Jr.

requests the pleasure of the company of

at a Reception

*honoring the occasion of the completion
of the degree of Doctor of Philosophy by*

Frances Bartlett Kinne

R. S. V. P.
5500-8020

Sunday, the eighth of September
From five until seven o'clock
Blue Room, Casino

was called to appear before the committee to receive my degree. No graduation ceremony, but a small group of professors sitting around a long table.

As I walked in the room I had mixed feelings — joy and relief, but frightened at the austere faces I saw before me.

The Dekan (Dean) read the doctorate in Latin and then handed me my diploma presented in German. It read:

Die Philosophische Fakultat Der Johann Wolfgang Goethe Universitat
Frau Frances Bartlett Kinne
Aus
Story City, Iowa, USA
Den Grad eines
Doktors der Philosophie

The "Story City, Iowa" stood out as I looked at my diploma. This was seven years after I had flown those long hours and never-ending miles to reach my father on his death-bed. I felt the presence of both my father and mother on that special day.

The hours following the ceremony are dream-like. Prof. Horkheimer later told me he watched me descend the staircase after receiving my diploma, and that I gave the appearance of a frightened fawn. Indeed, I was!

There was a flurry of publicity about my doctorate. The Frankfurt papers gave it extensive coverage, as did the Armed Forces publication of The Army Air Force Journal. What surprised me, it was carried in the New York Times and many Stateside papers.

One reporter queried, "Now what are your plans?" My immediate answer was, "I know I'll never open another book."

Harry was much wiser in his contribution: "I'll give her two weeks." That was right. And he hosted an elegant party for me which was attended by both Germans and Americans. One of the papers wrote, "The Frau Doktor brings us all together in peace."

I was deeply moved when the German-American Society honored me at a day-long celebration, but I was even more touched by the action of the Army. Major General Robert Porter and his Third Armored Division had a Review in my honor.

The day was sparkling and sunny, and the sight of th entire Division was an impressive one. As I was escorted to the Reviewing Stand it was comforting to have Harry by my side. However, the next part of the story came as a complete surprise to me.

Gen. Porter and I walked to center-field where he addressed everyone over the public address system. He spoke of my work in German-American relations and announced I was being made the first Honorary Member of the Third Armored Division. I listened in disbelief, as I recalled the proud history of this great Division.

When I returned to the Reviewing Stand I quickly glanced at Harry. He was smiling broadly, but I also caught a momentary glimpse of a tear in his eye.

The Army gave me the opportunity to live, work and study in two Occupations. Mother often quoted Emerson, and it came to mind that evening when Harry and I were discussing the post-doctoral events. "It is not by sitting still at a great distance and calling the human race 'larvae' that men are to be helped."

The Army also gave me a wonderful husband who would tease me about my wanting to "save the world," but encouraged me in my efforts to know better the peoples of other countries and cultures.

There was much for which to be thankful.

(center) Col. Harry Kinne presents 'Best Company Award.'

(left) Col. M. Worthington Bordley {Years later to become Fran's second husband}

Chapter Eleven:
New Eyes / New Careers
St. Augustine / Jacksonville

As our overseas tour was coming to a close in Germany, Harry was provided the opportunity of selecting his last assignment prior to retiring. Florida was his first choice, since he knew those freshwater bass were waiting for him in the waters of the St. Johns River.

The options were limited for a senior Colonel, but at that point the position as Senior Regular Army Advisor to the Florida National Guard became available. The headquarters was in St. Augustine, a charming and historic city.

The very first week we were in our new assignment an article about us appeared in The St. Augustine Record. Harry was enjoying his assignment in the National Guard office in the building that had once been a monastery, and I was looking forward to my first free time after my intensive doctoral studies in Frankfurt.

慶祝

Col. and Mrs. Harry Kinne, Jr.
"Celebrate" Harry's retirement and their
plans to move to California

But it wasn't to be, and answering the telephone that hot summer July day in 1958 changed my life. It was the Dean of the Faculty, Dr. William Highsmith, calling from Jacksonville University. He offered me a position as Assistant Professor of Humanities at the newly-created four year institution, an outgrowth of a well-established private junior college.

Harry and I discussed the challenge of a commute of 86 miles (round trip), along with a heavy schedule of social activities related to his position as Senior Regular Army Advisor to the Florida National Guard.

My visit to the campus in Jacksonville convinced me that the dynamic leadership of Dr. Johnson and Dean Highsmith would produce a winner out of this school. This resulted in my decision to "help them out" for a month or two while they conducted a search.

Something that did happen changed my life again, as the months turned into years. The golden thread found itself intertwining with a surprise I had not anticipated.

Three years as a Professor coincided with Harry's retirement, and our plans were to move to California. Harry favored Florida, but I was eager to spend more time with my only sibling, my brother in San Diego.

J.U. President Franklyn Johnson, and Vice President and Dean of the Faculty, Bill Highsmith, together, asked me to create a new College of Fine Arts — and I accepted the challenge.

Since I was the junior professor and lone woman in Humanities I had all the 8:00 a.m. classes those three years of commuting. There were many returning GIs from the Korean and Viet Nam Wars, and they were great motivators for me — many of them my age. The professors were young, enthusiastic and dedicated, and our President surely was the youngest (and brightest) in the United States.

Those few months I promised in 1958 have lingered on these many years. I wonder what would have happened if I hadn't answered Bill Highsmith's call that day so long ago!

One of the greatest joys is noting the growth and development of our graduates, and sharing in the lives of the hundreds who maintain communication with me. I read every excellent column graduate Bill Foley writes for <u>The Florida Times-Union</u>, and at the same time give thanks for the thousands of other students who have inspired me.

Colonel Harry L. Kinne, Jr., Banker

Harry's dream had always been to find enough time for all his hobbies: fishing, hunting, golf, tennis. It was a good friend who brought change. Guy Botts, who was CEO of the oldest banking chain in Florida, Barnett Banks, and also Chairman of our Board of Trustees at J.U., entered the picture. "Come into banking," he entreated Harry.

An interview in the paper quoted Harry: "I spent a year or two fooling around the house and doing all the things you do with a new house when I retired. But I got tired of saying goodbye to Fran in the morning and waiting for her to come home at night."

So when the banking opportunity came up, "I took it — and thoroughly enjoyed it."

Harry did exact a promise from Guy that he could spend Wednesday afternoons with J.E. Davis at the D-Dot Ranch. And on his way to the fishing paradise he would stop to check on his friend, Carl Swisher (King Edward Cigars), then in poor health and eager to talk fishing with Harry.

Before he started work Harry enrolled in refresher banking courses at J.U., and I warned him to produce, or it would be a reflection on me. He was proud when he made the Dean's list. This wasn't a surprise to me, as he had been an English major at the University of Illinois, the Cadet Colonel of a corps of 5000 students in ROTC. And as Captain of the Water Polo team he was selected for the Olympics.

I was in 1st and 2nd grade while he was a campus leader at Illinois. He would often point to a childhood picture of me and say, "What do you think my fraternity brothers would have said if I told them that was the girl I was going to marry?"

Harry receiving the 'Florida Distinguished Service' Medal from Major Gen. Mark Lance

(Harry was the first military man to receive this award)

(top-left) Fran welcomes
her old friend Arthur Fiedler
to the J.U. campus on his 16th visit.
They appeared in the Sept. 1977 issue of
<u>Southern Living</u> Magazine
(top-right) Harry and Fran on
their Cabin Cruiser "Ting Hao,"
which means "Very Good"
(bottom) Frances Kinne Garden,
"The Kinnegarten," at
"The Little People's School"

THIS PRESIDENT WEARS A SKIRT...

DR. FRANCES B. KINNE

Chapter Twelve:
The President, the Colonel, and the Surgeon

Harry's support during my many years as Dean were just as evident when I was asked to be President. I had no interest in being a college president and had indicated this on many occasions. There were so few women with administrative experience the field of applicants was minuscule, and one New York university offered me a presidency without even an interview.

If it hadn't been for Flo Davis, the first woman Chair of the Board of Trustees, the late Luke Sadler, former Chair, the late Bert Thomas, President Of Winn-Dixie Stores, Earl Hallow, Bill Hatcher and Alexander Brest, I wouldn't have agreed. Even so, I accepted with the understanding I would only hold the position for one year. Of course, that "one year" developed into ten years.

Harry Kinne provided great support for me, attending functions, athletic events, raising money and accompanying me at every turn. However, toward the end of my first year as President, Harry and I began to notice some unusual patterns in his speech.

There was a slight hesitancy and a search for words in a man who was brilliant with the English language — an English major who had a limitless stock of stories (mostly humorous) to fit any occasion.

He must have had an innate feeling something was wrong. Dr. Carl Mendoza, his close friend and fishing buddy, was always willing to assist, but Harry chose to go to a doctor who did not know him. This was an unfortunate decision, as the doctor made the judgment that the speech problem was the result of a stroke and prescribed a blood thinner.

In the meantime, I had observed other insidious developments, and I accompanied Harry to his next appointment. The doctor by that time had decided it might be a psychiatric problem.

This was ridiculous, for one couldn't find a better adjusted man. I kept insisting, "Could it be a brain tumor?"

One evening I joined Harry at the D-Dot Ranch, taking a picnic dinner and spending as much time as I could with him. As we completed our dinner, in one moment he looked at me and couldn't say a word.

He looked helpless as I asked him if he could speak. He shook his head. I was frightened but didn't want to panic. I do remember the tears were rolling down my cheeks as I drove him to the doctor's office at the hospital. But it took three months to convince the doctor to do a CAT scan. There it was, a massive brain tumor in the left frontal lobe. My worst fears had been substantiated.

The next hours were frenzied ones, in control on the exterior, but desperation tearing at my heart. My frantic call to J.E. Davis, Harry's dear friend, brought some comfort. A plane would be ready for us at 5:00 a.m. at the airport, and he had arranged for an 8:00 a.m. appointment at Mayo Clinic Rochester, Minnesota.

Harry and Fran at her Inauguration as President in 1979.

I drove the twenty miles from the hospital to our home with internal pressures catapulting thoughts through my brain. At the same time, I was assuring Harry everything would be O.K. — weak words of little meaning to a man who couldn't speak.

By the time I was able to assist Harry in getting to bed it was midnight. As I took a hurried glance at the mail, an IRS envelope on the top caught my eye. There was a disagreement on our Income Tax Return and I was to report that week for a meeting. Heartless Federal government, I thought to myself. And just as I pushed that from my mind, the burglar alarm started its harsh, penetrating sound. Income tax and a burglar paled beside the brain tumor that was growing in the left frontal lobe of the man I loved.

Harry came running from the bedroom with a gun in his hand, which frightened me more than the alarm. I had delayed too long, and the false alarm brought a patient policeman who recognized a drama in progress and didn't give me a ticket.

We flew out before dawn, and I cradled Harry's head in my lap as the sun rose to give us its promise of hope in a new day. Mayo Rochester was our destination.

The moment we arrived at St. Mary's Hospital I knew we were in the most competent of hands. Dr. Eugene Mayberry, CEO, met us with several of his staff. Dr. Mayberry's gentle and kind voice reflected those rays of the sun. "Don't worry, Col. Kinne will be in the hands of the finest brain surgeon in the world." I couldn't resist hugging that wonderful Dr. Mayberry!

But not only was Harry in the hands of the finest surgeon, Dr. Thor Sundt was a West Point graduate who had been an Infantry officer during the Korean War. Here was a man who spoke the same language as the Colonel who had commanded the 781st Tank Battalion in World War II, and the 4th Armor Group in post-war Germany.

The communication between these two men was electric — immediate empathy. Thor Sundt saluted Harry, put his hands on Harry's shoulders, and said, "Colonel, you have one more hill to conquer."

Actually, there were many more hills for each of us to conquer, for there were five more surgeries for him. For me, it was leading a small comprehensive university into a new era, with my heart torn between sadness in my husband's suffering and appreciation for the support of all the wonderful Jacksonville University Family and the entire community.

Dr. Eugene "Gene" Mayberry.

Certainly one of the most dramatic of the surgeries was the brain laser surgery. This had not been performed in the United States, so it meant purchasing a laser and building a cooling tower at St. Mary's Hospital. We knew it was experimental, but we had nothing to lose.

The night before the laser surgery, the light-sensitive drug hematoporphrin was injected, and the surgery then had to follow within 72 hours.

I arrived early the following morning, after a sleepless night at the Kahler Hotel, to discover a drama had been taking place throughout the darkness of the long night.

Dr. Sundt, his Senior Resident, Dr. Robert Wharen (another wonderful surgeon who entered my life later in another dramatic chapter), and others had been up all night trying to get the laser to work. It was only a brief time before the appointed time of the surgery. They worked their magic. The laser was ready for the exploration into the left frontal lobe of the Colonel who was ready for battle, as was the case on so many other occasions as he led his 781st Tank Battalion through combat.

The years of 1980-1981 reminded us of the importance of living each day to the fullest. We filled each moment with energy and significance. Certainly there were times of discouragement but never despondency. And each of us grew with the challenge of every surgery.

Fran's beloved Harry as he will always be remembered

I presided at the Commencement ceremonies at J.U. on April 26, 1981 and hurried to St. Luke's Hospital to stay with Harry each night as I had always done. Shortly after midnight he slept away quietly, and I reinforced my vow to fulfill one of his last requests:

"Fran, please get the government to recognize the serious health problems resulting from the atomic test drops where so many of us were exposed to radiation."

I fought my way through committee after committee. Even an appearance in Washington, however, brought no results. And I was sad. How quickly we forget the combat veteran in the time of peace!

But Harry's legacy lives on in the lives of all those men who fought with him in the preservation of freedom.

Letter from Thor Sundt

Thor Sundt's letter to me after Harry passed away expresses well the bravery of those combat veterans who escaped death from enemy fire:

Dear Fran:

I must apologize for taking this long to write to you regarding the loss of your most wonderful husband. There is little that one can say at this point in time that has not already been said, and the written word offers only minimal solace for wounds associated with the loss of a very special person such as Harry.

I never cease to be amazed at the incredible courage some of my patients have as they face high risk situations and in some instances terminal disease processes. Often this courage is born of a conscious or unconscious effort to ignore the illness and neglect its presence. I had the definite feeling that no such detour or escape route was accepted by Harry, and in fact, I am quite certain that he fully understood every day his ultimate fate and looked it squarely in the eye as he would have were his regimental commander to tell him that it would be necessary for him, Harry Kinne, to take his battalion into the jaws of certain death.

I thought many times to myself that here truly was "one hell of a soldier and one hell of a man." I am very certain that all who served under him were proud to do so and he is the type of individual I would have loved to have had as a commanding officer.

Well, the future will not be easy for you but hopefully you can keep yourself so totally occupied that you have little time to reflect. This is not to say that you do not wish to keep the wonderful memories that you have shared, memories which are in the bank just like a savings account.

Obviously we are all so very sorry we could not do more for him but such is the way.

The last two lines of the West Point alma mater are certainly applicable to Harry. They read as follows:
And when thy work is done,
Thy course on earth is run;
May it be said well done,
Rest thou at peace.

Sincerely yours,
Thor
Thoralf M. Sundt, Jr., M.D.

Dr. Thor Sundt and Fran shortly before Thor's death in 1992.

Letter from Al Haig

Among many other letters I received shortly after Harry died, in addition to the wonderful letter from Dr. Thor Sundt, was this from former Secretary of State, General Al Haig — who was a Major in Harry's 4th Armor Group:

"I will always cherish my memories of him and value the lessons I learned while under his command. Harry Kinne was an inspiration to all of us. My service with him in Europe is recalled for the leadership he provided and the standards he set. You properly nobilize his memory."

Dr. Thor Sundt's Boys

Time was not kind to the brillant surgeon, for some years later he was diagnosed with Carcinoma. During these years Thor, his wife (Lois) and I had become fast friends, and now we shared the pain of Thor's terminal illness.

After my farewell visit to Rochester to see Thor Sundt I spoke with him each day. Dr. Ron Reimer (a former Resident under Dr. Sundt) was being married that Labor Day weekend, and I promised I would call and describe in detail the wedding "of one of his boys."

I rode to the ceremony with Dr. Bob Wharen and his wife Mary Beth. The setting was the lovely Epping Forest Yacht Club, former DuPont Estate and earlier the home of Raymond and Minerva Mason. It holds so many happy memories, the most vivid of which was President Ford's kick-off for his Presidential Library.

Ron and Carol (a handsome couple) had selected the magnificent waterfront site for the outdoor ceremony, and everything was fun from the moment we were seated in the garden. A very articulate and interesting Chinese minister performed the ceremony, waving his arms in an all-embracing manner. Our only concern was he might fall backward into the little fish pond, on which edge he was precariously perched.

As promised on Labor Day I called Thor Sundt to describe the wedding, such a blessed and happy event. Thor was so excited and delighted to hear the details. When I described my concern about the precarious position of the pastor Thor started to laugh. "Oh, Fran, this is wonderful and I feel as if I were present."

I closed the conversation quickly as Thor's fragile bones could not even tolerate a laugh. When we said our farewells, I somehow knew it was the last time I would hear his voice. He died within 36 hours.

His Memorial service at St. Mary's Hospital Chapel was particularly poignant, since he had planned each minute of it. A West Point graduate, he had deep respect for the military. Of course, the famous West Point hymn brought tears to many eyes—*certainly to mine.*

When Ron Reimer completed his Residency, he had presented a desk pen set to Dr. Sundt. On my last visit to see Thor before his death he asked me to give the set back to Ron Reimer. After the funeral I did just that, knowing it would have special meaning.

It is ironic that Thor's wife Lois gave me great support, first when her husband performed six surgeries on Harry Kinne. And it was Lois who would sit with me while another loved one (about whom you will later read) was undergoing surgery.

Leslie Stahl interviewed Dr. Sundt for "Sixty Minutes" the last year of his life, and the program has been shown three times. The last was a New Year's Eve special highlighting 25 years of the successful program.

Leslie Stahl said her interview with Thor Sundt convinced her he was one of the most outstanding of all the men and women around the world she had interviewed.

I flew to Rochester to see Thor the week before he passed away, and he repeated, "Harry taught us all how to die." I returned for his funeral with an ache in my heart.

(below) Dr. Jerry Knauer, Ash Verlander and Fran accompany Bob Hope on a flight from Miami to Jacksonville. The event: a joint Benefit for the Eisenhower Hospital, the Eye Research Foundation and J.U.

Jack Benny · *Press*

JACKSONVILLE UNIVERSITY
COLLEGE OF FINE ARTS

BOB HOPE — JACK BENNY

6 April 1972
Wolfson Student Center

12:30 P.M.

Admit One $10.00

Bob Hope

(above) A signed "Press Pass" for Bob Hope and Jack Benny's earlier visit to Jacksonville University.

Chapter Thirteen:
Bob Hope and Jack Benny Share the Stage with Fran at Jacksonville University

April 6, 1972, prior to awarding of Doctorates.

April 6, 1972. Very likely the largest representation of the media ever to visit Jacksonville descended on us that day. It was the only time Bob Hope and Jack Benny made a joint appearance on a college campus. And it was at Jacksonville University.

Since Jacksonville University is a private university, there are very limited funds available to pay celebrity visitors, so I pulled out all stops to arrange these appearances.

Bob Hope and Jack Benny, of course, had brought inspiration, humor and a touch of home to millions of GI's around the world. I felt they both deserved honorary doctorates. So I invited them to Jacksonville.

I first met Jack Benny when he appeared with the Jacksonville Symphony. We had dinner together that night with a small group of friends. Ira and Nancy Koger graciously hosted the dinner. And of course I invited Jack to the J.U.

campus. He gave me his telephone number and said we could discuss it later, and I added his number to my list.

I had met Bob Hope in Japan, and the next meeting was when our Alumni Association scheduled Bob for a Benefit. This cemented the friendship which has been very special to me throughout these many years. Of course, on his first visit to the J.U. campus I invited him to return.

"Would you be willing to come back? I really would like to honor you."

"Sure, I'll come."
And he, too, graciously gave me his telephone number.

After a little time passed I called Mr. Benny: "Would you be willing to share the platform with Bob Hope for an honorary doctorate?"

"I'd be honored."
I called Mr. Hope, and he answered, "I'd be honored."

There were devilish details to be worked out: my academic schedule, Mr. Hope and Mr. Benny's busy schedules, and, that was the year of one of J.U.'s most outstanding men's basketball teams. They were heavily scheduled that season for many appearances in addition to their games.

Ward Grant, who was Bob's Director of Bob Hope Enterprises and handled all of Bob's P.R., was priceless to me. He is an excellent writer and a delightful man. It was a disappointment to me he couldn't join us on the big day. Irving Fein, who handled Jack Benny's appearances, was present.

Bob Hope and Fran at the kick-off for the Ford Library.

Fortunately, I was scheduled to attend the annual International Council of Fine Arts Deans meeting in Los Angeles. You have already guessed it. I took two very important telephone numbers with me.

It all worked out for April 6!

Harry and I met the two celebrities at the airport — along with the J.U. pep band, 76 media representatives from around the world, and adoring fans. When I showed Bob and Jack the minute-by-minute itinerary I had prepared, they wondered if I would supervise their pre-bedtime activities as well! It turned out Mr. Benny wanted a glass of milk, and Mr. Hope wanted to drive golf balls.

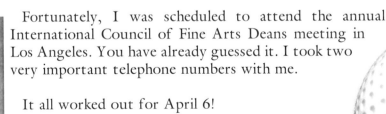

Fran receiving a phone call from Bob Hope indicating that he & Jack Benny would be coming to Jacksonville University.

Fran gets a kiss from Bob Hope during the Doctoral ceremony at J.U. in 1972.

I called a nearby golf range at 10 that night: "I have Bob Hope with me, and he wants to hit a few golf balls."

"Sure, Lady, I know you have Bob Hope with you. Everyone does when it's closing time and they can't think of a better one."

Conferring the doctorates was a formal affair, and the campus was beautiful with trees and flowers in bloom and their scent filling the air.

Bob Hope and Jack Benny were in rare form as well.

Bob had agreed that after I read his citation and he was hooded with the proper academic regalia I would reach up and congratulate him with a kiss. And since we were presenting the honors in alphabetical order, we could only guess what Jack Benny's reaction would be.

As I kissed Bob Hope's cheek, Jack Benny immediately jumped to his feet, displaying feigned indignation, and spoke just loud enough for everyone in the audience to recognize his style of wording and dramatic pauses:

Bob Hope and Fran chuckle at a comment made by Jack Benny during the luncheon at J.U.

"No one kissed me."

The attractive Flo Davis (from the J. U. Board) and I rushed over to Mr. Benny and kissed him on the lips.

Bob walked over and bussed Jack's cheek as well. And historic photographs were captured during those moments.

Only after a very long pause for the laughter to subside was the ceremony continued.

The luncheon was just as joyous. Jack related that this was one of his two greatest cultural experiences, the other being the naming of a junior high school in Waukegan, Illinois after him.

Bob Hope and Cindy & Jim Hoffren

Fran watches as Bob Hope makes an impression in cement to be placed in Swisher Auditorium.

Fran poses with two elephants from the Jacksonville Zoo. One accompanied her to the airport to meet Bob who adopted the elephant - not Fran.

Fran and Bob Hope with Minerva Mason flying from Palm Springs to Jacksonville. Bob played in The Players Championship (T.P.C.)

Fran & Bob pose for a photo during one of his visits to J.U.

Bob Hope pins an orchid corsage on Fran.

"I was thrown out of high school my first year for not studying. I was the most embarrassed honoree at that dedication service. I have always liked history, particularly about Abraham Lincoln, because anyone who would walk barefoot twelve miles in the snow to save three cents on a library book fine is my kind of man. And I recall a little girl asking me seriously, 'Mr. Benny, how come they named you after our school?'"

(top) Bob brings a laugh to the crowd at J.U. {l-r — Jim Winston, Ira Koger share a laugh with Jack Benny)}

(below) Bob Hope, Fran and Jack Benny on the two celebrities' April 6 visit in 1972.

Jack Benny then joked, "Bob Hope came to the United States from England to do a benefit show at Valley Forge, and after deciding we were going to win that war, he sent for his golf clubs."

Hope took his turn and joked about how many times I talked to him on the phone so he wouldn't let me down: "Fran Kinne called me so often and tied up my phone so much that this entire month it was necessary for me to go through her office to make a long distance call."

When both men were asked to autograph a giant 12-foot photo to serve as a memorial to our J.U. students, Jack Benny stood observing Bob Hope's efforts, and said, "My gosh, he can write."

Hope replied, "Not bad for a doctor, eh? He added, "This picture is big enough for Benny to write out his real name (Benjamin Kubelsky).

Benny said, "If I'd known I was going to be such a great violinist, I'd have kept the real one."

Hope chided Benny, "He played golf up to three months ago...when he lost his ball."

After the laughter subsided, Hope added, "The string broke."

When Mayor Hans Tanzler offered each of the two men a key to the city, Jack Benny bit his and said, "Thank you just the same." Bob's response was, "Fran, did you have to include a funny mayor?"

Jack Benny got another big laugh when discussing a Cosmopolitan magazine center fold featuring Burt Reynolds: "I didn't think too much of it one way or the other. I was offered the same kind of a job in Popular Mechanics. They wanted me to lie nude on a lawn mower."

During the Q & A time Bob Hope promised to make house calls, and Jack Benny appreciated the citation verifying his age at 39.

Benny quoted Hope: "It is a novelty to think you are honoring two recycled vaudevillians, honoring us in an election year when there are so many comedians to choose from."

My husband and I made separate trips to drive the two men to the airport. I was especially proud that Bob, flying off to another benefit appearance, flew in an Air National Guard plane with a crew who came to my rescue when Bob's scheduled flight was canceled.

Jack was sentimental as Harry and I drove him to the airport, obviously touched by his honorary doctorate. As we walked Jack down the ramp to the plane, Harry offered him one of his highest compliments: "Come back, Jack, and I'll take you bass fishing."

"I hate fishing!"

I answered Mr. Benny, "Come back, Jack, and we'll send Harry fishing."

After Jack Benny's well-known dramatic pause, he lifted his eye brows and responded, "That's funny, Fran!"

Bob Hope is given the key to the City of Jacksonville by, then Mayor, Hans Tanzler.

{Yes!, that's Fran sitting to the right}

He then tucked his beloved Stradivarius under his arm and blew a kiss with his other hand. And he was gone.

There are many of us who will never forget that memorable day and night in Jacksonville on April 6. 1972.

The Chicken and the Eagle

And there were many opportunities to enjoy these two gentlemen, for Bob and Jack returned to Jacksonville for other benefits.

On one occasion Bob appeared in a joint benefit for J.U., the Eye Research Foundation and the Eisenhower Hospital. Our Jazz Band had the unique experience of accompanying Bob, and our singing and dancing group (the Dolphinaires) gave a whiz-bang performance to open the show. This was a group I started, with the intention of giving students pop performance experience, serving as a public relations vehicle at the same time.

Moments after Bob made his appearance the lights went out in the Civic Auditorium and in the entire downtown area. One generator served the lone spotlight on the stage, but Bob never missed a line. This incredible man ad-libbed for one hour forty-three minutes, without a pause. The Jazz Band wasn't that successful as they couldn't read their charts. However, Bob's music arranger, who was at the piano, saved the day.

At the reception which followed, Bob said he didn't want to eat there. "Could we go home and eat at your house?" he asked.

All I could think of was an empty refrigerator, as I gasped, "Of course."

Harry came to the rescue, slipped away quietly and managed to stop at a Winn Dixie supermarket for some incredible edibles. In a photo finish he arrived at our home minutes before my car (with Bob) pulled into the driveway.

I invited Dr. Jim Hoffren (Chairman of the Music Division at J.U.) and wife Cindy to join us, and we all finally landed in the living room where Bob asked me to play the piano. Jim wouldn't sit down, excited at the presence of Bob Hope. Harry spoke to Jim, saying, "Sit down, Jim. Relax."

However, Jim was still in awe. Harry asked him again — and again.

Finally Bob spoke up: "Jim, when a chicken Colonel (the symbol for that rank is an eagle) tells you to sit down, you better sit down."

Saying Good-Bye to Jack

My last visit with Jack Benny was arranged by Jack. He called to inform me he was going to be in Des Moines for a brief time, since he was doing ads for an insurance company whose headquarters was in Des Moines. In fact, when Jack told me on the phone about the fee he received for representing them he laughed, "Now, Fran, you must admit that's pretty good pay for 15 minutes of work!" He stayed in character.

It was a coincidence I was going to be at a Drake University Board of Governors' meeting on the very day he mentioned. Since both Bob Hope and Jack Benny had met Mother, and she had charmed them (of course) I arranged for her to join me. My meeting had delayed me, and I became concerned we would miss Jack who had a close plane connection.

Jack and his manager, Irving Fein, were in the limousine waiting for us at curbside as I pulled up beside them. With a broad smile Jack quickly exited the limo and hugged me tightly saying, "We never did send Harry fishing. Too bad!" In moments he had gathered Mother into his arms with, "Hi, Mom. You have such big, beautiful blue eyes."

Mother was not to be outdone: "That's what I always say about you."

With that Jack and Irv were back in the limo, and we were left with our memories.

It is impossible to evaluate the force Bob Hope and Jack Benny have played in their blessings of humor to the world — and to me personally.

Chapter Fourteen:
Smooth Transitions and Innovations
Drake University, Jacksonville University and a Mayo Clinic Satellite

Dr. David Maxwell President of Drake University.

An artist rendering of the Frances Bartlett Kinne Alumni and Development Center at Drake University.

Fran stands in front of the Frances Bartlett Kinne University Center at Jacksonville University.

After the amazingly successful Hope-Benny visit to J.U. I received a telephone call from Mel Hickerson in New York. He was a native Iowan, had established a name for himself in the business world, and in retirement was involved in educational projects. The motivation for the call was to ask me to do a chapter in a book he was going to publish: How I Made the Sale That Did the Most For Me, a description of "Fifty Great Sales Stories."

It was a busy time for me (weren't all times busy!) and I declined. Another telephone call produced, "Will you allow me to write it?"

That did it. I agreed to add my chapter, and the book was published in New York. I attended the kick-off reception and luncheon at the Waldorf-Astoria, sitting at the head table with Muhammad Ali, Gene Autry, as well as other contributors. Ali amused and surprised me with his magic tricks. I was wearing a suit with a breast pocket, and he brushed his hand across the pocket pulling multi-colored, silk handkerchiefs he had brought forth from his own sleeve. What a delightful aspect of his personality. It renewed my parents' bromide, "Look beyond the facade and you will see much more."

The special treat for me was the inclusion of a chapter by Gov. Robert (Bob) Ray of Iowa. His record of achievement at that time (1981) was already remarkable. Since then he has been CEO of Blue Cross-Blue Shield of Iowa, Interim Mayor of Des Moines when Mayor Arthur Davis passed away while in office, Chairman of the Board of Governors at Drake, and Interim President while a search for a new president was launched.

Drake University

A dynamic Dr. Michael Ferrari had led Drake University through ten very successful years when we lost him to Texas Christian University, where he had accepted a position as Chancellor. At the same time, Drake lost its energetic

Former Governor (14 years) Robert "Bob" Ray of Iowa.

Vice President for Institutional Advancement, Jack Ohle, because of his appointment as President of Wartburg College. This left Drake University without its leaders.

Bob Ray assumed the presidency for a year and temporarily relinquished the Chair of the Board of Governors to a former effective Chair, Jack Rehm, CEO of the Meredith Corporation. Corporations and institutions of higher learning could learn a great deal from the organization of this change of leadership. The skill of this operation gave credit to these two gentlemen, and certainly a happy share to Donald Adams (Assistant to the President) whose influence on Drake goes beyond measure, and to the premier, dynamic fund-raiser Madelyn (Maddie) Levitt, Drake's "dollar a year woman."

This smooth transition within an institution was quite remarkable, and never once was history abandoned. Each President of Drake University has provided an exciting chapter, and I am very confident new President David Maxwell will continue this remarkable story.

President Maxwell made a remarkable introduction, indeed, when he bicycled across Iowa on RAGBRAI (<u>The Des Moines Register</u>'s Annual Great Bicycle Ride Across Iowa) — meeting alumni and parents along the way. And most impressive was his guitar performance for high school students. He will like Iowa and Iowa will like him.

<u>Hats off</u> to Drake University for providing an example for educational institutions and corporations to emulate.

And <u>hats off</u> to Dwight

Maddie Levitt — Drake's premier fundraiser.

Opperman, former CEO of West Publishing Company. It was he who recognized the vital role private education plays in our country — the balance of dual offerings, public and private, is uniquely American.

At the Board of Governors' meeting preceding our Drake fund raising campaign, I was sitting next to Dwight Opperman. He rose to the microphone and announced, "I would like to give (and I thought he said) 15 million to kick off the campaign."

I leaned over and kissed his cheek: "Dwight, you deserve a kiss for offering to give 15 million to start us off."

He looked at me and said, with a twinkle in his eye, "Fran, I said I'd give 50 million."

And <u>hats off</u> to Bill Knapp, a remarkable businessman and Board member who made a multi-million dollar gift that made possible the Knapp Athletic Center.

Jacksonville University

The late Dr. Felix Robb made frequent appearances for me at Jacksonville University, both official and unofficial. We had become friends throughout the years, and he was particularly helpful when he became the Executive Director of the Southern Association of Colleges and Schools (our accrediting agency).

I had scheduled Felix Robb during my tours as President of the Florida College Music Educators Association, and later as Chairman of the Independent College and Universities of Florida (ICUF). And when I became President of Jacksonville University. I spoke often to him of my dreams and aspirations for the institution.

Fran in her Chancellor's robe.

It was Felix who encouraged me to pursue my dream. I had founded the College of Fine Arts in 1969, but we had no College of Business. Since we represented the free enterprise system, located in a pulsating business community, I felt it was a "must." I managed to clear the hurdles and we added a College of Business my first year as President.

It took a short time thereafter to initiate a School of Nursing with splendid assistance from Baptist Memorial Hospital and the persistence of Dr. John Trainer, my Vice President for the Faculty.

We were determined to establish the Nursing School with a dynamic director, and we narrowed our selection to someone who hadn't even applied. Dr. Ruth Stiehl was the Director of Nursing Programs for Florida, and I suggested John call on her to suggest she consider our exciting project. She turned us down.

John came to my office to inform me of her polite but definite refusal. My reaction to him was, "Go back. Tell her she's making a mistake."

It was "No" again.

But persistence and patience paid off. John returned and the third visit brought a "yes" and the rest is history, thanks to John's charm and Ruth Stiehl's change of heart.

I have often said I am very much like a little dog chewing a pant leg. I won't give up. And I have been fortunate in having staff members who shared that trait.

And that was of prime importance when planning for the future of our private institution. I had learned a great deal serving on the Boards of private and char-

itable organizations.

I have always spoken publicly of the importance of the dual system of education in the U.S. It is unique to our country and important to retain and keep in balance. As a product of both public and private schools I support and lobby for both. As President of a private, independent University I was alert to problems on the horizon, both financial and enrollment.

"Planning is a pain in the neck," said one faculty member, but that is what we did. Each year a committee did both long-range and strategic planning, and I set out to discuss my ideas with Felix Robb. After all, in a sense, he was our boss as he sat in his Atlanta office directing accreditation.

Sec. of the Navy, John Lehman and Fran pose for a picture at J.U.

The first idea came about as the result of sitting beside a young man on a plane. Harry and I had attended a basketball tournament in Charlotte, N.C., and on our return became involved in the typical passenger conversation. Except this one set my brain on fire.

Our seat-mate was on his way to Atlanta to attend the weekend Executive MBA program at Emory University. On my return I was on the phone to Felix. "No, there isn't a program in all of North Florida or South Georgia. Go for it."

And that's what I did, sending Dr. Jim Brady, then Vice President of the Faculty, to schools where such a program existed. Executives who had seven years of management experience were eligible for the rigorous year and one half program we scheduled on weekends. My one recommendation was to make it top quality and tough. Our credibility rested on those points, as it does in any organization.

Another great matter of concern I felt deeply was the need to provide more service to young adults in the community who had been unable to complete their education because of obligations, lack of finances, interrupted academic careers, etc.

My own empathy for these potential students was very likely based on my own personal background. I initiated my own teaching career with two years and two summers of academic work, attending Drake University on week-ends until I completed my degree. Nowhere in north Florida or south Georgia was this possible.

There was a second factor of primary importance. Campus facilities were under-used on weekends, and a weekend program was a sensible way to approach the problem. Faculty needed to be convinced of the value of this "College of Weekend Studies," and the Dean of the College of Arts and Sciences, the bright and capable Dr. Joan Carver, expedited approval, and we were on our way with reduced tuition for the weekend student. There are certain acts in our lives that provide deep grat-

ification, and this was one of them for me.

Another program which brought foreign students to our campus to learn English was initiated by the International Students of English. We were one of three campuses in the United States to offer this program, and the students were housed in the same dormitories with regular students. The cultural exchange opportunities were manifold, and many of these students remained to pursue degree programs.

An exciting part of our J.U. program was a highlight for me — the NROTC program which always had one of the top ratings in the U.S. The strong Science offerings at J.U. were influential in these ratings, as well as the superb leadership provided by the assignment of outstanding Navy personnel to NROTC duty.

While I was President I invited the Secretary of the Navy, John Lehman, to campus to be honored. I wanted him to be aware of the superior quality of our unit. That proved to be a smashing success.

It wasn't long before the Secretary invited me to the Pentagon for lunch, and since I was a military wife one might well understand how much I anticipated this engagement in Washington, D.C.

On the appointed day I arrived at the scheduled hour.

Actually, it was the precise

NROTC graduates at Jacksonville University.

minute. (I had been trained well!) Much to my surprise we dined by ourselves in the Secretary's spacious private dining room. The gracious host led me to speak of our Army life, and then proceeded to tell me our NROTC unit at J.U. had just been listed as the tops in the country — a great tribute to the military leadership the Navy provided and the strength of our J.U. professors.

Mayo Clinic Satellite in Jacksonville

Smooth transitions can be maneuvered in all types of organizations, and another model is the prestigious Mayo Clinic. Each experience I had with treatment of loved ones over a period of thirty years was one of quality care. Over and above that, I observed the most remarkable philosophy of leadership I have ever seen anywhere.

When Harry Kinne was being treated I witnessed personal care and concern for every patient. From the moment Dr. Eugene Mayberry met us that desperate morning Harry Kinne and I faced the trauma of his brain tumor, I recognized something special about Mayo Clinic.

Certainly that year of Harry's multiple surgeries provided me with ample opportunity to evaluate the quality of his care.

I was at the side door of St. Mary's Hospital on a cold December day. Snow and ice made cabs scarce. I was returning to Jacksonville and my duties at the University, leaving my husband for further treatment. Harry's prognosis was dismal, I was discouraged and tired, and I was worried about making my scheduled plane take-off.

(above) *An artist rendering of the Frances Bartlett Kinne Auditorium at the Mayo Clinic, Jacksonville.*

(left) *Dr. Thane Cody and Carleton Rider during the construction of the Mayo Clinic Jacksonville.*

(right) Fran with Authur Fielder, Flo and J.E. Davis, who donated the land for the Florida Mayo Clinic site.

State of Florida
Executive Department

GOVERNOR'S AWARD FOR THE ARTS

Florida Women's Hall of Fame
Certificate of Recognition

Frances Bartlett Kinne

(top) Governor Reuben Askew and Secretary of State Richard Stone award Fran the "Governor's Award for the Arts" in 1973. (bottom-right) Governor, now Senator, Bob Graham hands Fran a Certificate of Recognition for her Induction into the Florida Women's Hall of Fame. (bottom-left) Fran and Katherine Graham. (<u>Washington Post</u>)

Fran stands with (l-r) Dr. Frank Johnson; Dr. Henry Randle; Dr. Paul Pettit and Dr. Bob Wharen.

A gentleman suddenly appeared from behind me. As he passed he said, "You look discouraged. Is there anything I could do to assist you?"

I explained my dilemma, and with a comforting voice, he added, "I have a station wagon out in the parking lot. I will get it and meet you here in several minutes."

In moments he was there loading my suitcase, several flowering plants and me into his wagon. On the way to the Kahler Hotel he introduced himself, "I am Bob Waller, and I am in Opthalmology." I liked him immediately, this "knight in shining armor" who seemed to have appeared from nowhere.

On my return to Jacksonville I wrote a letter about this man I had discovered was Chairman of Opthalmology - one letter to Dr. Mayberry, another to the Board of Governors, and one to the Rochester newspaper. Little did I realize Dr. Waller was designated to assume the CEO position on the retirement of Dr. Mayberry.

Obviously a superb selection.

During this time an historic decision brought the first Mayo satellite to Jacksonville, and later, the second one to Scottsdale, Arizona. J.E. Davis donated land for the Florida facility, and Dr. Thane Cody and Carleton Rider were sent to Jacksonville to plan and supervise the construction and initial organization. They did this with panache.

I was sent to Rochester to speak to the families and doctors to convince them Jacksonville was a great city. That was easy.

Since those early years in Rochester, Dr. Waller has now retired and Dr. Michael Wood has assumed the supervisory position. Likewise, in Jacksonville since Dr. Cody, smooth transitions have occurred, with a strong period of growth under Dr. Leo Black, and now to the new CEO, Dr. Denis Cortese.

The Mayo founders would be proud of the development of the finest health system in the world.

And I am so grateful to have been made an Honorary Staff Member in 1993. I cannot diagnose any health problems (although my good doctor friends tease me about trying) but I can be admiring of the great Mayo system of health care.

The Mayo Team — First Hand

I had first been a patient at Mayo Clinic Rochester forty years ago, with Dr. Hugh Bett as my Internist; when he retired he arranged for my transfer to Dr. E.R. Dickson; when Mayo Clinic Jacksonville was built, Dr. Dickson referred me to Dr. Richard Fleming; later he became terminally ill and arranged for Dr. John Cangemi to be my primary physician — all a reflection of managed transitions, to include surgeries by Dr. Paul Pettit and Dr. Mark Broderson. The team included consultations with Doctors DeOrio, Van Den Berg, Pearson, Liesegang, Lundy, and I am a healthy woman.

Mayo Clinic is a team!

Fran surrounded by J.U. Baseball players.

Dr. Robert Waller

(l-r) Barbara Hazlehurst, David Miles, Fran and Dr. Michael Ferrari cut ribbon at Dedication of Frances Bartlett Kinne Alumni and Development Center at Drake University.

Fran landing on the Saratoga.

Dr. Mark Brodersen, a native Iowan at Mayo Clinic Jacksonville.

Chapter Fifteen:
FRANTASTICS! — Cast Call

As the Dean and founder of the College of Fine Arts at Jacksonville University I was fortunate in being able to make contacts in the entertainment industry. I was determined to schedule celebrities who would "rub shoulders" with the students, as well as provide career guidance. And an equal motivation was to share these celebrities with the citizens of Jacksonville.

When I became President I broadened invitations of the guests to include great men and women in many disciplines outside the entertainment field. As a private, independent institution there were no funds for my ambitious plans. Dr. Frank Johnson had set the pace as President in inviting Lord Montbatten to campus.

Frank Johnson had developed a friendship with Montbatten while working on a book on "Government by Committee." No stranger to fine writing, Frank's book on World War II, <u>One More Hill</u>, was later selected as one of the 50 best books about that conflagration.

Montbatten's appearance in Jacksonville inspired a flurry of excitement, and the question arose as to where he should dress for the ceremony, since his uniform would need to be removed for the gown. My office was in the Green Room on the second floor of Swisher Auditorium, and I happily volunteered my space. It was at the time

of the scandal in London involving a member of Parliament. Aside I asked Frank if he minded if I put a little sign on my desk which would read: "Lord Montbatten dressed here."

After our guest's remarks, Frank drove Montbatten and me to the ballfield where the helicopter awaited. (I do remember how handsome our guest was, but I always did have a weakness for uniforms.)

As the helicopter lifted off we were all caught in the whirling dust, turning away to protect ourselves. Dr. Sydney Lefkowitz, the endeared Rabbi who was an Adjunct Professor, turned his back and loudly proclaimed, "This is the first time I have ever turned my back on the Lord."

And this has been an oft-told story by Frank Johnson, as well as Dr. Dan Thomas (who later became Vice President of the Faculty), and yours truly.

—Sir Rudolf Bing

I worked for years to schedule Rudolf Bing to visit us. With the assistance of many I finally made it. For 23 years Sir Rudolf Bing was General Manager of the Metropolitan Opera, and I was a great admirer of his. On his arrival at the Met he had taken over the management of temperamental stars, labor problems, public relations difficulties, and disagreements among the board of directors. It is quite amazing Sir Rudolf endured the 23 years, and I wanted to honor him.

Every spring the Met would go on tour, and Flo Davis and I would trek to Atlanta to enjoy at least five operas. Flo would often host parties after the performance, and the stars would join us for a midnight supper. It provided a splendid opportunity to become acquainted with the great opera singers, as well as Sir Rudolf and Francis Robinson,

Sir Rudolf Bing
and Fran

who handled public relations for the Met.

One of our favorite stars was Franco Corelli, the great tenor, and certainly one of the finest of his era. He and Fereni sang the lead roles in "Romeo and Juliet," and we looked forward with the greatest of anticipation to this opera.

At the party two nights preceding the performance, we were all invited to visit a pig farm. Betty Talmadge (wife of Sen. Herman Talmadge, and a charmer) had convinced us we would have a unique experience. The invitation included the opera stars, and Franco Corelli and his wife joined us for an unusual afternoon.

The limousine called for us at our hotel, and the number of people attending required our using the jump seats. Corelli had held back while I sat on one of those jump seats, and he then insisted we change places so that he would be sitting on the uncomfortable seat. I felt guilty about this, since he would be singing in "Romeo and Juliet" the following day. But the afternoon was a great success, and I never gave it another thought. That is, until the next day when I heard disturbing news.

Corelli's back was the problem. The morning after our trip he could not stand up straight. He was in the hands of doctors and massage therapists most of the day, and we were finally informed we would hear his golden voice at the performance. However, there was much misgiving about whether he would be able to lean over the canopy bed to lift Juliet.

Flo and I went backstage to wish Corelli well, and I felt even more guilt when he so graciously welcomed us prior to his performance. And when the decisive moment arrived, I silently gave a sigh of relief when he leaned carefully over the bed singing his song of love, and then straightened up to recognize the warm response of the audience.

Franco Corelli and Fran.

The post opera performance party was a gala affair. Flo and I had decided this was the night to convince Sir Rudolf he should visit Jacksonville University. The problem was to find enough time to explain the importance of his visit, while his fans would be crowding around him at the party. With the help of Flo, Betty Talmadge and Rosemary Smathers (then wife of Sen. Smathers) we managed it. Whenever anyone would approach Mr. Bing, one of the three of them would engage that person in conversation. In the meantime, I had Mr. Bing in a corner.

These were the early years of integration, and we knew that Mr. Bing supported this long overdue effort. I explained to Mr. Bing I would like to have a White-Black Festival, with his appearance at both Jacksonville University and Bethune-Cookman College in Daytona. Also, we would schedule events at both schools, using our student groups. He seemed responsive to the idea, but he explained his year was totally booked. Would I stay in touch? That was the only encouragement I needed, plus his private telephone number.

The following year I continued to write and call his office and home. I was scheduled to attend a meeting of the International Council of Fine Arts Deans in London, and he suggested I stop in New York to make final arrangements. When I arrived in New York, there was a note waiting for me at my hotel asking me urgently to call Mr. Bing. On doing so he explained there were strikes by the various unions involved with the Met. He asked me to take a cab to the lower parking lot within the building, and he would meet me there and take me up the back stairs to his office on the mezzanine. He explained this was the only safe way to maneuver my visit, as there were picket lines everywhere.

As the cab pulled into the parking lot, Mr. Bing was waiting for me, took me by the hand and led me up the emergency stairs. I was astounded to see a large lead screen behind his desk. He noticed my glance and explained he was the target of what could be some violence, but for me not to worry. I wasn't quite as confident.

We were able to schedule a satisfactory date in March of the following spring, and I was ecstatic. I explained to him we would be performing our first major opera at J.U. I had already been in touch with Bethune-Cookman, and great plans were underway for our Black-White Festival.

I scheduled a major Fine Arts Festival each spring, and for this occasion in addition to the appearance of Mr. Bing we featured all of the arts, which was our custom. Because we received a matching grant from the National Endowment for the Arts through the Fine Arts Council of Florida and the Florida Department of State, we included an art lecture-demonstration by the fine artist, Fred Messersmith; a drama presentation by Ruby Dee, a recognized star of the stage, films and television; appearances in the opera by Carol Bayard of the New York City Opera, and Randolph Symonette from the Met; Larry Riddle (one of our J.U. graduates), a superb designer and technical director; the outstanding sculptor Duayne Hatchett; as well as experimental film showings.

The celebrated Festival arrived with a great deal of fanfare. The Governor and Mayor were to attend; the President, Bob Spiro was to present an honorary doctorate to Bing, with the assistance of Flo Davis from the Board, and me as Dean of the College of Fine Arts.

Little did we know that Joe Williams (our great basketball coach) would be leading our

team to the finals of the NCAA basketball tournament at the same time. Yes — we were playing UCLA in the finals! So, the Governor, Mayor, President and most everyone else decided to attend the game. I must admit, as a basketball fan, if there had been any way in the world for me to attend that game, I would have been there.

Sir Rudolf Bing was not a basketball fan. Every student- musician playing in the orchestra pit was a fan, and little radios were tucked away hidden in accessible areas. How was I to know that Artis Gilmore and his teammates would be making history at the very moment we were presenting the opera?

It is fortunate we had a cast of real troupers, or we wouldn't have made it. Included were members of our own J.U. family: Ellen Frank (wife of our Dean, Sam Frank), as a lovely Zerlina, George Massey as Leporello, Gustavo Halley as Don Giovanni - all of whom now sing professionally. It is unfortunate we lost the basket-

ball game in the finals, but I'm convinced we won the Arts Festival for the many art lovers who attended. Also, I know we created a great deal of goodwill from a racial standpoint — and that certainly was one of my goals. Even the stunning program reflected the Black-White theme so effectively.

I kept in touch with Mr. Bing for years, and he graciously invited Harry Kinne and me to be his guests in his box at the Met. I treasure that evening, and I shall always have fond memories of the distinguished Sir Rudolf Bing.

—Richard (Dick) Boone

I had always been a great admirer of Richard Boone, a gifted actor. One evening I was returning to our home in St. Augustine after a day of teaching. Much to my surprise he was on a neighbor's porch and spoke to me as I pulled my trusty Volkswagen into our driveway.

Dick and his wife Claire were visiting her parents, and later chose to

Richard Boone and Fran
"Have Gun Will Travel"

live in St. Augustine. Since we had developed a strong Theatre program in our College of Fine Arts, my very first thought was to have Dick lead a Master Class in Drama for the students, and my invitation was graciously accepted.

There was a stir of excitement when I announced our plans for Dick's appearance. Students were admiring of his fine stage background, as well as the critical acclaim for his TV role of Konrad Styner in "Medic." They recognized that any actor nominated for the best-actor Emmy on five occasions had a great deal to offer.

He was so warmly received by our students, Dick returned several times to lecture, critique and motivate the Drama majors. But it wasn't just our students. Dick had a major following among adults for the many years he appeared in TV as Palladin in "Have Gun, Will Travel." And right at the top of the list of admirers was my mother, B.B.

One of the most amusing incidents occurred one evening at the Women's Club of Jacksonville. They were honoring me with a "Fran Kinne Day." The Mayor, Hans Tanzler, awarded me a key to the city, and the ballroom was filled with guests who had paid a handsome sum to attend. My mother, the great leveler, was astounded: "Did all these people pay that much to honor you?"

Before the program started I greeted Dick and Claire, who had driven from St. Augustine to share the evening with me. I took Dick by the arm and guided him to the table where Mother was seated, saying, "Mother, I want to introduce your hero to you."

Mother looked up and fixed those big, blue eyes of hers on Dick. After the warm hug he gave her, Mother quipped, "Now I know why all these people are here."

Dick was on the program to speak at my Inauguration as President, but he had already become ill. At the time, I did not realize how very soon his life would end with cancer. Nor did I realize that Harry was beginning to show symptoms of his own fatal, malignant brain tumor.

Dick Boone enriched the lives of tens of thousands of people, maybe millions. I know this seventh-generation nephew of frontiersman Daniel Boone made a valuable contribution to my students, as well as my family, and I am grateful.

— Alexander Brest

"Dollar-a-year-man Citizen-Soldier," recipient of the Legion of Merit Award, civilian engineer, U. S. Army engineer, military aviation engineer, co-owner and originator of Duval Engineering and Contracting Company, and philanthropist — Alexander Brest was truly a town father for Jacksonville. These accomplishments, as well as his lifeblood contributions and support of Jacksonville University, are legendary.

Harry said of Mr. Brest: "One of the main reasons we won World War II was because of the citizen soldier. Alex Brest is the perfect role model, providing brilliance, expertise and skills we did not have in the Regular Army. That's quite a bargain for the services of a 'dollar a year' man!"

Mr. Alex Brest and Fran.

While serving J.U. as Chancellor,
I included these remarks in a letter
I sent to Mr. Brest on February
11th, 1991:

Dear Alex: Shakespeare said it so well — "What a piece of work is man." Indeed, what a piece of work is Alex Brest, and the very finest role model for all of us!

In the countless times I have introduced you throughout the many years, it has always been a delight to discover some new facet of your wonderful character. You are truly "Alexander the Great." You have what Dewey described as "audacity of imagination," and you are inspiration in its finest definition.

Your brilliance has been of inestimable value to all of us at Jacksonville University, and your generosity speaks for itself. In your quiet but persuasive manner you have guided and counseled us, and with patience, dedication and perseverance you have led us through both difficult and exciting times.

And it has been wonderful to share with you so many splendid occasions, both on and off campus. This certainly includes getting to know your wonderful sons and their fine families. This is a privilege I have enjoyed — memories of which I shall forever treasure.

Alexander the Great, I write to you in humble appreciation and gratitude for your friendship and support. Your faith in our Jacksonville University (and in me) ignited that precious lamp of learning. You taught us to dream and to test our limits. Because of <u>you</u>, the future is ours.

*Alex Brest and Fran enjoy a
chuckle during Fran's
"30th Anniversary at J.U." celebration.*

I love to tell the story about Mr. Brest of that pivotal time in the history of Jacksonville University when a donor was needed to improve facilities to insure our accreditation would not be lost.

Alex Brest wrote modestly in his book about his role at J.U. All of us knew, however, that he was a dynamic force in the history of J.U.

I invited Alex to my home for dinner one evening, and, in Alex's words, "Fran gave me two drinks of Scotch and a good dinner and I volunteered to provide $37,000 for the plans and specs for the College of Fine Arts building. Those were the most expensive drinks I ever had."

And it was worth it. Famed historian, Sir Arnold Toynbee, assisted Alex and me with the ground breaking for the building venture. And Maestro Arthur Fiedler made one of his frequent visits to the J.U. campus to dedicate the new Phillips Fine Arts building, a great gift from the Phillips Family.

—Winston Churchill

A celebrity who caused a great deal of excitement, not only at J.U. but in our community as well, was Winston Churchill, grandson and namesake of the great Prime Minister. And the historians weren't the only ones who hung on his every word. We all did.

Because of his extensive experience in Parliament, students, faculty and community leaders alike recognized the grandson as a figure who was in touch with history. In fact, he was a part of history. His brilliance as a speaker, as well as his personal charm, made it a unanimous decision to invite him for as many return visits as he was willing to schedule.

One of these visits was to speak at the Colonel Harry L. Kinne Free Enterprise Award Luncheon. The occasion was to present the annual award to W.W. (Bill) Gay, because of his individual commitment to the American ideals of free enterprise and independent higher education. Bill was a natural selection to be the recipient. A noted civic leader, philanthropist and CEO of W.W. Gay Mechanical Contractor Co., Bill is a self-made man. The previous recipients were national success figures: A.D and J.E. Davis, Alexander Brest, W. Ashley Verlander, Billy Walker, Herman Terry, Norwood Sandifer, Bertram Reid, and Jacob Belin.

At the W.W. Gay award luncheon Churchill spoke to a standing-room-only audience about "Churchill As a War Leader: Lessons for the Future." It was a magnificent history lesson in itself, not only about the amazing service of his grandfather, but also addressing the challenges of the years ahead in our complex society. Certainly he is one of the great orators of our time.

Carrying the Churchill name has been both an advantage and at times a disadvantage; this quote from his address is an amusing and true anecdote:

Winston Churchill, grandson and namesake of the Great Prime Minister and Fran at J.U., after he dons the JU jacket she presented to him.

Arriving hotfoot from covering wars in Viet Nam and the Middle East, I found myself (25 years old) covering the Democratic National Convention in Chicago in 1968 as a young journalist. As I was approaching the convention hotel where I was staying on Michigan Avenue, I was surrounded not only by a sea of anti-war protestors, but by a phalanx of the Chicago Police Department and National Guard — many hundreds strong with their nightsticks drawn, plexiglass shields in place, and weapons at the ready. All of a sudden I found myself lifted bodily off the ground by two rather burly members of Mayor Daley's police department who inquired, "Where do you think you're going, Mister?"

I replied, "I was going to my hotel."

*To which one rejoined: "You're not in this hotel.
        What is your name?"*

You guessed it! Like an idiot I told them!

*They put me down only long enough to draw
        their nightsticks and gong me over the head.*

But I have to say that it is a special pleasure to be back here at J.U. in the land of Dr. Fran Kinne where the warmest of welcomes is assured. Yours is an excellent university which combines a wonderfully happy atmosphere with standards of academic excellence across a wide spectrum of fields, a university that goes from strength to strength, as Minnie and I have seen with our own eyes, coming here at least a decade and a half since our first visit under the guidance of your wonderful and inspired Chancellor, Dr. Fran Kinne.

Another of Churchill's highly successful visits was in 1993 when he returned to the campus to dedicate the Frances Bartlett Kinne University Center. On this occasion he spoke at the dedication ceremony, and again at the luncheon which followed. On this occasion he launched the publication of his excellent book, <u>Winston S. Churchill, Memories and Adventures</u>. His other books — <u>First January, The Six Day War</u> (written with Randolph Churchill), and <u>Defending the West</u> — had already been widely accepted. His new book presented a warm and loving relationship with his grandfather, and their time together at Chartwell.

Fran and Winston Churchill cut the ribbon at the dedication of the Frances Bartlett Kinne University Center.

As I am writing this, I have been reading his latest — THE GREAT REPUBLIC: A History of America (by Sir Winston Churchill, edited by Winston S. Churchill) — featured on the November 28, 1999 C-SPAN program, "Booknotes," hosted by Brian Lamb.

On one occasion I visited the Churchills in London. My one and only Concorde flight produced an amusing conversation with the pilot. It was obvious everyone else was a seasoned Concorde flyer, for I seemed to be the only passenger excited about Mach I and Mach II.

The pilot was taking a break and stopped to chat with me. "Is this your first flight on the Concorde?" (Was it that obvious?!) I was enthusiastic, "It's wonderful."

His smiling query, "Is it the most exciting thing you have ever done?"

And my answer — "No, it's the second most exciting!" — invited his question of what that could possibly

be. He asked for it, and he listened with an amazed look on his face.

My story described my adventure landing on the Aircraft Carrier, the Saratoga.

I was at a party one evening with the late R/Adm. Jerry Paulson. In one of those "off the top of my head" conversations I said, "I have always wanted to land on an Aircraft Carrier and take a high line transfer between two ships."

Adm. Paulson's answer was immediate: "Well, we can't do the transfer, and we have never landed a civilian woman on a carrier in the Atlantic; however, I'll try to get permission for the latter."

Several months later (and when I had forgotten my conversation with Jerry Paulson) I was surprised to receive a telephone call. It was the Admiral.

"Fran, we have permission from the 'powers that be' in the Pentagon to land you and several others on the Saratoga. It is about 100 miles out in the Atlantic now. Could you arrange to be here at the Naval Air Station at 7:00 a.m. tomorrow? Oh, by the way, wear pants, and it might be better not to wear your contact lenses."

He had heard my story about wrapping Christmas presents when we were stationed in Germany. I sneezed and one of my lenses flipped out of my eye and into the wrapping paper. Someone received it along with a Christmas present. In this case of landing on the carrier, I knew I should be prepared for a jolt when the plane caught the hook.

Winston signs a copy of Winston Churchill, Memories and Adventures during his visit in 1993.

When I boarded the plane Adm. Paulson called out to me, "Fran, I hate to tell you the plane is older than the pilots."

The flight across the calm waters of the Atlantic increased my eagerness to experience this new adventure, and I am confident the pulse was keeping pace with the excitement I felt.

I was wearing ear-covers and strapped in securely as the Saratoga came in view. We made the approach to the carrier, I felt a jolt and thought we had caught the hook. That is, until I realized we were leaving the deck and ascending. How delightful, I thought. The pilots want to give me a thrill.

We circled again and came in for a second try. The same jolt. The same ascending over the bow of the ship. Again I thought, "Adm. Paulson has told them of my love of adventure, and this is great."

That wasn't the end, and when we had a third bolter I realized the pilots must be "up tight" about landing a woman, and we had missed the hook.

When we finally made it on the fourth attempt I admitted to a sigh of relief — probably a minor sigh compared to that of the two pilots. The door opened, and there stood one of my graduates, now a Lt. Commander assigned to the Saratoga.

It was in a strained voice the young man said, "Dr. Kinne, the Skipper wants me to accompany you to the Bridge."

When we arrived at the hallowed spot, the Skipper, Capt. Ready (later a four star) apologized profusely, and informed me he had already called ashore to tell Adm.

Fran and Winston Churchill walk together during his October 4, 1984 visit.

W. Churchill and Fran pose for a photo at the dedication.

Winston Churchill (center) with (l-r) Fran, Minnie Churchill, Alice Verlander and the late Frank and Helen Sherman in Fran's office at JU.

Paulson of the experience I had just had. I assured Capt. Ready I had enjoyed every moment of it and "Please don't discipline those two nice, young pilots."

This story I related to the pilot of the Concorde. When he left me he laughingly said, "This flight is tame compared to your landing on the Saratoga. Do you mind if I send back the Co-Pilot to hear the story?"

And I told it again between the third and fourth courses of our airline dinner — unlike any dinner I had ever had on any airline. So that was a first for me!

After my one and only Concorde flight I had taken a cab to the Churchill's flat, which was close to Parliament. The flat was filled with the possessions of the Prime Minister, willed to the grandson. They certainly must continually remind young Winston of beloved circumstances of his childhood, and I sensed a wistful tone in his voice when he lovingly passed his hand across his grandfather's desk.

It reminded me of the story Bob Hope had told Jack Benny and me in 1972 when I asked Bob if he had ever met Winston Churchill. His answer was, "I did and I didn't." And he proceeded to tell the story about him and his troupe in England on their way to North Africa to entertain the troops.

Bob Hope had seen a Senator friend of his ("Happy" Chandler) in his hotel room. The Senator suggested Bob accompany him to see Prime Minister Winston Churchill at #10 Downing Street. Bob and Jerry Calona joined the party, but unfortunately the Senator hadn't informed the Prime Minister of the added guests.

Bob's eyes would crinkle up in a delightful way as he related the story. He joined the receiving line, and when he reached Churchill, the latter did a double-take. Churchill suggested the invited guests go into the rose garden for tea and conversation, but both Bob and Jerry felt they very likely wanted to discuss business. So what did they do but go into Churchill's study, try on his hat, and Bob picked up a half-smoked cigar. He also pocketed several of the blank note papers with Churchill's name on them.

When I visited Bob in his home in the middle 1980s, he proudly displayed the "artifacts" he had taken from the Prime Minister's office.

Of course, when I related this story to young Winston we both laughed at this image of the world's leading entertainer.

And when Bob showed me his "memorabilia" it was obvious what admiration he had for the Prime Minister.

And I am sure it has been difficult for "young Winston" to wear the mantle of the name. However, the grandson himself is brilliant and is writing his own chapter in history.

—*General Bruce Clarke*

A gentleman of whom Harry and I became very fond was General Bruce Clarke. A brilliant military record included outstanding success in WWII, Commanding General of the 2nd Constabulary Brigade and the 1st Armored Division. He was Commanding General of the 1st Corps in Korea and the 7th Army in Germany, and later Commander-in-Chief of the United States Army Europe.

It was while Harry commanded the 4th Armor Group that we first met Gen. Clarke and his lovely wife, Bessie. Gen. Clarke had come from the 7th Army in Stuttgart and was on an inspection of Harry's six battalions in the 4th Armored Group. The units were in various sections of Germany so it was necessary to helicopter in to the remote areas.

Gen. Clarke was a stickler on morale, and his first question to each Battalion Commander was, "How is morale?"

He had heard each Commander say, "Sir, it is excellent."

When Gen. Clarke and Harry boarded the helicopter for the return, both of them bonded as Gen. Clarke laughingly commented, "It's obvious there are different grades of excellence."

General Clarke was highly supportive of German-American cultural exchanges, and one of the very rewarding Army programs in Germany was the Seventh Army Symphony. It was a successful effort to mold German-American relations, since the Germans were and are great lovers of classical music.

The Clarkes had Goering's train, and they invited us to eat dinner with them on their train prior to the symphony concert. This impressed me, and when I discovered we were the only guests I was even more impressed.

Bessie Clarke wanted to continue her interest in the piano. It provided an opportunity for us to discuss adult learning methods and appropriate music, while Gen.

Clarke and Harry discussed military matters. While eating dinner at a bounteous table in the elegant dining car, Harry and I couldn't help noting the nine full bottles of vitamins neatly placed in front of Gen. Clarke's plate, and it became an amusing point of conversation for us.

That is, until some years later when both of us started adding our countless vitamin bottles in front of our own plates.

President Dwight Eisenhower said of Gen. Clarke: "The Army had two great trainers, Von Steuben and Clarke." A splendid book about Gen Clarke, <u>Clarke of St. Vith, the Sergeants' General</u>, written by William Ellis and Colonel Thomas Cunningham, is the story of a brave soldier.

As I look through my thick file of correspondence to and from Gen. Clarke, the educator in me recognizes how important it is for us to study the past. It is helpful to do this with heroes such as Bruce Clarke.

When Gen. Clarke returned to a Stateside assignment at the Pentagon we were nearing the completion of our German assignment. Harry was determined to retire in Florida where he knew the large mouth bass were awaiting his lethal lure. He had already pursued what assignment would be available for a senior Colonel, and a highly prized slot awaited him as Senior Regular Army Advisor to the Florida National Guard.

It was then Gen. Clarke approached him, indicating Harry was Clarke's choice for a staff position which would mean Harry's promotion to Brig. General. At dinner that evening we discussed the problem at length. It was obvious to me 33 years had taken its toll on Harry and his decision when he said, "If we go to Washington I'll have an ulcer or a heart attack."

Both Gen. Clarke and the bass lost out in that decision.

However, our friendship with the Clarkes was just beginning and we enjoyed their visits to St. Augustine. After I became President of J.U. we had an extensive correspondence

about leadership, morale and his passion — "How to Study and take Examinations." Many ROTC college units used (and still use) the latter as a text. He also published numerous articles and maintained a weekly posting to my office.

I was flattered when he wrote to me:

Dear Frances:

You have the real approach to leadership. Congratulations on your success. You should be in Reagan's new cabinet.

Love,
Bruce Clarke

—Aaron Copland

When I was a Professor of Humanities there was one burning question my students enjoyed debating. Does the need or the time make the man, or does the man himself create an era?

As I have enjoyed Aaron Copland's music throughout the years, I recognize the wonderful American flavor of his compositions. As much of an American patriot as I was when I went overseas to live and study, I returned with a deeper love and understanding of my country. So it was with Copland, and he did influence his time.

Copland's study with Mlle. Nadia Boulanger in Paris exposed him to the intellectual life of Paris, as well as an immersion into every facet of musical life. When he returned to the States, Aaron was recognized as a bur-

Aaron Copland and Fran take a quick photo opportunity

geoning talent, and his music was intoxicating and American in character. He was excited by the jazz rhythm, and the folk music of our country. But whatever his music is, it speaks of our land. He is one with our broad expanse of prairie, the towering mountains and flowing rivers of our country.

Betty Mendoza and I were in attendance at the annual London Symphony concert in Daytona Beach when Aaron Copland was the guest conductor. This was my first experience with the Copland phenomenon. It was both American and highly personal, all at the same time.

We went backstage after the concert, and wonder of wonders, he gave me his home telephone number. I was so electrified by his conducting, I almost forgot this was the composer of so many American favorites - whether in the concert hall, the ballet stage or the background music for movies.

That was 1966, and by the time Aaron Copland had returned to his home in Peekskill, N.Y., I was on the phone with an invitation. His answer was affirmative, but we must wait until the following spring. Wow! The Dean of American Composers would visit

us for three days, and now all I needed to do was raise the funds to support the entire production.

The telephone was my salvation. I called the Dean of Music (Bill Lee) at the University of Miami and suggested a joint festival. With the assistance of the Florida Development Commission, as well as other donors, the festival took shape. I was proud of our thriving College of Fine Arts — as music, dance, theatre and visual arts combined to produce two days of Copland and his music.

It was called "The Contemporary Music Festival Honoring Aaron Copland," April 6-7, 1967. The dance program included original works by our own faculty. Copland was fascinated by the outstanding work of the combined areas: dance choreographed by our dance director, Christa Long; set design, costumes and sculpture by Steve Lotz (now a well-known artist); music composed by various members of our own faculty and students.

The climax of the evening was "Contrasts," a Copland composition, choreographed by our faculty, and the set design by the late Memphis Wood, already a recognized artist.

This was the beginning of a strenuous schedule, followed by a convocation the next morning at which we presented Aaron Copland with the Degree of Doctor of Fine Arts, "Honoris Causa." Ed Bryan directed our J.U. Chorus (over 100

voices) in a rousing interpretation of Copland's "Stomp Your Feet," during which an unexpected spontaneous reaction had the audience clapping in rhythm to the music.

That evening Aaron conducted our orchestra in a wonderful concert of his own compositions. Later I drove him back to the Thunderbird Motel after a reception at which he greeted hundreds of guests and students. I accompanied him into the hotel lobby, thanking him profusely for the sparkle he had brought to us.

"Do you go like this every day?" was his question as I hugged him goodnight. When I nodded, he smiled wearily and said, "I am going to rest up before my next visit."

When I took him to the airport the next day, he invited me to meet him in Washington for a concert. I knew full well he would be back in Jacksonville for another visit. And he was.

But we had to wait until 1972, at which time I had scheduled our annual Fine Arts Festival for March. I wanted something unusual for this special week, and conferring with Copland we determined we should do the "Lincoln Portrait," which had never been performed in Jacksonville.

I persuaded the great actor, John Carradine, to fly from Hollywood to narrate the work. Professor Bill McNeiland prepared the J.U. Orchestra, and Professor Bill Vessels was the baritone soloist. Carradine was in the twilight of a brilliant career, having done more than 400 motion pictures. Copland was still in his prime, and the two wove a magic spell as they performed in the Civic Auditorium.

Fran, Aaron Copland and John Canarina (former Jacksonville Symphony Conductor) in front of the Delius House.

But I didn't let either one of them rest the next day, as Copland spoke at our "Day of Concern," a student convocation, and Carradine did theatre workshops for the Drama majors.

The next morning I drove Aaron to Gainesville where he was to appear at the University of Florida. Mother accompanied us, as she had already won Aaron's heart. As we said our farewells, he turned to Mother and said, "I have found someone who has as much energy as I. Maybe more. It's your daughter."

I did go to Washington to meet Aaron at a concert at the Library of Congress. As he was honored by dignitaries, I couldn't help but recall his tremendous rapport with young students at our J.U. He was the Dean of 20th Century musicians and composers, but he was also a good friend.

He told me he would leave some of his books and music to me when he died, and I encouraged him to remember J.U. instead. He did precisely that!

When the call came from his attorney informing me of Aaron's gift, I thought of this dear man. The last paragraph of the doctoral citation I read when we conferred his degree explained it all:

Aaron Copland - student, pianist, composer, musicologist, editor, author, lecturer, executive, conductor, Gold Medalist, Oscarist (Yes, actually he won an Oscar) - you are universally recognized as the dean among present-day American composers. You are the representative genius of modern America, the quintessence of democratic creativity, a towering Brooklyn Leonardo.

Yes, he was all of that.

—Dr. Mark Coventry of Mayo Clinic Rochester

It is fascinating to note how a chance meeting with another individual may become another thread in one's fabric of life. It was so for Harry and me when Senator Margaret Chase Smith visited Jacksonville.

Dr. Mark Coventry and Fran.

Sen. Smith's visit was prompted by her acquaintance with Bill and Helen Mills. We were all entertained one evening on Franklyn and Katherine Russell's luxurious yacht. The Senator had recently had a total hip operation and her success prompted Harry to consider this new surgery for his battle-weary, painful hip.

In his usual meticulous manner he surveyed the surgical field and discovered that Dr. Mark Coventry of Mayo Clinic Rochester was the man he must convince to perform the surgery.

Our connections with Mayo Rochester were great men Doug Milne and Joe Adams, both of whom had pioneered the Mayo Jacksonville connection by waving their magic wands; and J.E. Davis graciously arranged for a plane to fly Harry to Minnesota.

Harry's surgery was such a success that Mark later would teasingly encourage Harry to come to the waiting room, jog around and announce that he had just received a new hip from Dr. Coventry. Mark had performed the first total hip replacement in America the previous year, after he went to England to observe the surgery developed by Dr. John Charnley.

The orthopedist and the Colonel often fished together, the two of them sharing a love for the great outdoors. All of the trips spawned numerous stories, but one particular week-end became legendary.

The two adventurers departed one day in Harry's Air Stream Trailer. I teased Harry about this, as his "roughing it" meant enjoying as many conveniences in his Air Stream as the luxuries of a Ritz-Carlton suite.

The destination this time was a familiar one for Harry — the Swisher farm, approximately 80 miles from Jacksonville. We had often visited Carl (the Swisher Cigar tycoon) and Amy Swisher, and the lakes were loaded with large-mouth bass.

Carl was Chairman of the Board of Trustees when I was first appointed a professor at J.U. After Carl passed away, Harry continued to fish the lakes and knew where the grandfathers of the fish population were hiding.

Bass don't stray far from home base, and Harry knew precisely where one of those trophies was waiting for him. In fact, that very fish had struck his lure, a fancy Hula Popper, and broke the line. So this was the "fish of all fishes" Harry was saving for Mark.

When they arrived at the lake, it was late afternoon, that time between dusk and dark when the tree toads sing in chorus. The time when man becomes minuscule in the cathedral-like presence of weathered oaks dressed in Spanish moss. The time when God surely meant for us to recognize our place in the grand scheme of things. And part of that scheme included a trophy bass at the end of Mark's line. If Harry couldn't have this treasure, then it was OK for his special friend to capture the honors.

Mark cast. In a split second the giant struck, leaping high, and just long enough for them to see this silver beauty before it took off. The line on the reel was moving as fast as the heart beat, as Mark cried, "I've got him!"

(above)
Dr. Mark Coventry.

(right)
Col. Kinne with his hunting dogs.

But not for long. Suddenly the line broke, as the physician and the Colonel looked at one another in disbelief. They didn't see the bass again, and very likely that wise, old fish eventually died of natural causes, and probably with a sore mouth.

Disconsolate, the two men decided to travel to the D-Dot Ranch where Harry and I had spent so many happy hours with J.E. and Flo Davis.

It was a 50,000 acre paradise with deer, buffalo, alligators, wild turkey and even a panther Harry was convinced he saw one evening. J.E. never believed it, and the two good-naturedly argued about it for years.

And so it was natural for Harry and Mark to leave the scene of their disappointment and look for greener pastures. The many lakes at D-Dot had been lovingly stocked by Harry, and he kept a log of every fish he caught in the main lake and transported to a new lake.

It was a ritual for J.E. and Harry to "ride the ranch" almost every Wednesday afternoon. While Harry fished, J.E. worked on his mail. At an appointed hour, Harry docked the boat, rang the huge bell at the ranch house, and the two men happily drove from lake to lake leaving the newly-caught fish to explore their new surroundings. In the meantime, the men would feed the alligators and often follow the buffalo.

It was 11:00 p.m. when Mark and Harry parked the Air Stream adjacent to the ranch house and the feeder filled with corn for appreciative game. As the men undressed in the light of the full moon and returned to their respective bunks, there was an ominous sound. Suddenly the thunder of hoofs on sod echoed through the night air, increasing from forte to fortissimo.

The men looked out the window and saw 125 buffalo headed directly toward the feeder. And the Air Stream was the only obstacle between the buffalo and the food supply…

At the last moment the thundering herd split, one half moving to one side, the other rounding the trailer at the other.

The bulging bodies of bison had given the men the second rush of excitement for the evening. Harry, in his humorous manner, addressed Mark, "You don't need to tell all your famous buddies at Mayo Clinic about losing the trophy bass. Why don't you tell them you're the first one to have been in a buffalo stampede?"

When I lost Harry, Mark was helpful. In the meantime, he had lost his dear wife, Betty, and we shared our grief. When visiting Mayo Rochester I would always stay at the Coventry home.

After one of these visits I discovered gossip pronounced a forthcoming wedding for us. When I called Mark and disclosed my concern, his answer satisfied me: "Fran, we know we're just dear and fast friends. Isn't that all that is important?" I agreed.

We lost Mark to cancer, and the world lost a great orthopedic surgeon.

—Composers: Frederick Delius and Eric Fenby

I never met Frederick Delius, but his amanuensis, Eric Fenby, became a close and devoted friend. It is difficult to determine where Delius ends and Fenby begins, but surely the latter made it possible for the world to hear and appreciate the haunting themes of Delius' music.

As a music major in college I had enjoyed Delius' music, but I was unaware of the fact Eric Fenby transposed the music of the paralyzed composer from 1928 to 1934. The musical world owes Fenby a great debt of gratitude.

Cousin Phyllis (Malmanger-Hermanson) is a Delius devotee, and when I first mentioned our Delius connection, she introduced me to some compositions of which I had no knowledge. Phyllis is a composer and performer in her own right, and one who has provided me with a childhood story.

When she was born I was four years old. My mother, recognizing my excitement and curiosity about the new baby, said, "The Easter bunny has just left a baby at Aunt Petra's (Petra Olson Malmanger). Would you like to see what the bunny brought?" Since the baby's birthday was October 25th, it didn't dawn on this four year old's mind that logic didn't apply.

And as I "fast forward" to the announcement by Dr. Franklyn Johnson of the appointment of me as the first Dean of the College of Music and Fine Arts at J.U., my life seriously becomes entwined with that of Delius and Fenby.

In 1961 the very first annual International Delius Festival was held at Jacksonville University at a much-publicized banquet. It was on that occasion Frank planned to make the surprise announcement about my appointment as Dean, and the renowned British conductor, Sir Thomas Beecham had accepted the invitation to attend. Unfortunately, he became ill and telegraphed his regrets, and it was our loss.

Prior to the banquet the Delius Association of Florida had been chartered as a not-for-profit organization, with Mrs. Henry Richmond as honorary chairman, Frank as president, and subscribed to by the late Hugh Alderman and C. Edward Bryan, Mrs. Walter F. Rogers and Mrs. John Donahoo, all of whom were splendid supporters of the cultural climate in Jacksonville. And it was Frank and Richard Suddath who engineered the moving of the Delius House from its original setting. The latter, the owner of a large moving company, accepted the challenge to float the house up the St. Johns River.

Delius had composed some of his most beautiful music on the east bank of the St. Johns River at Solano Grove Plantation at Picolata. The influence of the slave songs, the fragrant jasmine, the syncopated rhythms — all combined eventually with his love for Scandinavian music in unique and exquisite compositions. The ensuing Delius Festivals have provided a rich array of these musical works.

My files are filled with an abundance of correspondence with the members of the Delius Trust in London. The late Dr. Phillip Emanuel, the first trustee of Delius' music and co-trustee of

(Background) Delius House.
(above) Mr. & Mrs. Eric Fenby (center) with Delius supporters gather on the porch of the Delius House for a photo. (right) Sir John Barbirolli, left, former conductor of the Houston Symphony visited the Delius House with John Canarina and Fran.

the Delius Trust, received an honorary doctorate at J.U., an honor for which for which he was particularly grateful. Mother and I visited him and his wife, Miriam, in London some years later. We were amused by his reference to the very modest Delius House: "My, I wish we had it here in London. A flat like that would bring a fair price."

The following evening the Emanuels took us to dinner at a lovely restaurant. When the gourmet food arrived, Phillip said, "Now, isn't this much better, having each vegetable and the entree in separate dishes? You Americans mix everything up on one plate, and you don't know what you are eating." He laughed as he teased us good-naturedly. Mother, with her sparkling sense of humor, replied, "You see, it's because we value time so much, as well as informality. It all gets mixed up eventually anyway." From that moment on Phillip would always write, "Give my special love to that wonderful mother." Phillip was only one of Mother's long list of admirers.

It was a 22-year old Eric Fenby who left his home in Scarborough in England to live with the elderly Delius, who was then failing in health. Delius had responded to an admiring letter Eric had sent him, and there the friendship started. Eric describes it beautifully in his book, <u>Delius as I Knew Him</u>.

Fenby offered to go to Delius' home in Grez-sur-Loing in France to assist the composer, and the immediate acceptance by Mrs. Delius initiated a chapter of musical collaboration unique in history. And that chapter of his life was followed by a life of promoting the music of Delius.

Fenby received the "Order of the British Empire" in 1962 and Sir Malcolm Sargent wrote, "No honor has been more merited."

*Fran presents
Duke Ellington
with gift.*

Recommending Eric Fenby for an Honorary Doctor of Music degree at J.U. seemed to pale in comparison to his OBE, but he and his wife, Rowena, were deeply grateful. They followed this with other visits to Jacksonville, and our extensive correspondence throughout the years will undoubtedly document his American connections for the archives.

The late Eric Fenby will surely be known for his selfless and dedicated service to Delius, but also for his role at the Royal Academy of Music, his own compositions, and his gift as a conductor. Certainly my life has been made richer by our own association with the many friends from England who have attended our

Delius Festival — too many to list here, but always in my affection.

—Duke Ellington
*(awarded a special posthumous
Pulitzer Prize in 1999)*

"Satin Doll." And every woman in the audience thought the Duke was playing it for her. But on this one occasion he actually was playing it for me.

For two years I had been attempting to schedule the Duke for a concert, but the double problem of minimal funds and his inten-

Artis Gilmore and Fran.

J.U. Speaker Henry Cabot Lodge.

Artis Gilmore, movie, TV and Radio personality- Jay Thomas, Dr. Kinne and Frank Pace, Executive Producer of "Suddenly Susan", "For Your Love" and other hits.

Bob Hope signs a plate for Fran.

Fran poses with Doc Severinson.

A little kiss from Don Ho in Hawaii.

Frank Pace and Fran at Warner Bros. Studios.

Fred Seely escorts Fran when Florida Publishing Company names her it's first Eve of the Decade (1970-80).

Professor Dr. Max Horkheimer and his wife. (University of Frankfurt, Germany)

Flo, J.E. Davis and Col. Harry Kinne at the D Dot Ranch.

Dr. & Mrs. Phillip Emanuel (Delius Trust, London) and Fran.

sive concert schedule had brought what seemed to be insurmountable barriers. A concert I finally scheduled was canceled because of Duke's hospitalization for cancer. But I continued to call him after he was released from the hospital, and he very graciously agreed to include the concert in a tour previously scheduled for the South (and at a reduced fee since my funds were limited).

I had first met Duke Ellington when our Symphony commissioned him to compose a composition for concerts in Washington and New York. He produced a superb work, and I understood why for years I had been so fascinated with his distinctive style. Certainly his orchestra could not be matched. Duke possessed one of the greatest talents of the 20th Century, and he served as a magnet for the great jazz musicians who worked with him, names every jazz musician recognizes.

There were multiple parties for the Duke, and it was a delight getting to know this amazing man. I had always respected and admired his musical abilities, but now to recognize his charm and intellect was an added pleasure.

He was fascinated when I told him I was playing one of his standards, "In a Sentimental Mood" when Harry entered the door to call on me for our first date, a blind date it was. I was unaware Harry was standing behind me at the piano. This was his first glimpse of me, and his reaction was ambivalent, he later revealed — anger because I had broken two prior dates with him, but on the other hand thinking, "I may marry her."

Duke Ellington was amused at the story, and responded, "That's the magic of music." And until

Harry died, the Duke's number was "ours," and I played it for Harry each evening.

On one occasion while attending a cocktail party at the home of Symphony supporters, Ira and Nancy Koger, the Duke had inquired as to the date of my birthday. It was casual conversation, and I forgot all about it. Some months later I had been invited to a birthday luncheon in my honor, and as I walked in the door of the Phillips Fine Arts Building my secretary rushed out to greet me: "I didn't know you knew John Wayne. He sent you three dozen long-stemmed roses."

"I don't know John Wayne," I replied. But the mystery was solved as I looked at the card she had already read: "Love, peace, joy. (Signed) The Duke." Of course, it was Duke Ellington, not John Wayne.

The Duke's appearance at J.U. had extensive advance publicity, and it pleased me he was bringing his star performers. I arranged to meet him at the motel so that I could escort him to the concert. Their travel schedule was tight, since the Duke had added our concert to his already packed schedule, a generous act on his part since he was ill. How ill, I didn't realize until I called on him at the motel.

Information had been given prior to the Duke's arrival indicating he was not strong enough to walk any distance. It was arranged for him to dress in my office, which was adjacent to the gym, the setting for the concert. But when we arrived, Duke indicated he couldn't manage the steps. The dressing rooms in the gym had steps to a lower level and the only alternative was the janitor's broom closet. The idea of the "Jazz Great" dressing in the

broom closet wasn't a thought to savor, but there was no choice. I scrambled around trying to find someone with a key to the closet while the Duke good-naturedly stood by apologizing for any inconvenience he was causing. He was a sick man, and I even had to assist him in walking to the stage.

That is where the magic of this man seemed to take on the miracle of a sunrise. As he seated himself at the piano the dynamic Duke was himself, and the audience seemed to catch the electricity of the moment.

I had worried that the "streakers" who were rumored to be planning a prankish evening in the dorms would reduce the size of the audience. But once the rhythms of the music pulsated across the valley, our Pied Piper had attracted musicians and non-musicians alike to a "standing-room only" gathering.

The Duke announced there would be no Intermission, and he seemed to gather energy with each number. When he dedicated "Satin Doll" to me I was happy I had worn my black satin formal for this historic evening, but I was sad because I knew this farewell would be the final one.

As he entered the car to drive on to Tampa that same evening he kissed my cheek and said, "Come see me in New York."

He passed away soon after that. But Harry and I did go to New York to see his son, Mercer. The Duke Ellington Orchestra was appearing at Lincoln Center with the Alvin Ailey Dance Theatre. Prior to the concert Mercer entertained us at cocktails and we drank a toast to the man who remembered my birthday — and changed music forever.

—*Maestro Arthur Fiedler*

Arthur Fiedler was like Santa Claus to me. He was immortal, or so I thought, and his sixteen visits to Jacksonville and J.U. only substantiated the belief that he would always be here.

I didn't approve of most of the biographies written about the Maestro. Of course, we often judge celebrities by the tabloid stories, or by authors who have but brief opportunities to know the "real" person about whom they are writing.

It is worrisome to realize that some history as we know it is written and preserved in the same manner. I recall the visit of a distinguished author to Japan, when he stayed three weeks at the Imperial Hotel where we were living. It was incredible to me when some months later his book appeared — an analysis of the "Oriental mind."

Fiedler's personality very likely engendered some of the less than complimentary comments about him, but to me they weren't valid. "Parsimonious" they said. Quite to the contrary with me. The Maestro would be showered with gifts by his admirers, but when he left Jacksonville he would present them to me with his usual salutation, "For Fran, the Fan."

In the early Seventies the Maestro invited Harry and me to Boston for a Pops Concert. Due to a prior commitment it was impossible for Harry to accept, so I invited C. Edward Bryan, our superb choral director, to accompany me. Coincidentally, Alex Brest's son Paul (later Dean of the Stanford Law School) and daughter-in-law

Fran listens attentively as Arthur Fiedler speaks at JU luncheon.

Iris were being graduated from the Harvard Law School the same weekend. Peter, Paul's younger brother, was not present, but he could tell this story by memory.

Of special interest was the appearance of the Chair of my Division of Music, Dr. Gerson Yessin, as a soloist with the Pops. As a gifted young man he had performed with them many times, and I recommended to Fiedler that he invite Gerson for the concert we would attend. Complications arose because Gerson was not a Union musician, but Fiedler maneuvered that in his usual persuasive manner. Gerson's performance was a stellar one, as I knew it would be.

Danny Kaye was a guest conductor for one of the symphonic selections. His entrance caused a stir as he appeared in black tails and white sneakers. There was laughter as he pirouetted his graceful frame to the lectern, picked up his baton, tapped his music rack for attention, and the musicians responded enthusiastically. From that moment on it was serious business for Danny Kaye, and the audience showed appreciation with a standing ovation.

Later I attended an intimate reception as Fiedler's guest, and when the Maestro introduced Kaye to me my first words were, "Symphonic music lost a fine conductor when the movies won you." His gracious response was a modest one, and I hastened to add, "But millions of people are happy you chose the cinema." With that I received a warm hug.

I had first met Fiedler when he came to assist in the dedication of the Phillips Music and Fine Arts Building. It was a French impressionist sort of day, with the sun playing leap-frog with the dancing leaves of the great oaks. Fiedler, Mrs. J.E. Davis (Flo), Alex Brest (our patron) and I were seated directly in front of a lectern at the entrance to the building.

A respectable crowd of guests and students had gathered as we initiated the brief program. Fiedler's remarks were appropriate and inspiring as he spoke in his articulate manner. When he sat down he looked at Flo who was wearing a stunning hat with colorful peacock feathers, and queried of her, "Did you shoot that bird?"

I could write volumes about this gentleman who became one of my dearest friends, so I selected carefully the more colorful stories about this conductor who introduced the joy of music to millions. From 1930 until his death, the Maestro challenged the musical world with his phenomenal success with the Boston Pops. But it wasn't just Boston, for he was an intercontinental "jet setter" with unflagging energy — tireless at the lectern and uncompromising in his musical demands of orchestras. His recordings are still heard everywhere there is radio communication.

On one occasion I called him in an emergency. Our Jacksonville Symphony was in difficulty, and a benefit concert with him at the lectern would sell out the house. But the window of time was short for us, and his schedule was completed at least a year in advance.

When I reached him at Symphony Hall at Boston, my voice must have had a pleading tone, a sense of urgency, for he responded, "What can I do for 'Fran-the-Fan'?" He managed to shift a San Francisco engagement, and we did sell out the house.

Jacksonville adored Fiedler. It was several years later we had a "We love you, Arthur Fiedler Day," and with the cooperation of the City Fathers it was a smashing success.

The evening of the concert, the Maestro had his baton raised, ready to initiate the evening's festivities with a rousing version of "The Star Spangled Banner." All of a sudden,

in the hush of the concert hall, a male voice cried aloud from the balcony, "We love you, Arthur Fiedler."

There was a ripple of vocal disbelief from the 3200 members of the Symphony audience. I reached for Harry's hand and held my breath. Fiedler was not known for his patience in such matters, and time and again he has said to me, "Perhaps the only place left for a dictator in this world is the symphony conductor, poised on the lectern, baton in hand."

My concern was short-lived. The baton was quickly lowered, as he did an about-face, nodded, smiled broadly and blew a kiss to the audience. The applause that followed was deafening, and the National Anthem followed with an added burst of enthusiasm.

Fiedler's favorite diversion when in Jacksonville was to come to our home after the rehearsals and concerts, but he didn't want a party. We would only invite the symphony conductor, John Canarina, William McNeiland (our J.U. conductor) and later Willis Page. Willis had played in Fiedler's Boston Pops Orchestra, and it was Bill McNeiland who came to the rescue of the Symphony during a year in which there was a crisis.

I had no choice about our midnight menu, as Fiedler liked my baked bacon and scrambled eggs. While I was preparing the food I was constantly checking, and I overheard the stories these men would relate. Harry was also a master storyteller, so he wasn't intimidated by the musical emphasis. Fiedler had a treasure trove of experiences which he related with delight. The others would match him story for story.

The only problem for me was trying to get to my office at 8:00 a.m.

Usually around 3:00 a.m. I would indicate it was time to adjourn, and the Maestro was going strong.

I am well aware of my gift of energy, and I recognize it is in my genes. I also believe the more energy I give away, I am gifted with more in return. It is interesting so many of the professionals with whom I became good friends seem to have that same philosophy — Fiedler believed it and certainly Bob Hope and Copland were also role models.

When the Maestro and I were discussing this magic energy between bites of bacon and eggs one mellow midnight — I queried him about his amazing level of energy. He pulled a worn newspaper clipping from his jacket and handed it to me. It read, "He who rests rots."

On several of Fiedler's visits, J.E. and Flo Davis graciously offered to assist us in entertaining the Maestro, inviting us to the magnificent D-Dot Ranch, just thirty minutes from downtown Jacksonville. Fiedler was fascinated by the many alligators, particularly so when J.E. and Harry practiced their grunting-alligator mating calls. Many gators glided swiftly across the lake to the dock on which we were standing.

Fiedler was astounded, and with a twinkle of the eye and a laugh at his lips, Fiedler offered, "I'm going to practice that on Mrs. Fiedler when I get home." A year later we returned to D-Dot Ranch with the Maestro. As we stood on the dock, he volunteered in a cryptic voice, "I tried it on Mrs. Fiedler, and it didn't work."

One of my gifts to him was a scrapbook with a letter from the Governor of every state. And so many of them wrote, "He and his music changed my life."

Fran and Arthur Fiedler sit in the living room at Fran & Harry's home.

Fran and Arthur Fiedler on his return to JU.

Arthur Fiedler, Fran and Fran's mother, Bertha at the Jacksonville Airport.

Former Jacksonville Symphony Conductors celebrate a 2000 Symphony Reunion. (l-r) Willis Page and John Canarina.

One of Fiedler's many letters to me is this one of March 28, 1977:

Dear Fran-the-Fan,

It was fun to be with you and Harry, and I always enjoy the bacon and eggs after a hard rehearsal. Spring was all around us, but then disappeared with a tremendous storm of snow and rain. I hope you are faring better.
With my very kindest regards to you and your mother and Harry.

Love,
  Arthur

I still miss Arthur Fiedler after all these years, but his magic lives on. And when I hear his rousing version of the "Stars and Stripes Forever" — every day is the 4th of July.

—Malcolm S.(Steve) Forbes, Jr.

The Forbes name has been legendary for three generations, playing an important role in the publishing business. However, it took Malcolm (Steve) Forbes, Jr. to toss his hat into the political arena.

My first meeting with Steve was some years ago when he spoke to business leaders, and I was mesmerized by his speech. His philosophy was that on which I had been raised: Look beyond the surface of things, always emphasizing the importance of ideas. His message is always clear and compelling: "Less government rather than more." From the beginning, I knew we were singing the same song. It was a message I wanted students to hear.

I invited him to speak at J.U. His acceptance was very likely prompted by his interest in the Free Enterprise program we had been developing. In addition, he learned of the award J.E. Davis had established. It was in memory of Harry and was called "The Colonel Harry L. Kinne Free Enterprise Award," presented at an annual luncheon to an outstanding business leader.

Steve Forbes

It was appropriate to give formal recognition each year to an individual who represented the finest qualities in a world hungry for strong, ethical leadership. And it was also entirely appropriate to name the award after Harry, a gentleman who had fought in two wars to preserve our system of government and to promote freedom for others. Steve Forbes recognized our efforts to remind people of how proud and appreciative we are to live in this great country.

Steve's next visit to Jacksonville gave us the opportunity to present him as our Commencement speaker, as well as to award him our Honorary Doctorate. He charmed the graduates, as I knew he would. His brilliance was warmed by his splendid sense of humor. His introductory remarks on that April 29, 1989 day included a delightful story:

About a year after I joined the company, one of my younger brothers also joined the family welfare roll. In those young and naive days we used to tease my father. We called it teasing; he called it something else. We used to tell him how good he would look with a gold watch. We urged him to spend more time in sunnier climes outside the headquarters in N.Y., and subtle hints like that. One day he had enough and he called my brothers and me into his office and told us a story about a family out in Oklahoma.
A father out there owned several newspapers and he brought his son into the business. The father was in his fifties; the son was in his twenties. Nonetheless, the son suggested they put in a mandatory retirement age of 65. (This was before Claude Pepper.) The father said, "Gee, son, that's a splendid idea. We'll put it in for everybody but me." The father proceeded to live through his 60s, 70s, 80s, and when he was 97 years old (he was still running the company and he still had that 51 percent), he toddled into his son's office one day and said, "Son, you're 65, you're out."

Several days after Steve Forbes returned to N.Y. I received this letter (dated May 1, 1989) which was generous on Steve's part:

Dear Fran:

There's no way to thank you adequately. Saturday was one of the most delightful days I've had. I've never been so honored! Moreover, the graduates were a very nice and responsive group — a great tonic for a speaker!

I enjoyed also the Friday night dinner. Those fireworks (I'll give you credit for them!) were a great way to end the evening.

You are obviously one of the most extraordinary people in the world today, and it is a great privilege for me to be able to know that I am one of your many friends.

Thank you again for everything — including the rides in your sensational new car!

You might get a chuckle out of the enclosed, which has on it the motto of Forbes magazine.

Cordially,
/s/ Steve

Bill Gay, Steve Forbes and Fran. Forbes receives his Honorary Doctorate while at JU as the Commencement speaker.

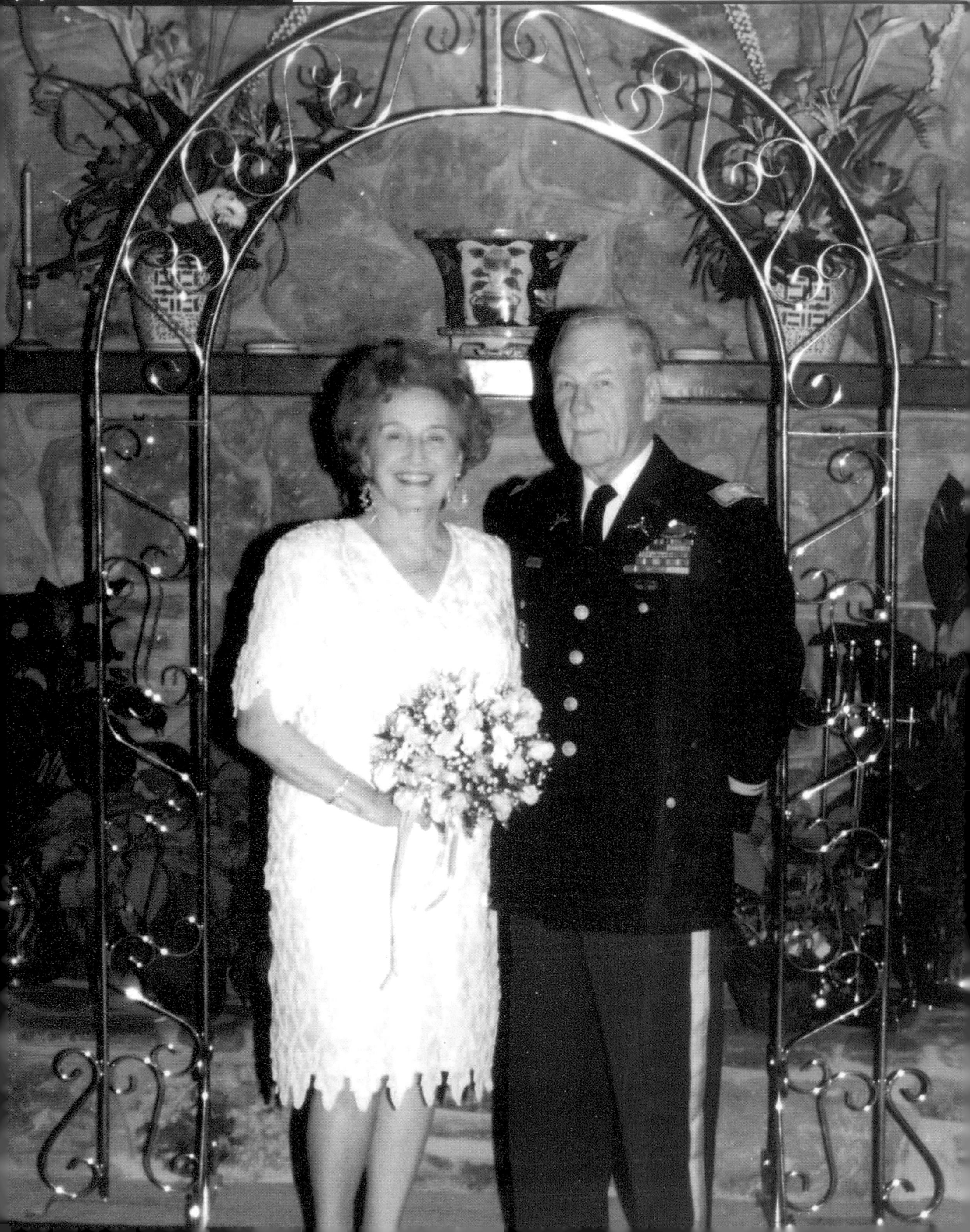

Later, the Vice President of Development, Don Ames; the J.U. Business Dean, Felix Livingston; Chairman of the Board of Trustees, Ash Verlander; and I called on Steve at his office in the Forbes Building on Fifth Avenue. When we departed he insisted on accompanying us down the stairs and out on the street. Wherein he walked into the busy traffic of that famous street, raised his hand and hailed a cab for us. I have learned a lot from this fine gentleman, and much of it is a review of what my father and mother taught me.

When Wordy (Col. M. Worthington Bordley, Jr.) and I were married in 1992, Steve sent us a set of exquisite, hand-painted plates. Each was an image of a different Forbes property. But the Forbes Building is my favorite. Built in 1925 under the direction of the future British Prime Minister, Harold MacMillan, the building is a handsome structure.

But that is not why the Forbes Building plate is my favorite. It is because it reminds me of one of my favorite friends, standing in the middle of busy Fifth Avenue and hailing a cab.

— Charlton (Chuck) Heston

One of the most intelligent and articulate figures in public life is Charlton Heston. He is the actor <u>par excellence</u>, a superb writer, a man of political conviction, honest and forthright, who has courage to stand up for his strong set of values.

I first met him when he was playing in a benefit tennis tournament, and of course I invited him to J.U. I arranged for an Honorary Doctorate to be awarded at an all-school convocation. Heston's speech was a college professor's dream of the perfect world. "Learn your English well. It is a pathway to the stars."

As he spoke he gathered each one of us into his brilliant symphony of words — students, faculty and community guests alike. And as he built to the climax he raised his arms, covered with the sleeves of the black doctoral robe. From his lips came Prospero's farewell speech from Shake-speare's <u>The Tempest</u>:

Our revels now are ended.
These our actors,

As I foretold you,
were all spirits, and

Are melted into air,
into thin air.

And, like the baseless
fabric of this vision,

The cloud-capped towers,
the gorgeous palaces,

The solemn temples,
the great globe itself —

Yea, all which it inherit
— shall dissolve

And, like this insubstantial
pageant faded,

Leave not a rack behind.
We are such stuff

As dreams are made on,
and our little life

Is rounded with a sleep.
Sir, I am vexed.

Bear with my weakness,
my old brain is troubled.

Be not disturbed with
my infirmity.

If you be pleased,
retire into my cell,

And there repose.
A turn or two I'll walk,

To still my beating mind.

(page 124) December 12, 1992 — Fran marries Col. M. Worthington Bordley in a private ceremony at the Verlander home.

(left) The Forbes plates that Steve gave Fran & Col. Wordy as wedding gift.

(above) Charlton Heston at JU.

(below) Chuck & Fran pose for a photo

As he stood transfixed in the last word, there was a penetrating silence — a minute of timelessness. And then after the dramatic pause the audience broke into enthusiastic applause, students whistled, stamped their feet, and yes, they even screamed.

That moment alone made years of educational effort worthwhile. It was Shakespeare, instead of a basketball game. And it was Heston who worked the miracle.

We have continued a lively correspondence throughout the years, and one of his letters came at a strategic time in Wordy's fatal illness. Chuck sent his book <u>In The Arena</u> to me and autographed it, "To Fran, who knows the arena well." And it was the note he enclosed in the book that inspired hope to Wordy and gave courage to me: "May God hold you in the palm of his hand."

And indeed he did!

—Jerome Hines

We had many talented and gracious vocal stars who appeared for our students throughout the years. However, none worked under such difficult circumstances as the great Metropolitan bass, Jerome Hines.

Arrangements had been accelerated by Ruth and Paul Conley. Both were patrons of the arts. Ruth's splendid musical knowledge and Paul's support opened the doors for us to share in the remarkable talent of Jerome Hines. He graciously agreed to do a Master Class for our Voice

Jerome Hines and Fran.

majors in the College of Fine Arts, as well as a concert. Unfortunately, his appearance was on the coldest day of the year, and Florida isn't accustomed to the problems arising from a rare night of icy temperatures.

The heat in the auditorium was minimal, and Jerome Hines sang a magnificent concert to an appreciative (but very small) audience. My teeth were chattering from the cold, but this artist managed to fill the auditorium with his rich, full bass voice.

After the concert, I apologized for the freezing weather, the very small audience, and everything else for which I could apologize. The goodness of this man matched his artistry: "My dear, I sing the same, whether I am singing for one or one thousand. If I provide joy for one, that is meaningful to me." A great philosophy.

— Juilliard String Quartet

For years we scheduled the famous Juilliard String Quartet for an annual concert, and it was always a sell-out.

After Joel Krosnick became the cellist, a new spirit prevailed. Joel is the brother of Aaron Krosnick, the fine violinist I had the good fortune of employing at J.U. That was a coup, for that meant we captured Aaron's pianist wife, Mary Lou Krosnick. Each has a magnificent talent, and their lives are filled with the giving of that talent.

I invited the Juilliard to J. U. to receive Honorary Doctorates. I had wanted us to be the first school to recognize them, but Michigan "sneaked in" before us. However, on this particular visit the four members of the group led Master classes for our students and presented a superb concert.

It was a unique setting to present the doctorate, but we had done this on several previous occasions.

However, it is the only event where a humorous situation developed, and I came very near to losing control. I had asked Aaron Krosnick to read his brother's citation, and we were concerned Joel would be called to New York at any moment to be present at the birth of his first child.

Some bantering went on between the two brothers, and the serious moment suddenly seemed ludicrous to me. We all started to giggle — then outright laughs erupted. It took every ounce of control I could muster

(left) The Juilliard String Quartet pose with Fran in her home.

(below) The Quartet in the concert attire.

to take command of the situation.

The very distinguished and dignified Juilliard String Quartet suddenly seemed to resemble four young boys who had just pulled a prank on Halloween, and I wasn't much better.

It was a year later on a return concert I invited them to my home post-concert for beverages and food, prior to their return flight to New York. We all made conversation about the historic night of the doctorates. In the meantime, the airline kept reporting a delayed flight, so I kept the bar open for several more hours.

Before they left I took a picture of them. I have the "Before" and "After" pictures, side-by-side on my wall, and they have prompted amused reactions from the many music admirers of the Juilliard!

(above) Dear Abby, Abigail VanBuren and Fran in 1980.

*(right) Ann Landers (below) Ann Landers and Fran at the
1998 Commencement where Ann received an Honorary Doctorate at Drake University.*

I have a vivid and happy memory of the four of them and their instruments as they crowded into the departing car, merrily waving farewell, laughing and singing their way to the airport. Four fine men who play the music of angels.

— Ann Landers and Dear Abby, The Iowa Twins

Iowa is proud of the twins who "made good." And Sioux City is known for something in addition to the war-time song of "Sioux City Sue." These remarkable women have made a difference. Each has a strong sense of ethics and is dedicated to assisting others.

Because of our Iowa ties I invited each of them to our campus to receive an Honorary Doctorate, and each was warmly received.

Intelligent, petite and pretty Ann and Abby have been the conscience

of America. While mores of society change, the twins have not been hesitant about reminding us of civilized standards of conduct. Likewise they are willing to go out on a limb to do it, and, wonder of wonders, America listens.

Perhaps I have developed a closer friendship with Ann (Eppie) because each of us is without a spouse. Professional women who are called upon for public appearances and social engagements share similar problems.

I also nominated Ann for an Honorary Doctorate at Drake University and had the pleasure of introducing her for the award at the 1998 Commencement. After the Recessional one of the graduates pulled me aside and said, "She changed my life. I wouldn't be a graduate if I hadn't read her column. I'm a single mother and —" Just then a beautiful curly-headed girl pounced on her mother, pulling her away, and I never heard the rest

of her story. However, similar stories may be heard on every campus across the United States.

I don't know who wrote the script for the unauthorized movie about the twins, but it is unfortunate the writer never was privy to the countless stories students revealed to me throughout the years.

Those columns continue to be dynamite, and we thank the twins for not only reminding us how very beautiful life may be, but for our responsibility to make it so for others.

Fran and Patrice Munsel.

—Patrice Munsel

One of my early guests was the beautiful Metropolitan Opera soprano, Patrice Munsel. She presented a Master Class for the voice majors and sang a concert for a large audience.

After she departed I spoke with the students, inviting their reactions. One obese freshman female voice major responded, "I learned two things. First, I need to relax my chin when I am singing."

Since she didn't offer her second point, I said, "And?"

She looked embarrassed but determined, "I am going to lose 40 pounds. You just wait and see. When I do my Senior Recital (a requirement) my waist will look like hers. And I'm going to wear false eye lashes just like hers."

Three years later she had lost the weight and she did wear the false eye lashes at her Senior Recital.

I sat there and felt a little guilty about my own waistline!

— Patrica Neal

One of the ancillary benefits of scheduling great talents is observing the exciting changes that take place in the audiences who are able to enjoy the first-hand experience. This is valid whether it is an audience living through the aesthetic or the one-on-one association. My 18 years as the Dean of the College of Fine Arts, and my 10 years as President, provided rich opportunities to offer a plethora of stimulating "stars" from varying disciplines.

Patricia Neal, an actress whose dramatic gift has succeeded in spanning several generations, visited campus soon after her much publicized stroke. To this day she continues to give generously of her great ability to mesmerize her audiences.

As a beautiful young star and the object of the movie magazines' concentration on her love life, she convinced her audiences there was much more to her than what the tabloids wrote.

Certainly her association with our students taught them the importance of dogged determination and discipline. "You can overcome," she told them. Indeed!

—Dr. Linus Pauling

Because Dr. Linus Pauling was the only double Nobel Prize winner in the world (Medicine and Peace) my goal was to honor him. He was very much in demand, and I knew I would need to use every creative resource to capture him. I had never met Dr. Pauling, but I relied at first on the U.S. Mail and my trusty telephone.

After the faculty gave me enthusiastic support and the Board of Trustees approved the Honorary Doctorate, I sent the invitation Special Delivery Air Mail. My follow-up telephone call was to Dorothy, his talented and dedicated secretary.

"Watch for my letter, and please be sure Dr. Pauling sees it."

She assured me he would read it, and indeed he not only read it but called me personally to accept. I was astounded and ecstatic, all at the same time.

Fran, with the help of Dr. John Trainer, honors Dr. Linus Pauling with an Honorary Doctorate, which was approved and enthusiastically supported by the Faculty and Board of Trustees at JU.

Dr. Linus Pauling on his visit to JU.

Shortly after that his wife, life partner and co-worker, passed away, and I called to express my sympathy. As time passed I was concerned that in his grief Dr. Pauling would change his mind.

Since I had a speech and meeting in San Francisco I decided to ask him for an appointment at his office at the Linus Pauling Institute in Palo Alto. On arrival in San Francisco I rented a car and drove to the Institute to meet the distinguished gentleman.

As I entered his office I was met by this very handsome and kindly elderly gentleman. Beret perched jauntily on his shock of white hair, smiling broadly, eyes twinkling he extended his hand.

"Dr. Kinne, you didn't need to come clear out here to ensure my visit to Jacksonville. I made a promise to you, and I will keep it."

As he said this, he held the chair for me to be seated. I said to myself, "I like this man."

He called his assistant in to meet me, and as he shook my hand there was a note of nostalgia in his voice. This Austrian gentleman had his eyes riveted on a gold coin I was wearing on a chain.

"Franz Joseph — where did you get that?"

And it was a 1915 gold Austrian coin with the likeness of the Emperor.

Dr. Pauling was a charmer, and he seemed to enjoy our visit. I determined I must leave for the drive back to San Francisco, and as I reached the door I said, "Your secretary told me how many invitations you receive each year. Why did you accept mine?"

His response was immediate: "Because you sent your invitation Special Delivery Air Mail, and I liked your persistence." Then he added with a chuckle, "And you have such a pretty voice on the telephone."

Of course, I melted.

We had agreed that Dr. Pauling would speak to community leaders and local physicians at a reception I would host. This was highly successful, and he won over the non-Vitamin C believers as well as many of the military men. My dear Harry had already passed away, but I am confident he would have shared my enthusiasm.

Dr. Pauling was a guest in my home, and my maid of 20 years was aflutter. I had a full refrigerator with both nutritious food and cholesterol-laden bacon and eggs. Since I had to leave the house early in the morning to prepare for the Convocation, it was Estelle's duty to feed Dr. Pauling the nutritious food for breakfast. Not so. He preferred what the Verlanders call a "farmer's breakfast."

Estelle served the bacon, eggs, grits and buttered toast. Later her description covered the second serving she gave him on his request, "And he ate and ate and just ate some more."

I always used student assistants in the office, and they had a game of Lotto to see which one would assist Dr. Pauling. When it came time for the Processional, however, there were dozens of "assistants" just waiting to rub shoulders with this great man.

The students fell in love with Linus Pauling. As one student remarked, "He's like everyone's grandfather, only everyone's grandfather doesn't have two Nobel prizes."

There were more than five thousand in the audience who must have rushed out to buy Vitamin C, as the next day it wasn't available on any shelf in Jacksonville.

I continued to stay in correspondence with Linus Pauling, who would always sign his letters "Linus." I nominated him for a prestigious international science award for which he was selected, but he was unable to attend the meeting. However, his son repre-

Fran and Dr. Linus Pauling pose together for a photo.

sented him and accepted the award in his absence.

He made a lasting mark on the young students who were fortunate enough to hear him. He made a lasting mark on this writer. But more importantly his lasting mark was much larger — the world.

—H. Ross Perot

In an effort to expose students to a wide and diverse selection of public figures the name of Ross Perot kept surfacing. J.E. Davis knew Mr. Perot, and a telephone call to him initiated correspondence which brought positive results.

I had launched an Executive MBA program several years earlier, and I felt it was important for the class of 30 successful business men and women to hear Perot. In addition, I wanted him to be the Commencement speaker.

On the day of Commencement Mr. Perot left Hawaii in the middle of the night on his own plane, arrived in ample time to robe for the ceremony, and presented a thoughtful speech to the graduates.

Immediately after the two hours of Commencement I took him by the hand to the Executive MBA class, where he lectured to the students, in between bites of our picnic baskets of chicken. He really came into his own in the hour of questions and answers. That was the real Ross Perot, the free enterprise success story.

A reporter was covering Mr. Perot's visit, and the paper quoted him the next day: "It was amazing to see so many students hugging the President. I have never seen that before."

(above)
Fran & Ross Perot enjoy a laugh together at JU when he visited as the Commencement speaker.

(Inset)
Ross Perot in his JU Dolphin's hat.

— Royalty

The many years in the educational field have been rewarding in so many ways. If one is motivated by teaching and enjoys students, the profession is highly gratifying. Even as Dean and President I kept an "open door," so that I wouldn't lose touch with the reason universities exist — for the students. It is unfortunate some institutions and corporations become so involved with aesthetics and superficial appearances. In so doing they forget the heart of what it is all about, and lose the fun of it.

I could write books about the students who touched my life; I truly cared for them, and I still do. It is a rare day I don't get a letter, card or phone call from one of the thousands, and there isn't a week that goes by that I am not writing a reference or recommendation for a graduate or faculty member.

Prince Khalid (Son of King of Saudi Arabia) and Dr. Kinne.

One of my interesting graduates was Prince Khalid, son of the King of Saudi Arabia. He arrived with his entourage while I was Dean of the College of Fine Arts. Perhaps because of my years of overseas experience I was selected to advise the Prince. He was a tall, handsome man and was gracious in entertaining faculty and students.

On one occasion the Prince and his staff had a Saudi dinner prepared for us, and a mock Saudi wedding was performed with music and dress. The reaction of over 300 American students was a genuine appreciation in understanding the cultural differences.

The Prince flew to Saudi Arabia for special holidays, and he always returned with a lovely gift for me. On one occasion it was a black and gold ceremonial dress, and a perfect size. When I commented about the proper fit he responded, "That was easy, you are the same size as my mother."

I always sent a modest gift to the King, and I often thought he must have thought his son's Dean must be a crazy American. On one occasion I sent gold paper clips (one could not send plain paper clips to a King), and on another I gift-wrapped wooden book-ends in gold paper. After all there isn't much wood in Saudi Arabia, I rationalized.

I became very fond of Prince Khalid, and I look forward to his return visits. It is always a delight to welcome him with his friend (also a J.U. graduate) Fahad, and my early graduate and long term friend, Karim Cadora.

In saying farewell to students after four years of association I have always concluded my remarks with the following: "You are initiating a new phase of your lives. We are changed because of you, and you leave a part of yourselves here. Likewise, you take something of us when you depart, and you are changed as well."

Certainly the daily dynamics of our lives deal with our interconnection with others. We grow and add another fiber to that "Golden Thread" with each relationship.

Because of Prince Khalid I understand more about Saudi Arabia and its people. I am so happy he wants to return to Jacksonville to see me, and our warm friendship allows me a feeling of sadness when he leaves.

—Dr. Charles L. Schepens

Dr. Charles L. Schepens must surely be recognized as one of the most outstanding scientific figures of this Century. As the Father of Modern Retinal Surgery, he has received world recognition for his many achievements, as well as the devotion of thousands of patients.

Certainly he changed my life with his very special surgical skills, and the ensuing friendship with him and his wife, Cette, has had very treasured meaning for me.

I had learned about Dr. Schepens when we were stationed in Germany. My eye problem was worsening, and I saw Professor Dr. Thiel, a distinguished ophthalmologist in Frankfurt. He informed me that eventually I would need surgery and told me about Dr. Schepens, a name recognized by every eye doctor around the world. Dr. Schepens had invented the prototype of the indirect binocular ophthalmoscope, the instrument used by eye doctors internationally.

When I arrived in Florida several years later my own very fine ophthalmologist, Dr. Jerry Knauer, indicated he was a friend of Dr. Schepens and recommended I fly to Boston when the time for surgery would be needed — to "get away" from well-meaning students, faculty and friends. The iridectomny was the accepted procedure at that time, requiring the surgical removal of a small part of the iris and the lens. I respected the talent and expertise of Dr. W.J. Knauer and his son (my doctor) W.J. Knauer Jr., and now the latter's son, Dr. W.J. Knauer III. Because of this I followed the advice to go to Boston. The surgery was a great success — congenital and senile (I objected to that word) cataracts.

There have been so many times in my life when my destiny seems to have been taken care of by a higher order. Perhaps it is that angel I feel is always present. I was in Boston presenting a speech at a meeting, looked up Dr. Schepens' telephone number and called his office. The secretary responded, "Dr. Schepens just walked in. Would you like to speak to him?"

When Dr. Schepens answered the phone, I explained my situation, and he said, "Could you come to my office right now?" I was astounded, as I knew this gentleman was booked many months in advance for his appointments.

I walked briskly from my hotel to 100 Charles River Plaza on Cambridge Street, and was ushered into Dr. Schepens' office on my arrival. The moment I met this gentle, brilliant man I felt assured that my future was in his hands.

I had not been able to drive at night, and the musical notes on the page were getting more difficult to read. His prognosis was guarded. (One must recognize that most of the advances in eye surgery had not been developed in the late Sixties.) He suggested I return to Jacksonville, discuss this surgery with my husband, and decide whether or not I wanted to attempt something which had some

doubt as to its success.

Several months went by during the period of time Harry and I discussed the ramifications of the surgery. Of course, the alternative was bleak, and we both decided to "go for it."

I was Dean of the College of Fine Arts at the time, and I kept my plans secret until the day of my departure, because the results were questionable, and I did not want to distress the many people who were supporting me. I was particularly grateful to Harry, as he desperately needed a total hip operation, but he insisted that my surgery had priority.

Dr. Schepens determined that he would do one eye on a Monday and a second eye on Thursday. It was easy to see where my priorities were, as my first question was, "How in the world will I eat with both eyes covered?"

Harry's response was immediate: "You can stand on your head that long if it means you are going to have successful results." I have repeated his statement over and over to students who faced crisis and were reluctant to take action.

When Dr. Schepens carefully lifted the bandages that following week, jubilantly I said, "Dr. Schepens, you have a beautiful tie, and I can't believe the colors in it."

*Dr. Charles Schepens
and Dr. Kinne.*

(l-r) J.E.Davis, Grace Osborne, Bob Hope, Fran and guests listen attentively as President Gerald Ford speaks at Epping Forest, former home of Mr. & Mrs. Raymond Mason.

(l-r) Former Mayor Ed Austin, Eloise Gay and her husband Bill Gay, Fran and Mayor John Delaney at a Ronald McDonald Benefit.

Count and Countess Amadeo Zedtwitz, a very proud cousin of Mark Twain.

Pres. Gerald Ford with Mrs. Walter Rogers (left) and Fran.

Pres. Ford and Fran at his Rancho Mirage office.

Pres. Ford gives Fran a kiss good-bye after visiting Jacksonville.

Pres. George Bush and Fran.

In the meantime, Harry Kinne had to return to Jacksonville, and I spent several weeks in the hotel with daily visits to Charles River Plaza. I took a taxi to and from the office, and the results were both exciting and traumatic. I had lived in a myopic world, and suddenly everything seemed of gigantic size to me. I had lectured on color, and suddenly the magnificence of the spectrum exploded in front of me. The stoplight! The sky! The trees!

Student unrest at that time was certainly prevalent in Boston, and a sit-in in front of my hotel presented a problem on one occasion. A taxi driver (who seemed to be accustomed to handling eye patients) graciously took me to the back door and led me through the kitchen to the elevator. I had learned where the 4th floor button was, and that was my security blanket.

Returning to Jacksonville, I experienced many of the same reactions as that of my father (whose story is in Appendix "A"). It seemed I was appreciative of the simple things in life and grateful for every moment.

Returned to Jacksonville, my post-operative visit to Dr. Knauer was early on a rainy morning, and by that time I was driving with great joy. I parked my car. Suddenly noticing the raindrops on the leaves of the trees I rolled down the windows of my car. It was a scene of thousands of scintillating diamonds to me. Tears rolling down my cheek I dashed into the office crying, "Have you ever really looked at raindrops?" They all knew what I was talking about and smiled at my reaction.

Yes, Dr. Schepens changed my life.

Is it any wonder that this giant of a man is my idol?! But Dr. Schepens is also Monsieur Perot, and both Army husbands shared my admiration for his remarkable Resistance activities against the Nazis in World War II. He was arrested in Belgium by the Gestapo in 1940, and without any apparent reason was released several weeks later — and imprisoned again. He escaped to France, but the Gestapo were relentless in searching for him. At this point Dr. Schepens became Monsieur Perot, instead of Lt. Schepens.

In the Pyrenees Mountains near the Spanish border he performed a miracle, rebuilding a cable car on the mountain. In his Underground activities, this served as an escape route for the Resistance.

Perot became a legendary figure, arrested and imprisoned again and again. His escapes are an amazing story in themselves. Cette (his wife) walked eleven hours over the mountains to see her children who were with a babysitter in a vacant hut. She was captured by the Germans and returned to her home. But she escaped again and with the children, one on her shoulder and the other on her side, made a long march into the mountains through wind and storm and made it to Spain.

When World War II was over, Dr. Schepens resumed his practice, and fortunately for us, he and his remarkable wife came to the United States in 1947. He provided the first retina service, and initiated a center to do both clinical and research work. He did this with the same tenacious manner in which he became the legendary Perot, and the great Schepens Eye Research Institute now is the largest and most productive in the world.

Indeed, Dr. Schepens is one of the great scientific figures of our age, and I was fortunate he answered the telephone that day in Boston. And I am also grateful I was able to confer an honorary doctorate on this distinguished gentleman.

He continues to see patients and hold Emeritus status in the Schepens Eye Research Institute affiliated with Harvard University. A splendid selection to lead the Institute in the new millenium is the brilliant scientist, Dr. Wayne Streilein. No better team anywhere than Dr. Schepens and Dr. Streilein.

— *Frank Skinner*

In presiding at ceremonies one may expect the unexpected, and so it was for me at a Commencement on the lovely green on the campus of Jacksonville University on April 26, 1986. It was a strikingly beautiful day filled with the excitement of that special time of accomplishment in the lives of the graduating seniors.

I always had ambivalent feelings at graduation: joyful because of the achievements of young men and women who were my friends; but also a time tinged with a bit of sadness, for I knew there were many final farewells.

The setting for such a ceremony was always the consummate, outdoor arena. We rented 5000 chairs for graduates, family and friends, and constructed a stage for the platform party. On this day, the band had accompanied our processional, the mace had been placed in its holder with great ceremony.

Our guest speaker, who would also be the recipient of an Honorary Doctor of Laws, was B. Franklin Skinner, President and C.E.O. of Southern Bell. Seated beside Mr. Skinner was Jack H. Quaritius, Chairman of our Board of Trustees.

I was at the microphone welcoming everyone, when I was stunned by the loud crash directly behind me. Startled, I spun around and was horrified to see our guest speaker sprawled on the floor, all 6 feet 5 inches of him. Of the 5000 chairs, how could this one chair have broken into splinters?

Bob Phelps, columnist for the <u>Jacksonville Journal</u>, covered the story in a column three years later (Saturday, Mar. 25, 1989):

After three years, Atlanta resident, B. Franklin Skinner, President and C.E.O. of Southern Bell, has sufficiently recovered from his visit to J.U. to make a return visit. He was seated on the platform during his introduction as the Commencement speaker in 1986 when his wooden chair collapsed.

"I was flat on my back," he said. I remember looking up at palm trees and clouds."

J.U. President Fran Kinne was speaking at the moment. Assured that Skinner wasn't injured, physically anyway, Dr. Kinne said to the crowd, "Now I hope you'll believe me when I say we need donations."

Skinner made a grand recovery. (For his speech) he said he had taken a poll of his family, including his daughters who were recent college graduates, and none remembered the Commencement speaker or what he had said. Skinner said, "I suspect 35 years from now, you won't be able to recall who the speaker was, but you'll never forget he fell out of his chair."

Later, Skinner sent Dr. Kinne a wooden chair, painted J.U. green and gold, with a seat belt attached. Skinner returns today to present the Colonel Harry L. Kinne Free Enterprise Award to community leader, Ash Verlander. That safety chair awaits Skinner.

Along with that chair came the accompanying note:

Dear Fran,

Since I destroyed your folding chair when I was on campus for your commencement exercises I wanted to replace the loss. This one should be sturdy enough to hold your future speakers.

Warmest regards,
Frank

(above) Ann Sothern & Fran with JU students.

(right) Ann Sothern in Fran's office.

— *Ann Sothern*

When the Thunderbird Dinner Theatre was in its hey day, Harry and I frequently were guests at the Opening Night productions. A highlight was the appearance of Ann Sothern starring in I Remember Irma. I had admired her on the screen, not only for her natural gift for comedy, but also as a musician and painter.

On the evening of the production we went backstage prior to the curtain to meet her and invite her to J.U. She graciously accepted, and, at the same time charmed us with her gracious and warm personality.

We had front table seats, only several feet from the stage. Moments into the production the audience was caught up in Ann's role as the bag-lady, but in a moment of surprise and concern we saw part of the set fall on Ann as she was descending a few steps. Unfortunately, the damage was

done, and Ann's visit to the E.R. revealed damage to her back.

The ensuing years have meant countless hospital visits and surgeries, but the injury took its toll. However, Ann kept her promise, and she did return to Jacksonville to work with our Theatre Arts majors, as well as to attend a Friends of the Fine Arts function.

After Harry passed away I visited Ann in Beverly Hills, and she took me to dinner at a restaurant frequented by the Stars. In a black jersey pants outfit she wore a dramatic scarf folded around her shoulders, with a flair movie actresses of that period did with style.

As we stepped in the door the maitre d' greeted Ann with obvious admiration and recognition, then led us to a window table. Ann and I are products of the Middle West, and our conversation certainly reflected our respect for its work ethic. A great place to raise

children we agreed, a fact the Children's Rights Council (an advocacy group) recognizes each year.

Ann drove me back to my hotel, and on the way I asked her to stop at a mailbox for me to mail my letters. As I got out of the car she said, "You've got good-looking legs, 'Fraunces.' You'll be re-married in a year." (I loved the way she pronounced my name.)

"Not me," was my answer. "I had a great marriage, and I won't gamble on another." Famous last words. When Wordy and I were married 9 years later I called her, and she answered, "I only missed it by eight years."

Ann presented me with a valuable gift of 120 of her TV films of "Maisie" and "Private Secretary." And these films are now in the archives of the J.U. Library.

She is a great lady, whether on or off the screen.

— George Steinbrenner and The Yankees come to town

It was a gala day and night for us when George Steinbrenner and the New York Yankees came to town. On March 9, 1983 a paid crowd of 11,119 established an attendance record for a game involving a collegiate team from the state of Florida. Approximately 1000 additional fans had to be turned away. Also, the event set a record for the city baseball center, Wolfson Park. And it was a Benefit, proceeds of which were to provide lighting for our baseball field at J.U.

Steinbrenner had brought the first string Yankees, which was the realization of my dream. This was all made possible by the superb assistance from Carl Ogden, who

George Steinbrenner and Fran.

was our initial contact, and the former U. of Florida athletic figure, Ray Graves.

The game started at 6:00 p.m., and one may only imagine the fever of excitement in the J.U. dugout. Coach Terry Alexander described it as a life-changing experience for all 30 J.U. players - and the weather allowed everyone the opportunity to play at some time during the game.

Steinbrenner seemed to enjoy it as much as the thousands of fans. And as I sat by Steinbrenner I was constantly entertained by the good-natured banter between him and Billy Martin.

On the field the Dolphins battled the Yankees through four scoreless innings, after which George Steinbrenner turned to me and said laughingly, "Fran, that wasn't part of the bargain."

Pitching for the Yankees were Ron Guidry, Rudy May, and Dave La Roche — to catcher Rick Cerone. The Yankee lineup also included: 1B, Butch Hobson; 2B, Willie Randolph; 3B, Greg Nettles; SS, Bobby Meacham; LF, Dave Winfield; CF, Oscar Gamble; RF, Brian Dayette; and DH, Don Baylor.

Our J.U. pitcher, Larry Heise, will certainly have something to tell his grandchildren, for Larry struck out Dave Winfield, Butch Hobson and Don Baylor in one inning.

The Yankees scored a lone run in the top of the fifth, and J.U. tied it at one in the bottom half of the sixth. The J.U. Dolphins had their

opportunities to take the lead, but they had two runners gunned down at the plate.

The New Yorkers scored one run in the seventh to take a 2-1 lead, before breaking it open with five runs in the eighth. Particularly exciting was the three-run homer by Butch Hobson.

Terry Alexander was in his fifth season as a coach with the J.U. Dolphins, having experienced many accelerated-pulse games. But that night was one that didn't end with the game. His friend Tommy Zimmer, a scout with the San Francisco Giants, had told his father, Don Zimmer, a coach with the Yankees, to spend time with the J.U. Coach.

Terry found himself invited out to dinner with Don Zimmer, and ended up sitting by Billy Martin, the colorful manager of the Yankees, and Yogi Berra, Jeff Torborg, and Art Fowler.

Terry told me he was floating on air all night long as Martin and Berra told story after story. Meanwhile I was having a late dinner with the Ogdens and Steinbrenner at the University Club.

I thought Steinbrenner was a charmer. And I wish the media could see this side of the Yankee's much-publicized owner.

What a great experience this game was for Terry and me, as well as for 30 young men and for thousands of spectators.

When I drove home I thought of my father when he coached the amateur American Legion team. I thought of his allowing me to sit on the bench with the players. I thought of my brother who had such promise as both a shortstop and a pitcher. And I thought of my father's good friend, Hank Severeid, who was Story City's own fine major league player in the Big Leagues.

Most of all, I was thankful I chose the great rewards of working with young people. This was one of hundreds of wonderful days and nights - actually thousands.

— Mel Tormé, The Velvet Fog

The late Mel Tormé was performing in the Venetian Room at the Fairmont Hotel in San Francisco, and I was an admiring listener at a front table. Since it was a pops concert, it caught me by surprise when he sang two of Delius' compositions. He then proceeded to explain to the audience his admiration for Delius music.

As presented earlier in my writing about Eric Fenby and the Delius Trust, the Delius cottage (where Delius had resided in the Eighties) was moved up the St. Johns River to Jacksonville University shortly before I founded the College of Music and Fine Arts. I was confident Tormé would enjoy seeing the Delius House.

After Mel Tormé's smashing performance, I went backstage to thank him for including the Delius songs. He was aware of the interesting history and colorful life of the composer, and naturally I invited Tormé to visit campus. Later we were able to schedule him for a concert with the Jacksonville Symphony. This was 1994, and the artist was still to have five more productive years before his death. Tormé's visit to the Delius House

was an emotional one for him. Dr. James Brady (then President of Jacksonville University), Sheila Brady and I stood quietly by while the musician whispered, "I am so honored to stand on the floor where Delius stood, and touch the piano on which he played."

That was a poignant reminder to me that every moment of our lives provides a meaningful opportunity for belonging to a place, a person or an experience. It is a linking process that suggests a transfer of energy.

Since music is such a compelling part of my life I experience a reaction every time I hear a familiar strain of music. It may be an appreciation for pure form in sound (Mozart). It may be the magnitude of a symphony (Beethoven). Or it could be the delicate perception of artists' unusual talents (Juilliard String Quartet). Or it could be any one of the thousands of melodies which are a part of me.

In Germany, when I visited "Linderhof," one of King Ludwig's castles, I was asked if I wished to play on the piano Wagner had used. I was honored but I declined. I felt it was more appropriate for me to absorb the moment by merely touching the instrument of the great operatic composer. That transfer of energy was present for me merely by touching the piano. Playing it after Wagner was unthinkable to me.

I understood what Mel Tormé meant when he expressed his emotions while standing on the floor in Delius' cottage.

It is safe to assume the tens of thousands (perhaps millions) of Tormé's admirers would feel the

same about the late musician. But he hasn't really left us. Our hearts will undoubtedly be warmed each Christmas as we sing along to his wonderful Christmas Song of "Chestnuts roasting on an open fire." And we'll remember someone or some place where we first heard this magical music.

—Arnold Toynbee

While I was Dean and founder of the College of Fine Arts at Jacksonville University, Franklyn Johnson invited this great historian to our campus. I was very taken with him, and we carried on a correspondence after his departure.

He had been invited to assist in the ground-breaking for our new College of Music and Fine Arts Building, and we were to dig the first spade of earth. The soil had not been prepared, and my spade refused to penetrate the dry, hard soil. Toynbee smiled and spoke quietly to me, "I thought you said you were from Iowa." This had meaning for him, since he left J.U. to spend four months residency at Grinnell College in Iowa.

As a Humanities professor I had often used Toynbee's brilliant works for required reading as we studied the epochs of our Western civilization. He taught us, "We can't really judge the importance of our own times." We are not in a position to answer for the future.

Fran's Valentine to the last Century's great historian.

In my own discussions with him, as well as in his speeches, he pointed to the various paths we could take toward the future. In my idealistic state of mind I asked, "Don't you feel the burden of what influence you have on this generation of students? You could change the course of history."

His response was that of an understanding and perhaps indulgent parent. His hand rested lightly on my shoulder, his voice kindly responding, "You place far too much importance on my influence, but thank you, my dear."

Valentine's Day has always been one of my favorite holidays. In bidding farewell to Toynbee, I had said, "Oh, You will be in my home state of Iowa on Valentine's Day."

His response was, "I have never received a Valentine, nor have I ever seen one." And I knew at that moment I would be searching for a beautiful and appropriate Valentine for this great historian.

A few days later I signed a Victorian Valentine, all hearts and flowers, sending it post-haste to Iowa. His response came by return mail: "I was deeply touched by your thoughtfulness, and I now have my first Valentine. Signed, Arnold Toynbee. P.S. You were correct about Iowa, and I am grateful for this experience."

— Paul Volcker

Paul Volcker was an interesting and warmly received guest. Since he was Chairman of the Federal Reserve Board, community leaders and students were equally enthusiastic about his appearance at J.U. In fact, they tried to analyze and "second-guess" Volcker's every word. (*Jacksonville was fortunate to have one of its leading citizens as Vice Chairman of the Fed, Fred Schulz.*)

"Is the Fed. going to raise interest rates?" The one question was on everyone's lips.

The next time I saw Paul Volcker we hardly recognized one another. Hospital gowns are great levelers and camouflage our identities.

And so it was as he and I sat in the Xray-waiting room at Mayo Clinic Jacksonville. He is 6 feet 5 inches and I am 5 feet 4 inches, and each of us was wearing the same length gown.

My question of what the stock market was doing that morning seemed a bit ludicrous under the circumstances.

— Many Distinguished Guests

There were many distinguished men and women who stimulated students and members of the community through the years.

Knight Kiplinger spoke at one of the Colonel Harry L. Kinne Free Enterprise Award luncheons. I am confident his list of subscribers to the "Kiplinger Letter" received a boost.

And a charmer was the late Charles Kuralt who spoke to our Fine Arts majors about the importance of communication. One student remarked, "He was like everyone's nice neighbor." I was able to schedule Kuralt because I was President

Charles Kuralt

of the St. Johns Dinner Club and had presented him to the membership.

On another occasion at J.U. I was introducing Dr. Joyce Brothers. I went to the hotel to call for her, and she appeared in the lobby in her long, formal gown, wearing heavy walking shoes: "What should I do? I forgot my shoes."

My response: "Never mind, you will be at the Head Table and no one will see your feet."

But, of course, we had to walk into the large room, so her shoes were very obvious. Later a student asked me, "Is that the fashion in New York?" Well, hardly!

The list goes on — Edward Villella (great ballet dancer), Leonard Pennario and Mark Frampton (pianists), Giannini (composer), Olivia de Haviland (I spent hours working with her on what spotlights were the most becoming to her skin. She didn't need to worry. As I stood beside her I was the pale-face, and certainly I should have worried more about spotlights.)

Certainly a distinguished guest on many occasions was Dr. Alton Ochsner, founder of the Ochsner Clinic in New Orleans. Our Board member and good friend Dr. Carl Mendoza was Dr. Ochsner's prize medical student. Carl and Betty Mendoza hosted Dr. Ochsner

on these numerous occasions and arranged for him to speak at J.U.

We were not generous with our honorary doctorates at J.U., usually awarding but one a year, and in some years none at all. However, it was a distinct pleasure and honor to recognize this gentleman who was among the very first to identify the dangers of tobacco.

When I was a member of the National Council of the Arts, I became acquainted with my favorite jazz pianist, Billy Taylor and he was one of my frequent guests.

— U.S. Navy/Admirals

The U.S. Navy in Jacksonville has played a dramatic role in this entire area, including J.U. — as it does in Norfolk and San Diego. Great leadership has been demonstrated by the Admirals and Captains assigned to the bases. I was always deeply grateful many of the Admirals sent their sons and/or daughters to Jacksonville University. This includes V/Adm. Michael Kelleris, who also was vocal throughout the country in his support of J.U.

I had seen the superb development of leadership while my husbands were on active duty with the U.S. Army. And equally impressive is the input of these officers and enlisted personnel of the various Services whenever they retire.

One of the happiest for me was the return to Jacksonville of V/Adm. Joseph Moorer, a distinguished officer and a member of an Alabama family which boasted two Admirals — the other Admiral Thomas Moorer, former Chairman of the Joint Chiefs of Staff.

(l-r) Betty Mendoza; her husband, Dr. Carl Mendoza; Ann Landers; Dr. Charles Schepens and, his wife, Cette.

The Blue Angels pose with Fran
during a show honoring her.

Fran, Rear Admiral Bert Chase and
Congressman Charles Bennett at the
Blue Angel show honoring Fran.

I had met Joe and Eleanor Moorer on a previous assignment, and when he called me on his return I knew it was imperative we capture him at J.U. My philosophy was to surround myself with capable people, let them run with the ball, and then give them credit. The only question was where to place him and where would I get the money for the position? We operated on a tight budget with no frills.

And I had to convince Joe Moorer he should join our team and great cause. He quotes me as saying he could golf as he pleased and he wouldn't be compelled to be present every day, but it didn't evolve that way. We decided on the title of "Visiting Distinguished Professor," which is precisely what he was.

On the receipt of my calls to friends I managed to scrape together enough for his salary, and the major donor was Bob Davis (Winn-Dixie) who said, "If you don't get him at J.U., someone else will!"

V/Adm. Joseph Paul Moorer needs no one to "sell" him, as his background speaks for itself. A graduate of the U.S. Naval Academy, he participated in WWII operations in the Philippines, Borneo and Okinawa campaigns — resulting in the Distinguished Service Medal with Gold Star, Legion of Merit with Two Gold Stars, the Purple Heart, etc.

Vice
Admiral
Joe Moorer

Admiral
"Snuffy"
Leighton Smith

R. Adm.
Kevin Delaney

After WWII Joe Moorer completed flight training, and his career took off in one command after the other. In 1977 he assumed duties as Commander in Chief, U.S. Naval Forces, Europe, and he retired in 1980. That is when he brought his expertise to our institution. A man of such background is able to fit in anywhere, and when the Vice President for Operations position became available I offered the position to Joe. Again I told him he could keep his golf dates, and he reminds me to this day the position turned out to be much more time consuming than I had described.

I completed our team with Dr. James (Jim) Brady as a very capable and dedicated Vice President for Academic Affairs (a Notre Dame graduate, Jim had pitched for the Detroit Tigers), and Don Ames, a J.U. graduate and effective fund raiser as Vice Pres. of Development. These appointments assisted in softening the loss of Dr. Dan Thomas (who returned to the classroom) and O.D. Barksdale; whose untimely death left a void.

An incentive for all of us was to provide a quality education and be fiscally responsible at the same time. With the assistance of a highly-supportive Board of Trustees, the Jacksonville University Council, faculty, administration, students and alumni — the City of Jacksonville opened its arms to us.

Joe Moorer worked with Bert Thomas (President of Winn-Dixie), Norwood Sandifer (Chairman of the Finance Committee) — and the finance report I received each month didn't stop at my desk. I sent it on to J.E. Davis (Chairman of the Board of Winn-Dixie) who offered to analyze it each month and grade me accordingly. He used his red pen, and I am happy to say we never were graded lower than an "A-/B+."

The faculty caught the fever with such enthusiasm that our popular Liberal Arts Dean, Joan Carver, predicted to me we would be listed in <u>U.S. News and World Report</u> as one of the outstanding small comprehensive universities. She was right. It happened year after year. We were motivated.

And during those years one of my favorite Navy friends told a story about motivation I have often used in my speeches.

(Sir) Admiral Leighton (Snuffy) Smith, now retired, had a brilliant career. His last overseas Command was as Commander-in-Chief of NATO's Southern Command in Naples, directing the Multi-National Peace Implementation Force (IFOR) in Bosnia.

Because Admiral Smith provided such inspiring leadership in 1998, Her Majesty the Queen (Elizabeth) made him an Honorary Knight Commander of the Most Excellent Order of the British Empire. The award was bestowed at an audience with the Queen at Buckingham Palace. Accord-ing to the release, Adm. Smith's "skill and perceptive judgment earned the respect and admiration of the 12,000 United Kingdom troops under his command, and greatly contributed to the overall success of the mission."

Certainly he is a master of motivation, and now the story he related to me some years ago:

As a young Midshipman at the Naval Academy, Snuffy Smith knew he had to produce. What inspired him to achieve? "I knew if I didn't I would be back in Alabama on the family farm taking care of 75 pigs. Also, I didn't want to go back to plowing and look at the south end of a north bound mule."

We all have our motivation — pigs, plows or promises. However, I am confident this great military man didn't need <u>anything</u> to motivate him. What a leader!

— *Blue Angels*

R/Adm. Bert Chase arranged for the famous Blue Angels to dedicate their show to me with 80,000 spectators present. He called me forward to meet them and be photographed with them as we exchanged gifts.

Included in the program, the Parachute Team for Fort Bragg presented me the baton they exchanged in midair. Thanks to R/Adm. Chase, that baton is now attached to a plaque, and part of the inscription is:
Passed in Midair
By Members of
The U.S. Army Parachute Team,
The Golden Knights

The Blue Angels provided a thrill for all of us as we observed their maneuvers. They were flying my favorite plane, the F18. It is no wonder I went through the Simulator experience with such delight. Only I didn't know my squeals were going over a public address system.

*Army
Parachute Team
at the show in honor
of Dr. Kinne.*
(pictured in the ever popular red)

— *Miss America Scholarship Pageants*

Perhaps because of the strength of the J.U. College of Fine Arts, talented students flocked to the Miss America Scholarship Pageants on our campus.

We were fortunate to have the Farrell sisters — all beautiful, bright and gifted pianists. For the only time in the history of the National Pageant, three sisters (Mary Ann, Monica and Kathy) competed in the Atlantic City competition. And another lovely J.U. student did become Miss America — Leanza Cornett.

Monica Farrell in Atlantic City at the Miss America Pageant.

Miss America, Leanza Cornett.

Kathy Farrell in Atlantic City at the Miss America Pageant.

Mary Ann Farrell at the Miss America Pageant.

— *Meeting Liberace on a Very Memorable Night*

Just before her appearance in the Miss America finals in New York, Mary Ann Farrell was visiting me at J.U. the same weekend Liberace was appearing in Jacksonville. I thought this would be an opportunity for Mary Ann to receive a lesson in Showmanship. She agreed to accompany me to Liberace's performance.

Liberace's manager was aware we were attending, and arranged for front row seats. We were charmed by Liberace's presentation, as he graciously referred to us during his program. And after the performance we were invited to be guests backstage to have

Cokes with Liberace.

When it was time to depart, Liberace's attendant offered to accompany us to our cars in the parking lot. But we had parked in opposite directions. I said I could find my own way since I was familiar with the area.

I had parked in the farthest, darkest part of the lot. And I soon realized I was being followed, then chased. I made it to my car, got in hurriedly...and flooded the motor. Harry, fortunately, had warned me repeatedly to count to 60 before trying to start a flooded car. It worked.

I managed to shift the car into gear, as my assailant was banging on the window with his fists, evidently under the influence of drugs. I was frightened as I backed directly over the curb. I wasn't particular about finding the proper driveway.

This was one of the very few times when I feared for my life.

Dr. Kinne, Liberace and Mary Ann Farrell during his appearance in Jacksonville.

Billy Walker, Alice Verlander, Doc Severinson, Ash Verlander, Fran, and Nettie Walker at Doc Severinson's concert at JU.

Fran (in green) and Olivia de Hauiland

Jay Thomas & Fran celebrate a reunion.

John Connally and Fran

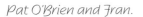

Pat O'Brien and Fran at JU luncheon.

Pat O'Brien and Fran.

Actress Ruby Dee at JU.

Fran a guest of honor at the wedding of Willie and Shata McDuffie.

Fran's mother, Jim Drury "The Virginian" and Fran.

W.W. Gay speaks at the Dedication of the Frances Bartlett Kinne University Center.

Bill Knapp (Drake philanthropist) and a surprised Fran.

(left)
Pat Summeral,
Dr. Fran Kinne and Artis Gilmore at a convocation where Pat is awarded an Honorary Doctorate.

Chapter Sixteen:
Looking Back on Lifelong Loves of Reading, Music, Arts, Humanities, Medicine, Museums, Libraries and Learning

I had always been reluctant to remarry. My first marriage of almost 33 years was a very happy one, and eleven years as a "single" hadn't changed my mind. I was married to the University and didn't even date.

Early in October of 1992 I gave a speech for a women's group, and the question and answer session that followed evoked a personal question: "Why haven't you ever remarried, Dr. Kinne?"

"Oh, I will never remarry," I answered with confidence. "My marriage for almost 33 years was a great one. My life is too busy for a second marriage."

In that same month I had a telephone call from Virginia from a dear and old friend of ours. "I am going to attend a wedding in Jacksonville. Could I come to see you?" It was Colonel M. Worthington Bordley.

"Wordy" had been Harry's Executive Officer when the latter commanded the famed 4th Armor Group, with six battalions in various areas of Germany, defending our position in the Cold War. During this time, Wordy and his wife, Dale, became close friends of ours, and after a year Harry rewarded Wordy's efficiency by appointing him as Commanding Officer of one of the six units, the 510th Tank Battalion.

The Cold War brought one crisis after the other, which only served to cement our friendship with the Bordleys, and Harry kept in close touch with Wordy after they both retired. The two men shared so many experiences, both of them having been "old Cavalry."

Wordy's visit to Jacksonville renewed our friendship, and we spoke lovingly about Dale and Harry, who had both lost their lives in a brave fight against cancer. And Wordy himself had already had several cancer surgeries. I was shocked to learn that he too had been exposed to radiation at one of the atomic test drops.

Wordy — The Colonel Winner of The Grand National as a "Gentleman Jockey" riding "Clifton's Duke."

Before his return to Virginia, Wordy asked me to marry him, and I replied with a resounding, "No." His quiet persistence resulted in repeated telephone calls at all hours of the day and night, and I finally succumbed to his charm. I wonder how much significance I placed on his love and knowledge of Shakespeare. One evening we were discussing life, and he made reference to Prospero's farewell speech in "The Tempest." I was impressed.

My good friend, Dr. Richard (Dick) Fleming agreed to examine Wordy under the latter's insistence: "What is my life expectancy, given the exposure I experienced?"

Dick's answer was, "You will very likely have three to five years — no more."

Nevertheless, Wordy and I decided to proceed.

B.B.
at 99,
"Queen
for a Day"
May 1, 1987

Flag
Day
and B.B.
reaches 100.

"B.B.'s good friends help her celebrate"

(l-r) Alice Verlander, Nettie Walker and Betty Mendoza at B.B.'s 100th birthday, June 14th, 1988.

We knew it was necessary to have a private wedding, as it would be impossible to include all of our friends and associates. Ash and Alice Verlander invited us to be married at their home in a private ceremony. They also indicated they had planned a cocktail party for that evening, so we scheduled an early ceremony with no one to be present except the members of the wedding party.

J.E. Davis and Alex Brest had offered to "give me away," but unfortunately, J. E. was in the hospital and could not be present. Ash Verlander and Billy Walker took J. E.'s place, and I was enthusiastically "given away" by three wonderful gentlemen.

A delightful pastor and good friend, The Rev. Dr. Jack Snell, performed the ceremony, and the doorbell rang at intermittent intervals while the surprised guests for the cocktail party became part of the wedding party.

Jack asked the question, "Who gives this bride away?"

Three answers followed, with Ash and Billy saying, "We do," and Alex Brest at 100 years old replying in a booming voice, "I do!" In the middle of this ceremony Jack offered, "It's obvious we haven't rehearsed this."

The following week I had a call from a <u>Florida Times-Union</u> reporter. "What happened? You said in your October speech that you would never remarry. What happened?"

My response was immediate: "Women's prerogative. My special right to change my mind."

—Wordy and B.B.

It is unfortunate B.B. passed away before Wordy and I were married. They had struck up a relationship when Mother and Cousin Olive visited Harry and me in Germany. At dinner one evening she sat by Wordy and amused all of us when she fixed her bright, blue eyes on him and said, "Col. Bordley, you're a handsome man."

Undaunted, he returned the gaze, grasped her hand and replied, "B.B. (her favorite nickname), you're a beautiful woman."

Dr. Elliott Richelson,
Fran and
Col. M.W.
Bordley (Wordy).

Dr. Richelson (Mayo Clinic) is a world
authority on antidepressants. His
favorite comment to Fran, "That's
something you'll never need."

She would have approved of our marriage.

But the life span for B.B. was ended August 27, 1988, a few months past her 100th birthday. She had celebrated that in style. Actually she had celebrated each day of her life with style!

At the funeral, the Rev. Tom Mundahl (married to Cousin Anne) gave a wonderful testimonial, Cousins Phyllis Hermanson, Hazel Nelson and Trudy Nelson sang an angelic trio, and Kay Munsen's lovely violin solo echoed her respect for B.B.

And with humor, Tom Mundahl related our favorite story about B.B. It was a tale she had often told her widow friends when she would drive her Buick to pick them up for a Sunday outing. This is the story:

The Davis Ranch (D-Dot) was an enchanting spot for B.B., and she was overjoyed when J.E. Davis invited her to join us to sit in hunting stands a sunny October afternoon. "Sitting" meant observing wild game from the stand as we were perched high in a tree, with only one person to a stand.

Harry and I tried to discourage it, since Mother was in her Nineties and didn't have appropriate clothing.

However, she was so excited we reluctantly agreed to what was to develop as a great adventure.

The three of us journeyed to the D-Dot — Harry and I in our outdoor clothes, B.B. in high heels(she didn't own walking shoes), a silk suit and a net around her freshly styled hair-do. Oh yes, earrings as well.

At the Ranch House, the guests were assigned to cars and several pick-ups, to be driven to stands.

As Harry and I watched Mother climb that tree we wondered what in the world possessed us to agree to this. Perhaps it was J.E.'s comment, "Oh, let her be happy."

The hours went by for each of us in our separate stands, as we watched the wild turkey and deer linger at the feeders located at the base of the trees.

At dusk each of us was picked up after experiencing four to 5 hours of exquisite stillness — one in which the only sound was the rustling of the leaves.

After returning to the Ranch House we didn't see Mother and queried, "Where's B.B.?" There was an immediate realization that Mother had been forgotten in the tree, and we were all in a panic. We piled into the cars and raced several miles to B.B.'s stand.

The rest of this story is Mother's — which she repeated countless times, and we all had it memorized:

After I climbed up that tree (and J.E. said I did it well) I sat quietly on that bench with camouflage netting in front of me. Of course I would peek around it once in awhile. (She didn't realize that was a "no-no.")

Pretty soon I saw this big thing crawling across the net. They tell me it was a scorpion, but I just knocked it to the floor and stepped on it. Then I started enjoying myself, and the hours flew by.

As it started to get dark something started buzzing around my head. I guess the bugs liked my hair spray. And just as the last rays of the sun dipped below the horizon I looked down. My heart was in my mouth. My pulse was racing. A mother bear with two cubs was munching on corn from the feeder.

It suddenly occurred to me — bears climb trees. So I stomped my feet on the floor of the stand to frighten the bears. They didn't look up — just lumbered away.

And I thought to myself, "You old fool, what in the world are you doing up in this tree in the middle of this wilderness?"

And just as I was thinking that, these cars came racing down the road, one of the cars with a spotlight on my tree stand.

J.E. later told me, "You shinnied down that tree faster than anyone I have ever seen!"

That was Mother's story, and that is precisely how Tom related it at her funeral. She would have liked that, and had she lived to see Wordy again, she would have told him word for word the same story. But perhaps first she would have said, "Col. Bordley, you're a handsome man."

Wordy and I had three and one half happy years together, although most of that time was spent battling his five primary cancers. It was fortunate I had made the decision to step out of the Presidency in 1989 to become Chancellor. This allowed me time to serve as Hospice for Wordy.

My recognition of Wordy's brain tumor came when we had driven to Georgia to the funeral of a beloved cousin, Kalah Knutson Hardy. She had been a baby-sitter for me when I was a small child, and we had often visited her and husband Max at their Georgia farm throughout the years. In fact, Harry and I left our hunting dogs with them when we were assigned to Germany.

While going to the Funeral Home

Dr. James Brady is inaugurated as President of J.U. and Dr. Frances Bartlett Kinne as Chancellor.

I noted erratic driving on Wordy's part, and a certain hesitancy in his speech. My experience with Harry's brain tumor so many years before made it possible to recognize similar symptoms in Wordy.

On New Year's Day, 1996, I called my good friend, Dr. Bob Wharen. It was a younger Dr. Wharen who had been a Senior Resident under Dr. Sundt, and had won my affection for his care and concern for Harry. Now I was calling him for assistance. I was in disbelief: "Bob, I can't believe this. Not again." It was my prayer that I was incorrect in my observation.

This fine doctor arranged for an MRI early the next morning. There it was - a massive brain tumor in the left temporal lobe. Within an hour Wordy was on the operating table.

For several years after Harry's death I had fought my way through committee after committee, finally testifying in Washington. Dr. Mendoza had been convinced Harry's tumor was the result of his being radiated at an atomic test drop, and Dr. Sundt was equally sure this was the case. Harry's last wish to me was that I do everything in my power to convince the government there were problems associated with the drops.

I now felt a sense of helplessness and a certain anger at the lack of recognition of what had brought suffering and death to so many. How much more was it necessary to prove?

It was a Navy Admiral who came to our rescue as we fought our way through surgery and the necessary post-operative radiation. R/Adm. Kevin Delaney, who is respected and admired by so many, was in daily contact with me as a concerned friend.

The weeks and months wore on with periodic hospitalization. Dr. Wharen and Dr. Paul Pettit performed surgery again (a shunt) to try to give Wordy more time. It was Paul Pettit who had done my hysterectomy, so it was Wordy's last bit of humor that brought a smile to his lips — my gynecologist working on him!

It was my dear friend, Kevin Delaney, who arranged for the military funeral at Ashland, Virginia.

And side by side in my home are the photos of two brave, handsome Colonels. It was a privilege and an honor to share a part of my life with each of them.

—Lt. Craig Munsen

Another tragedy occurred at this very time. Our dear J.U. graduate, Lt. Craig Munsen *(pictured left)*, was lost in making a night jet landing on a carrier. I had known Kay and Dick Munsen's son since he was born, and he had endeared himself to me even more as he worked in my office for four years. (He was one of five outstanding students I had recruited from Story City)

Wordy had difficulty speaking the last week of his life, but on learning of Craig's death among his last words were, "That is a tragic loss. He was a wonderful young man."

They were both wonderful men — one yet to realize his potential, one who had led a brave and full life.

Chapter Seventeen:
Married to Two Colonels, But Not at the Same Time

(right) Col. M. Worthington Bordley, Jr. receives the "Best Tank Battalion" trophy from (left) Col. Harry L. Kinne, Jr. — Fran's two Colonels.

It was lunch time, and my good friend, Dr. Henry Randle, at Mayo Clinic, was making a noble attempt to cheer me after Wordy's death. I don't allow many to move in beyond the cheerful exterior, as the inner self is very private, but I did with Henry.

"I was fortunate to have been loved by two great men and to have been married to them," I mused.

H.'s (Henry's nickname) immediate response, his penetrating eyes reaching me in comic relief: "Oh, Fran, you have been loved by a lot of men. You just didn't marry them all."

We both chuckled, and he helped me put it all in perspective.

At that moment, with Dr. Randle's use of humor to cheer me, I realized - an epiphany - the power that prayer had played (then and throughout my life) as I moved through each crisis. Of course, I realized, it was so true.

In retrospect I was very fortunate in many ways. The two officers taught me a great deal about living, and certainly how to die. Each of them was a true gentleman, and the epitome of both grace and bravery.

Harry Kinne was the ebullient one, full of personality and a master at leadership. He never asked a soldier to do something he

wouldn't do. And he had the courage to turn down an assignment which would have meant his star, because his 33 years of service had already taken its toll on him.

Born in the generation before me, he was a fun-loving story-teller who was an English major at the University of Illinois. As a senior he made his mark as the Cadet Colonel of the five thousand member Army ROTC. The same year he was Captain of the Water Polo team and was selected for the Olympics.

Wordy was the serious one of the two, a great horseman from his childhood days. As a student at St. John's College he was immersed in the "Great Books." While at St.

Johns he became a star in Lacrosse and was on the All-American Lacrosse team.

Col. M. Worthington Bordley "Wordy"

Both Harry and Wordy had brilliant combat records — the former in Europe, the latter in the South Pacific in WWII and in Korea during the Korean War. Each of them had Presidential Citations and Bronze Stars with Oak Leaf Clusters, and

Wordy had both a Silver Star and Purple Heart. The latter was awarded to him as a young officer in the 7th Cavalry Division fighting in the Solomon Islands.

A significant honor came to Wordy at the close of WWII when he commanded the Company selected to raise the first American flag in Tokyo. It was the reflective of his interesting military background — trained as a Commando, a helicopter and glider pilot, as well as a U.S. Army Parachutist.

Wordy was known internationally as an equestrian, achieving honors in point-to-point competition, and winning the Grand National as a "Gentleman Jockey."

I can well imagine how proud his mother was to receive a letter from the Commanding General of the 1st Cavalry Division:

Colonel Harry L. Kinne Jr.

It was my personal privilege to award your son the Order of the Purple Heart in recognition of his sacrifice and valor in sustaining wounds in action against the enemy.

It is most gratifying to me and to the First Cavalry Division that we have officers of his calibre and fighting ability. I am sure that you will share with us this pride, and that you will be pleased to know that Lt. Bordley has recovered completely from his wounds.

And one year later from the Brigadier General, U.S. Army, Commanding:

I recently have had the honor and privilege of awarding your son, Captain Marcello W. Bordley Jr., Troop H, 7th Cavalry Regiment, the Silver Star.

This award is authorized by Congress and presented, in each case, by direction of the President, to military personnel for gallantry in action against an armed enemy of the United States.

Harry and Wordy fought bravely in World War II and the Korean War. Their later peacetime commands were the 4th Armored Group for Harry and the 14th Armored Cavalry for Wordy— choice and happy assignments. However, the scars of war were never erased.

Fran and Wordy.

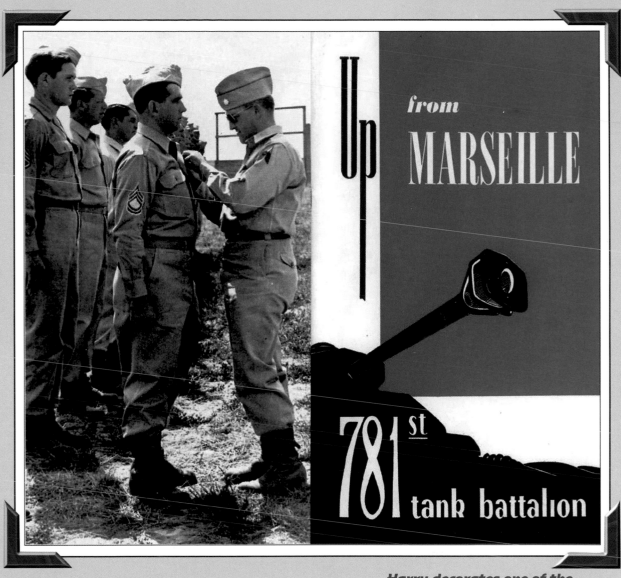

Up *from* **MARSEILLE**

781st **tank battalion**

Harry decorates one of the Sergeants in the 781st Tank Battalion in World War II.

Wordy as a young Calvaryman breaking wild horses.

*Fran gets a boost to cut down the net at the
Sunbelt Tournament win in Birmingham, Alabama.
This photo went coast to coast.*

Chapter Eighteen:
Father, Family, Sports — and Fracturing the Image of a College President

One of my deepest regrets is the loss of my father before I could share my career with him, and before modern eye surgery could have made a very different life for him. There was so much more I could have learned from him.

As the shadows gathered my father maintained his dignity further developing his phenomenal memory. He was able to play bridge by holding the cards a few inches from his eyes and winning each tournament he entered. And the billiard table provided equal entertainment, as his long, graceful fingers caressed the tapered cue. Yes, my dad was a sports fan. There were no talking books or low vision aids, but he had his bridge, radio, billiards and, most importantly, my mother to read to him each night.

I realize now how much of my philosophy and behavior were shaped by the examples my parents set. And they used interesting and exciting ways to educate and impart knowledge, with such inventive and innovative methods. My brother and I didn't recognize we were learning ethics, etiquette and a cornucopia of valuable information.

My father never came to the table without his suitcoat, and dinner was always served at 6:00 p.m. No matter where my brother and I were, when the six o'clock whistle blew we better be prepared to sit down at the table. This was imperative since three evenings a week Mother had to return to the library at 7:00 p.m. It provided a superb lesson in discipline, one from which we learned so much; the conversations included current events, humor and a share of sports stories particularly baseball — but no slang or gossip.

Dad managed the amateur American Legion team, and allowed me to sit on the bench at the start of the games. But my parts of the dinner table conversations, Arcadian as they were, must have elicited amused renditions from the adults. Naive and simple were my comments, but my opinions were respected. My brother was very likely tolerant, since I caught his pitched balls, moved the bar for his pole-vault, helped rebound his basketball shots, and assisted him in memorizing his quarterback signals. It is no wonder sports became a large part of my life.

When I became President of Jacksonville University, one sports writer inquired "Now that we have a woman President, are we going to forget about sports?"

I relished responding, "Not so. My brother was a four-letter man when 'four-letter' meant something different than it does now."

In ensuing years that same reporter wrote about my starting each game with a hug for each player. In fact, the basketball players soon became superstitious about the importance of that hug prior to a game.

— *Fracturing the Image*

It was Birmingham, Alabama, and we were playing in the Sun Belt Conference. Weather had delayed my plane, and the game had started by the time I arrived at the gym. We were down by one point, and it was half-time before I could get to the players to give them a hug. The response from the players was enthusiastic, and Willie McDuffie said, "Now we'll win!"

And we did, in the last few seconds of the game. Our team had just won the Sun Belt Conference, and our fine Coach Bob Wenzel and team were now in the national spotlight!

What I didn't anticipate was the immediate action of the players. They rushed to me where I stood near our basket, picked me up on their shoulders, and handed me scissors to cut down the net. And I did. Willie and Tom Terrell (now an M.D.) said, "Watch her skirt. Watch her skirt." At that moment a photographer snapped a photo from above me, and there I was, mouth open wide.

That photo went coast to coast, and a good friend in L.A. called me when I returned to Jacksonville, with this observation: "You certainly fractured the image of a college president."

— *Artis Gilmore*

But it was a 7 ft. 2 in. basketball player that put Jacksonville and Jacksonville University on the map. The City will never forget the Cinderella team that made it to the finals of the NCAA Basketball Tournament — to The Final Four. Joe Williams, great coach that he was, brought a magnificent team together, eventually to lose in the finals of The Championship Game against U.C.L.A. When Coach John Wooden later paid a visit to our campus he asked by name about the entire team: Artis, Pembrook Burrows (also 7 ft. 2 in.), Rex Morgan, Vaughn Wedeking, Greg Nelson, Chip Dublin, Rod McIntyre, Mike Blevins, Rusty Baldwin, Don Hawkins, Curtis Kruer and Ken Selke.

Artis Gilmore (later a star in the NBA, and now a Jacksonville businessman) led our Jacksonville University team to The Final Four. My Iowa friends and relatives remind me, however, that this trip to The Final Four was made possible at the expense of a crushing heartbreaker loss inflicted on one of the best Hawkeye teams ever at The University of Iowa — when Pembrook Burrows rebound-

ed/tipped in that last-second shot!

Artis Gilmore still calls me "Mom." His autographed picture on my wall draws comments from many of the visitors to my home. I do look quite small standing next to this 7' 2" superbly-conditioned athlete.

And I always enjoy telling the story about Pembrook Burrows' fine career as a highway patrolman for the state of Florida. A J.U. booster and friend of mine was speeding along one of Florida's highways when the light flashing in her rear-view mirror made her realize her predicament. She pulled over and noticed the seven foot two inch officer approaching her driver-side window. She recognized him before he said a word. "Why, you're Pembrook Burrows! You made that basket in the last second to beat Iowa and take us to The Final Four! And Dr. Kinne just loves you. She would want me to tell you 'Hello'."

After a friendly warning from a surprised and appreciative Burrows, the booster was sent on her way.

And I give grateful silent thanks to my parents and brother for those dinner conversations about sports and so many other topics so many years before. Certainly I am proud of Artis, as well as so many other J.U. athletes who have gone professional — Otis Smith, Dee Brown, James Ray, and Rex Morgan were among many.

Artis Gilmore and Fran.

Chapter Nineteen:
Looking Ahead/Influencing a
21st Century of Fine Arts and Life
Applying Charlie and Bertha's Bromides

—*"A Tribute to Librarians Like Mrs. Bertha Bartlett"*

I was very pleased a former Story City student, Barry Benson (now an editor, columnist and author) wrote a very touching tribute in the April 20, 1997 <u>Des Moines Register</u>. It is such a beautiful column I include it here:

The 1996 grand opening and dedication of the 2½ million dollar Bertha Bartlett Public Library in Story City — named to honor Mother — was a culmination of a great deal of hard work and multiple efforts at fund raising.

More than 300 local volunteers assisted in the effort, and around $500,000 came from pledges from people from Story City. Three people taking leadership roles were Story City natives and my good friends: John Egenes, Kay Munsen, and Thora Kinseth.

This modern, beautiful library stands as a tribute and legacy from all these volunteers, from hundreds of others who cared about the cultural life of Story City, and most of all to Mother for her 43 years of service as Story City's Librarian. She lived to pass the 100 year milestone on June 14th and passed away August 27 of the same year. In her honest humility she would have been surprised at her name being on the building, but she would be happy to see its growth and development.

As newer and more expensive technology fills classrooms and libraries, more problems regularly pop up: gaps between haves and have nots, plagiarism and censorship, copyright infringement, mechanical breakdown, power outage, long waits for access on overused lines, loss, obsolete parts, system shutdowns, etc.

A personal librarian and shelves of books, however, will always be there. They're approachable and transportable. There is a Human touch. They socialize instead of interface.

Esteemed Iowa poet, teacher, and Iowa Writers' Workshop administrator Paul Engle said: "A librarian can change your life by nudging you into the world of literature. It changed my life. It's amazing the power that a sympathetic, alert librarian or teacher can have...They can speed up your life by 20 years."

I know that without the personal interest and skills of Story City Librarian Mrs. Bertha Bartlett, I would not be a reader, writer and teacher today.

I don't remember what first nudged me to walk into the small public library in Story City as an elementary student on vacation. I remember how intimidated I was: "All those books. Where do you start? How could anyone read all these books?" Fight or flight feelings were pulling me back out that large, dark-brown oak door.

But Mrs. Bertha Bartlett took one look, recognized the feelings rushing through me, and quietly asked, "What do you like to read about?"

"Uh, sports and animals..."

She offered Walter Farley's The Black Stallion, *and Jackson Scholz'* Rookie Quarterback *and* Goal to Go. *By the next summer I had read all the Walter Farley and Jackson Scholz books. And Mrs. Bartlett stayed one book ahead of me, recommending "one more" author just when I was starting for the big oak door.*

Today the new million-dollar library in Story City, just across from where the small municipal library used to be, is appropriately named Bertha Bartlett Public Library. What joy that gives many of us who grew up where Bertha Bartlett was our librarian for 43 years.

Good guys can finish first! Mrs. Bartlett was always a good guy to thousands of patrons (including one-time street urchins like my brother Steve and me) who today are never without a book.

We developed a life-long love of reading and learning because of Bertha Bartlett's contagious dedication to books and education.

Mrs. Bartlett also gave me my first job. Her home was cater-corner from the library, a half-block from where I lived above Helland's TV Sales and Service. She offered me a job shoveling snow and carrying clinkers from her coal-burning furnace to her driveway. She knew I needed cash for sports shoes and admission to every movie showing at the Story Theatre/Grand Opera House. Bertha Bartlett was a real lady, not just the name on today's beautiful new library in Story City.

How many other Bertha Bartletts are there? Anyone who reads biographies of writers, authors or poets recognizes a motif of tribute to librarians like Bertha Bartlett.

What a wonderful choice when one becomes "a reader" and enters the never-ending world of learning and knowledge all found in books. Librarians change lives.

May there always be librarians to open those big, dark-oak doors to welcome us inside. I hope my writing is a down payment on the debt I owe Bertha Bartlett. When I see her painted portrait on the wall above glass-enclosed shelves of her childhood toys and belongings in Story City's Bertha Bartlett Public Library, I sense her presence.

Fran's niece, Ginger Shoemaker visits Bertha Bartlett Public Library, Story City, Iowa

B.B at Buckingham Palace in London.

Potrait of Fran's mother and some of "Her Favorite Things" (including toys) on display at the Bertha Bartlett Library in Story City, Iowa.

(l-r) David Nelson, Estelle King, Thelma Butcher and Harry Butcher help celebrate B.B.'s 100th birthday.

—Growing Up with Mother and Her Books

I was asked to write a column about Mother and the Library, and the following appeared in <u>The Story City Herald</u> and was reprinted in <u>The Ames Daily Tribune</u> (June 30, 1995, p. A6):

When I reminisce about the Story City Library, memories spark recollections beyond measure. Of course, "growing up" for me meant books, since Mother spent three afternoons and three evenings each week at the Library.

The most vivid recollections I have are of the Library's second-floor location, over what was then Jacobson's Drug Store — icy cold in the winter, since the heat didn't reach the second floor, and beastly hot July evenings when no breath of air seemed to move. But perhaps the winters were the most challenging. There were those days and nights when snow made it impossible for cars to conquer roads, but Mother dutifully kept the lights shining for those brave readers who could walk to the Library and navigate the steps to the second floor. And those wonderful books had to compensate for no bathroom facilities. Mother accepted all of this with her usual grace and sweet smile.

And what a celebration it was when the move to City Hall was accomplished. Here was clearly a recognition to Story City, for when a community opens its doors to a library something magical happens. So it was in Story City, as it has been all around the world. Chaucer described the ivory and glass of a library, and throughout the 15th and 16th centuries there were frequent free library references, including those found in Shakespeare. Of course, it had been a major decision in the '20s when Story City moved in the direction of a free library, and I am so proud my father was on the organizing committee and that Mother became the librarian.

I recall with some amusement the time Mother was asked if she would rather be called a "librarianess," and she answered with a very positive, unmistakable "No." (In 1734 the feminists insisted that female librarians be called a librariancss.) Thank goodness Mother said "No."

Librarians are often considered as the fount of knowledge, the resource for every fact, and amusing circumstances often presented themselves to Mother. On some occasions I recall her serving as a marriage counselor, adviser, comforter and baby-sitter. One evening three women visited the Library, not to check out books, but rather to request that my mother intervene in an argument they were having. They had been discussing the errant ways of a certain local gentleman, and they wanted Mother to settle the disagreement. The disagreement? Was the man going to the "lower regions" after his death, or could he possibly go the other way? Mother tactfully referred them to their pastor. Of course, librarians have been recognized in many ways, but perhaps Iowan Meredith Willson made the most lasting impression with his wonderful song from "The Music Man" — "Marian, the Librarian." I played that toe-tapping melody countless times for my dear mother, and she did hum along with me with an all-knowing smile on her face.

What a privilege we all had in Story City growing up in the midst of books. And with Charles and Bertha Bartlett as my parents, I not only read the books, but I learned to repair, accession the books and catalog while I was still in the lower grades. One of the most exciting times for me was when the new books arrived, and I was given the task of opening each book, a few pages at a time. Of course, this was to keep the back of the book from breaking. (To this day I can still remember the wonderful fragrance of a new book.)

An informed citizenry is what we desire for every community, and the Bertha Bartlett Public Library allows this privilege. It is inherent in the basic freedoms of the Constitution — a commitment to education from birth through senior citizen years; to growth, stability and a dedication to the values of learning from a plethora of ideas, philosophies, etc. There is an old Chinese proverb, "Learning is a treasure which accompanies its owner everywhere." Thousands of people who have enjoyed and appreciated the Library facilities throughout these many years are the living example of the important role the Library has played on all of these lives. Mark Twain so wisely wrote, "The man who does not read good books has no advantage over the man who can't read them." And Helen Keller wrote, "One can never consent to creep when one feels an impulse to soar." Story City chose to soar.

Mother was always proud of "her" readers. She watched with loving care the young children who developed good reading habits and skills, and she guided them throughout the years from easy reading to the great books of literature. I am personally grateful that Story City is recognizing my mother's selfless contribution by placing her name on this beautiful building. I am also very proud of my hometown for recognizing the importance of a Library.

The dedication of the Bertha Bartlett Public Library holds a special place in the history of this community, and indeed it holds a very special place in my heart.

J.U.'s First Legends Soccer Tournament, September 1999. J.U. and Drake (Fran's Alma Mater) in honor of FBK.

Doug Milne and Fran, New Year's Eve 1988-89. Member of the J.U. Board, Doug initiated the Jacksonville Mayo Clinic Rochester connection. Shortly after WW II the distinguished surgeon, Dr. William ReMine performed surgery on Doug, and every following year he and his friend Joe Adams flew to Rochester for their exams, and to see Bill ReMine.

Wordy feeding Craig and Emmanuelle's baby shortly before the death of both Wordy and Lt. Craig Munsen

Chapter Twenty:
Glass Ceilings, The River Club,
J.U, Rotary International and Free Enterprise

Being a first in men's organizations has never bothered me, as long as the action is followed by the admission of other women. As a professional woman, I found membership would often be very helpful in my profession. My mother was the trail-blazer for this in her generation.

Alex Brest came to my rescue after Harry passed away. I had always used my husband's membership at the Jacksonville Business Men's Club (River Club), but after his death my attendance was limited to a widow's membership for six months only. This was not acceptable to Alex, who conferred with his attorney, the late Ralph Martin.

The two gentlemen drafted a proposal to propose me as a regular widow member, without voting privileges. I was concerned, as I didn't want to harm Jacksonville University in any way, but the men had surveyed the situation and felt confident the vote would be favorable. Their strategy was to get it passed, wait a year, and then go for full membership with voting privileges.

As President, I chaired the Faculty-Administration Council, and one day I had just called the meeting to order when my secretary entered the room. She whispered in my ear, "I know you don't want to be interrupted, but Preston Haskell has just called and says it is imperative you come to the phone."

What kind of emergency might prompt this call! I was amused and relieved when the voice at the other end of the telephone said, "Fran, you know I am Chairman of the Board of the River Club. I want you to know you have just become the first woman member."

My thoughts returned to the annual meeting of the International Council of Fine Arts Deans where I was the only woman member for so long. When I was elected Chairman, I called my great leveler in Iowa to tell her about it, and Mother and I shared a hearty laugh when she responded, "Congratulations. I suppose they settled on you because different men want it, and it was an easy solution to elect you." I am wondering what humorous reaction my mother would have had to the River Club membership.

In the Rotary Club of Jacksonville two of us were inducted at the same time. The other woman was the late Sister Mary Clare, Chief Administrator of St. Vincents Health Center. When I was Vice President of the Jacksonville Chamber of Commerce I had enlisted her assistance, and I admired her fine leadership ability.

On the day of the induction Sister Mary Clare and I sat at the head table, and we were introduced to the membership. Ash Verlander was my introducer, and his sparkling sense of humor resulted in a challenge to us. As he was walking to the microphone, he leaned down and spoke quietly to us. "OK, now we have two women in the club. Don't screw it up." That elicited laughs from the both of us.

I had already known most of my wonderful Rotary brothers prior to membership, and certainly the motto of "Service Above Self" is a challenge to which each of us should subscribe.

During my second year of membership I was asked to be Program Chairman, and that was a stimulating assignment. Through the assistance of Vice Admiral Max Morris, we were able to schedule Ken Burns, whose Civil War Series had recently been aired. Other popular speakers were General Westmoreland and Ed Crutchfield, former CEO of First Union Bank.

Since Billy Walker, former CEO of First Union in Florida is a good friend, I had suggested I could introduce him, and in turn he would introduce Crutchfield. On the day of the meeting there was an excellent article in the Wall Street Journal about First Union, providing a perfect lead for my introduction.

"It is such an honor to introduce two distinguished financiers, who are known around the world for their banking expertise. The only thing I am going to be known for is being the first member of Rotary International to have a hysterectomy."

I don't know what prompted me to say it, and I certainly wasn't prepared for the spontaneous reaction. I do know I have a little pixie in me (thanks to my mother and grandmother) and once in awhile it bubbles to the top. The laughter continued for minutes, while Billy waited for the Club to come to order.

One of the speakers I presented was a dear friend. Herb Peyton (I call him, Herbie), who just happens to be one of my favorite public speakers as well. He is the epitome of the American Dream, and every school child should know his success story — a story with more chapters forthcoming. It is America come to life.

In my many years overseas it was always a distinct pleasure for me to speak of our great Republic, our democratic form of government, and the opportunities of a free enterprise system. Billy Walker says I never give a speech without inserting my philosophy, so obviously I promote speakers or writers who are fine examples of the American Dream. Lonnie Wurn is a splendid example of the writer who documents his travels with Emily around the world, always promoting the blessings of our country.

Long before I arrived in Jacksonville there were three local groups interested in starting a private University where such a philosophy would prevail. One finally emerged as Porter University (Judge William Porter) and it eventually became Jacksonville Junior College. The late Fred Noble, a distinguished attorney, became Chairman of the Board, and Guy Botts was a Trustee.

George Hallam's fascinating history of JU, OUR PLACE IN THE SUN describes the interesting saga of this independent, fledging institution of higher education as it grew from Jacksonville Junior College to Jacksonville University. After my arrival in Jacksonville, both Fred and Guy made history come alive as they related their great challenge in keeping open the doors of their educational venture. And it was my pleasure to intro-

duce Guy Botts as the speaker for the first graduation over which I presided as President. His address: "Too Much Government; Too Many Taxes".

This spirit was certainly reflected in the College of Business, which I had the pleasure of founding at J.U. two months after assuming office. Three years later the Executive MBA program was initiated, and Charlie Rice and Barnett Banks presented us with a $600,000 endowed Chair in honor of Guy Botts.

The growth of the programs in the College of Business inspired the Davis family to build the Davis College of Business Building. This also provided a home for the College of Weekend Studies program and was the catalyst in bringing it all together.

As one moves from one end of the campus to the other, it is obvious the names on the many buildings reflect the philanthropy of men and women who represent the American Dream. Surely it is an inspiration to live in a country where this is all possible. Although many other benefactors' names do not appear on these buildings, their names are also forever indelibly printed on my heart. Their great deeds supported a magnificent cause!

Some years later as I was asked to be first woman President of "Downtown Rotary" for 2000-2001 (Florida's first Rotary Club), I warned, "I don't think you are ready for a woman."

The comeback was, "Oh, we don't think of you that way."

I took that as a back-handed compliment, and I accepted. After all, my decades at J.U. provided me a

Herb Peyton, Jacksonville's "mover and shaker" and former J.U. Board member.

splendid opportunity to know the members of all the "Service" clubs in the area. In 38 years, I had given over 2,300 speeches throughout the United States, and many of them were to the members of these various clubs.

The support of the great Board of Trustees at J.U. made many things possible, both on and off campus. It was a happy adventure working with each of the Chairs of the Board, first while I was a Dean, then as President and Chancellor: Carl Swisher, Guy Botts, Judge William McRae, John Donahoo, Sr., Earl Hadlow, Luke Sadler, Florence Davis, Robert Shircliff, W. Ashley Verlander, Jack Quaritius, W.W. Gay, Tom McGehee, Billy Walker and William Nash.

And the membership of the Board was a "Who's Who" of wonderful examples of the free enterprise system at work. David Miller (former Board Member and COO of J.C. Penney) said it well, "This Board is full of Horatio Alger stories."

Chapter Twenty-One:
California Trip into Nostalgia:
President Ford, Bob Hope,
<u>*Charlton Heston, Frank Pace, Jay Thomas*</u>

My visit to California this past year was a trip into nostalgia. As the only surviving member of my immediate family, I feel it is important to honor and pay respect to those departed dear ones. I derive comfort in visiting their gravesites, and perhaps the main purpose of this book is to emphasize their influence in my life. My brother, Chuck, chose to be buried in the place that was so dear to him - San Diego.

And my visits to that beautiful place provided splendid "catch ups" with Dick and Laverne Warren and Ginger and Jim Shoemaker, as well as their families. In his early 20s, Chuck had married Thelma Evans Warren, who was a widow with two fine children, Dick and Ginger.

A fringe benefit was my stay in the queen of hotels, the Del Coronado. I have a penchant for historic hotels, allowing my romantic imagination to picture the elegance of the early years of our last century - the

Fran and Bob Hope in his Palm Springs home.

Broadmoor in Colorado Springs, the Brown in Denver, the Breakers in Palm Beach, the Waldorf or Plaza in New York. They were and are the grande dames of hotels, and I respect them.

The next stop was Beverly Hills, where Charlton (Chuck) Heston had invited me to breakfast. He had selected the dining room in the restored Beverly Hills Hotel, where we wouldn't be disturbed. I arrived several minutes early, so I had the pleasure of welcoming him as he entered the Lobby. Still handsome, still the ultimate gentleman, those several years in which I had not seen him melted away.

Seldom have I enjoyed as stimulating a conversation. We covered the gamut of politics, the entertainment industry, ethics, and his visits to Jacksonville. I reminded him of the enthusiastic reception he received at the close of his remarks on receiving the honorary doctorate. That surely would warm the heart of many a Shakespeare lover.

When we said our farewells, he presented me with his superb book <u>To Be A Man - Letters to My Grandson</u>. I like this gentleman for many reasons, but his respect for family touches the core of our society. This book should be required reading for all of us.

That evening, J.U. graduate Frank Pace hosted a special dinner party

President Gerald Ford at Rancho Mirage.

with graduate Jay Thomas in attendance. Frank has been highly successful as a producer, and his awards include seven nominations for an Emmy. In fact, one nomination was for a pilot of "Murphy Brown." The previous evening I had visited his office and the Warner Brothers Studios, and he arranged for me to attend the taping of one of his shows.

Since I was on the Warner lot Frank then accompanied me to the taping of the Drew Carey Show, since the writer and originator of the show is a former J.U. Theater Arts major, Bruce Helford. That very morning the headline news was, "Helford of a Deal," announcing his 20 million dollar contract.

Frank has this past year successfully produced two shows, Brooke Shields' "Suddenly Susan," as well as "For Your Love." What a delight it was for me to observe him in his element and to watch him in action. A bundle of energy and talent, it is so

(l-r) LaVerne Warren, Ginger Shoemaker, Dick Warren and Jim Shoemaker on Fran's visit back to California.

brainstormed about a gift we could give the President, and what we came up with was a hit.

I arranged with the Maintenance Department at J.U. to start with a golf club and create a monstrosity with a "P" trap (plumber's joint). I presented this to him after he had received the doctorate, with all the pomp and ceremony appropriate to this occasion. The Secret Service wouldn't allow me to tie the ribbon around the box for security reasons, but I placed an elaborate bow on the top. As he lifted the cover, out came the Rube Goldberg concept of a golf club, with much laughter from President Ford and the audience. The President still has this club in his collection, but it serves but one purpose - just for the sake of the story.

gratifying to follow his career. It has also been highly rewarding to me to note Frank's loyalty to his alma mater. Watch for the JU sweatshirts on his shows, and the many opportunities he has given our starry-eyed theatre majors looking for that "Big Break."

Exciting for me has been the growth and development of Jay Thomas. His pioneer work on radio and as a comedian was always recognized, but his gift has now developed him into a very fine actor. I have always felt the depth of his talent offers more diversification, and years ago I told him I felt he could do <u>Hamlet</u> beautifully. I was met by gales of laughter on his part. However, his recent work in <u>Mr. Holland's Opus</u> and his TV specials all confirm my belief in his abundance of creative talent. And who knows, I may have the pleasure of seeing this very talented actor do <u>Hamlet</u>.

Of course, a trip to California would not be complete without seeing my buddy, Bob Hope as well as President Ford. Frank drove me to Palm Springs for the visits already scheduled, and enjoyed teasing, "I'm Driving Miss Daisy."

It was gratifying to have a reunion with President Ford — after being ushered into his office by his gracious administrative assistant, Penny Circle. He was still youthful-looking and vigorous of mind. We spoke of our mutual friends, Raymond and Minerva Mason, and he entertained us with his stories about Bob Hope. He reminded me of the dinner at which I had presented an Honorary Doctorate to him. It was 1984 and the 50th anniversary of the founding of Jacksonville University. Bob Hope had intended to speak but he had already been committed to the Academy Awards Ceremony, so I flew to North Hollywood to his home in order to have him tape a message. Also, Bob and I

From President Ford's home Frank drove me to Bob and Delores Hope's magnificent home on the side of the mountain. It is an architectural wonder with its contemporary style. How wonderful it was to see Bob again. I had taken him a box of Lady Godiva chocolates, and at first he was reluctant to indulge himself. After several minutes he said, "Fran, would you please open that box for me?" The top level soon disappeared. The wit is still there. The charm is still there, and history certainly is still there.

When we departed he gave me his last book which was edited by Ward Grant. Ward is Director of Hope Enterprises and has been a good friend of mine these many years. Bob and Ward compiled this historic coverage of Bob's amazing association with eleven Presidents. One of the highlights of my trip was having brunch with Ward and reminiscing.

Frank Pace, Fran and Jay Thomas.

Jack Benny & Bob Hope give the "Iowa Girl" a kiss....

Charlton Heston and Fran

Fran in front of Bob Hope's Palm Springs home

Bob's ecumenical approach to politics made him loved by all political parties. In the dedication of his book, Bob writes, "To all the Presidents who have extended me friendship and tolerance, who have shared a day on the golf course, a night in the White House and an afternoon in the Rose Garden...and a lifetime of laughter." He goes on to write, "A joke has always been a safety valve, even jokes about our Presidents. Thank God they had a sense of humor or I would probably be writing this book on Leavenworth stationery."

I know that I had a tear in my eye as I said good-bye to Bob. "It has been so long since you visited Jacksonville — why don't you come and see me? Jacksonville is not the end of the earth, you know."

A twinkle in his eye appeared as he grasped my arm and said, "Well, almost."

I couldn't help but think of the many telephone calls throughout the decades Bob and I have been friends. When Harry died, he remembered to call me on that first Christmas Eve I was alone. When Mother reached her 100th birthday, there was that telegram of congratulations. When Wordy died, there was Bob again extending his words of support. His friendship has meant a great deal to me. Emerson said it and so did my parents: "The only way to have a friend is to be a friend."

Jacksonville Jaguars owners, Delores and Wayne Weaver.

Fran meets with the Story City Historical Society in the Bartlett Museum. (l-r) Fran, Cheryl Eddy (President), Cousin Arvin Nelson (1917-1999), Gary Griggs (Architect).

Chapter Twenty-Two:
<u>Iowa Girl—My Iowa</u>

And so I reminisce about a life of incredible adventure and my good fortune along the way.

China was my destination, and I was filled with anticipation. I was joining my bridegroom who preceded me to that country by one month. But as the ship glided through the blue waters of the Pacific I looked back. There was the Golden Gate Bridge fading in the San Francisco fog. It was that moment it all came together. It was also that moment I faced the reality of years away from family — years away from Iowa.

Perhaps I had begun to feel those pangs when I first took my Army Colonel to meet my parents and introduce him to Story City and my Iowa roots. We drove from Fort Leavenworth, Kansas into Missouri and then across the Iowa border. As we crossed the border I shouted, "Stop. Pull over!"

The querulous look in Harry Kinne's eyes quickly turned to amusement when I exclaimed, "See. The Iowa sky is bluer, the grass is greener, and the air is fresher." I meant it.

For seven years those Army assignments took us to China, Japan and Germany. And I felt it was my duty to acquaint everyone with the incredible advantages of being born and raised in Iowa:

There was the Chinese General who queried, "I have always wondered how to pronounce 'Des Moines'." (And I thought to myself, I wish more airline pilots, flight attendants and travel agents would ask the same.)

There were hundreds of Japanese students I enjoyed teaching (as a volunteer teacher). They learned about the Iowa State Fair, the Carousel in Story City, and they lustily sang the Iowa Corn Song, although the "r" presented a challenge.

And it was in Germany while working on my doctorate that one of my professors questioned, "Where are you from?"

I answered quickly, "America."

That didn't satisfy him. "Which one?"

"North America, but <u>really</u> Story City, Iowa," I bubbled with enthusiastic pride.

It was in Tokyo I saw a Volkswagen, its driver making his way slowly down the Ginza. I chased that car for a block — a strange sight I must have been — because it had an Iowa license and an Iowa State University tag!

And it was the sounds of Iowa speech I missed in all those seven years. Much later my maid of many years, Estelle King, said, "You talk TV talk." The explanation was simple. Most of the TV newscasters hail from the Middle West — or have been trained to sound as if they do. I never fail to tell this to all my friends.

And now I continue my trek to Iowa, even though my parents have passed away. I still get that thrill of excitement as the plane circles the Des Moines airport, and I marvel at the well-patterned fields below me.

So what is the magic, the basic energy so contagious, the work ethic so taken for granted? My husband said it well shortly before he died, "It's the people."

And he truly adopted Iowa when in the last months of his life he chose to change his burial place from Arlington National Cemetery to the tree-shaded Story City Municipal Cemetery.

He remembered that in Iowa "The sky is bluer, the grass is greener," and the friendly folks find time to provide love and care to that final resting place.

There is probably something deep in the soul of each one of us that longs for the connection with the place of birth. It may be a fleeting memory of a loved one, the mention of a familiar name, a tug at the musical heart strings for no reason at all.

In no way does that diminish my love of Florida and its people, and I have chosen to live in this magnificent state since our return from Germany. There is an ever-present glow of greenness, with the contrast of seasonal flowers. Such harmony of color and form is always uplifting to me.

Nothing can compare with the full moon rising like a ball of flame over the Atlantic Ocean. Harry and I would often drive on the beach on those special nights, and he would look at me and always say the same thing: "Look out there, Francie, the next stop is Spain."

And for my Florida home, energy seems bursting from the Earth since Wayne and Delores Weaver brought the NFL Jaguars to Jacksonville. It is truly a city on the move. My personal acquaintance has been with each of the Mayors since Consolidation, and each of them has made a distinctive contribution to the great City of Jacksonville: Hans Tanzler, Jake Godbold, Tommy Hazouri (JU graduate), Ed Austin and the current Mayor John Delaney.

For me the nostalgia is for everywhere I have lived, for those are the places where memories were made.

But the fragrance of Iowa when the spring lilacs are in bloom — the crimson and golden leaves of fall — the thoughts of Christmas at Grandma's — that's Iowa to me, because I am an "Iowa Girl."

Addendum

*My father wrote the following after his eye surgery. The reader will enjoy
the elegance of his language and writing style...*

NEW EYES

by Charles M. Bartlett

"Seeing is believing" — the complement to realization. In the miracle of sight is a large part of the joy of living. My expressions of gratitude and appreciation for new eyes may seem extravagant. But were you ever in a "blackout" for more than three decades?

From gray skies to blue skies, from a dull, drab world to a brilliantly lighted one; out of a vague, colorless void into the effulgent glory of day, all in a very brief period of time — this was the rare and wonderful experience of mine a few months ago, after spending the early part of my life in gray mists and the later years in darkness.

No, it was not a miracle, but the work of the skilled hands of a master eye surgeon. On second thought, it is a miracle that man possesses the knowledge and skill to do such things.

In early childhood a severe illness had left my vision much impaired and, later, this trouble became greatly aggravated, and a gray fog began closing about me, growing thicker month by month. Letters faded from the printed page, and buildings, a short distance away, disappeared into the thickening gloom. The sinister shadows of darkness crept closer and closer until they entirely enveloped me.

In the earlier days of that period, as the realization of approaching blindness grew upon me, hope, at times, gave way to despair, but gradually there was the philosophic acceptance of "what can't be cured must be endured." In such hours of trial it seems that every individual has a reserve of spiritual, moral and physical courage which rarely fails him.

During those years of failing sight the other senses were learning how to substitute for the eye, and mighty well they performed. The hearing quickened and was ever on the alert. My ears became educated and learned to distinguish and catalogue sounds and to interpret their meanings. Walks, pavements and buildings were constantly whispering advice and warnings. I would not have walked into a stone wall or open excavation. Echoing footsteps would have proved an audible, red light and, by a slight tapping of a cane or foot, those echoes would become positively vociferous.

The ear associates voices of individuals in recognition just as does the eye the physical aspects. This faculty develops to an amazing degree. I knew many hundreds of people by voice alone. In conducting my business, a cash brokerage, it soon became evident that my memory had become remarkably retentive. Listening to radio broadcasts of the grain markets, both cash and future quotations running into a large number of figures and repeating them to customers by telephone — this was performed with no effort whatever. I just wrote those figures on memory's blackboard and there they were. My experience in memorizing has convinced me that the normal mind can absorb many times as much useful knowledge and also be taught technical skills far in excess of those possessed by the average, and this with only a little more effort.

In those days the radio was a cheering and comforting companion as it is to all shut-ins. It is such a chatty sort, right at one's elbow, friendly and informative, renewing and enlivening the association with the outside world as it sings, plays all the musical instruments, gives advice and preaches, too. To me it was newspaper, books, theater, pulpit and platform. It seemed a thing of life, animated by the ingenuity of man, and yet always so sensitive, it silenced at one dissenting move.

During all those years of gray mists and darkness I had long since abandoned all hope of ever regaining my sight. And then by chance there was an examination by an eminent eye specialist who expressed his belief that an operation might restore vision. I was overjoyed. It was only a slim chance though and I was warned not to pin my hopes too high.

When the bandages were removed there were the walls, ceiling and doors, and, through the windows, the world. The first thing I saw was the doctor's necktie, a thing of beauty, wonderful in weave, color and design. Sure! The doctor was a handsome man and the nurse beautiful! I made audible comment about the latter. To walk through doorways and around chairs and tables, unhesitatingly, unafraid, was a real achievement — my first adventure into a strange land. From that moment I became a jubilant, irrepressible and rejuvenated individual, as a perfectly natural result. Such an experience as mine creates a tremendous emotional upheaval in one, no matter how schooled in repression, unless the nervous system is wired similar to that of the turtle's.

Being only an infant in vision experience, everything proved of interest. My eyes were curious, questing and questioning, and I talked about everything I saw. No doubt such exuberant verbosity was trying to those about me. However, this new gift, the power of seeing, had opened up fields of marvelous interests, and exploring I would go. Dull, indeed, would have been one in like circumstances who would not have been thrilled mightily. New worlds are not commonplace.

Although my home is in the Middle West I was on the West coast when my sight was restored. For one who had undergone visual starvation for so many years, it was a fitting place to feast hungry eyes. There were the Pacific, the mountains, valleys and deserts, an elaborate course for a beginner.

It is amazing how lavish nature is with her colors and how generous with her varied scenic riches. Perhaps this is necessary as the average person is not easily impressed by such displays unless there is an exceptional arrangement of color and scene. To elicit a mild exclamation of appreciation it must be: "The pink fingers of dawn pushing back the velvet curtains of night"; the sun retiring in a night robe so red it turns the western sky to crimson flame, a moon at full resplendent in its silver setting; green carpeted fields; mountains hiding their heads in white clouds; "the funny old hills"; a bright and dewy May morning when every blade of grass is wearing a diamond; autumn bringing trees and shrubbery its gayest garb. But it was not so with me, for ever since they rolled up the curtain for me, letting in the light, I have gazed on these scenes with thankful and appreciative eyes. Thus it was borne upon me how color and setting enter into the scheme of things and it is with a passionate sincerity that I declare that of all the planets in the universe, the earth is easily the "best dresser."

Of color impressions there were only vague recollections from childhood. The operation had left the nerves of sight raw and quivering and acutely sensitive to color rays. At first these impressions were so vivid and intense I could endure them only a few moments at a time. The blue of the ocean was overwhelming, and a yellow cab appeared to be a gigantic gold nugget on wheels. The brightly colored dresses of the fair sex were too eye-filling for me.

About this time there was a visit to the sunken gardens at Exposition Park in Los Angeles at the time the roses were in bloom. There was such a profusion of buds, blossoms and blooms, it appeared a flame of flowers, a conflagration of composite colors, an efflorescent explosion, bewildering but beautiful. As we walked through that gorgeous flowerland surrounded by white palisades and buildings, it seemed to me the only things missing were the "pearly gates with parapets to match."

There were many pleasant days spent at the ocean shore gazing out over the Pacific, marveling at its everlasting restlessness and manifestation of power, especially when angry — conjecturing that if that power could be captured it would do the work of the world, and that in its depths more treasures for the human family will be found. Today it seems misnamed considering what the word implies. It has evil associates on the other side. Certainly they are not pacific.

Mountains
There were the mountains with all their kin folks: precipices, canyons and valleys, just as described and a lot

more so. True, those loftier peaks are solemn, somber and majestic, a thick green rug of cedar, spruce and pine thrown over each foot; deep purple capes over their shoulders; caps of white wind clouds or snow on their crests, a prevailing style at that altitude which, in the evening sun, gives them the appearance of having donned their night caps preparatory to retiring to that solitude of their isolated elevation. Nowhere on this earth does nature so strikingly assume such disdainful aloofness, such haughty reserve and such lofty dignity.

Desserts

Those "frying pans" of our Southwest, the deserts, are interesting places, even if uncomfortable. One can have a "hot time" with no effort at all. They are dry, parched and sizzling, and everything seems ready to voice that familiar complaint, "How dry I am." They are forbidding in their desolation, repelling with their scorching heat and threatening in their vastness — once deemed a trackless waste, now known to be a chemical laboratory. Even the reptiles and insects are vengeful and dangerous. The cactus bush and tree, a grotesque imitation of the real thing, and resentful of that fact, dares the human touch with its formidable collection of barbs and spikes.

Mountain home

There were a few days spent at a mountain home, one with a picture book setting: a swift mountain stream gurgling and giggling as it tumbled over the stones, its mossy banks bordered by bosky dells and leafy glens, a mountain with one foot in the back yard, live oak trees with limbs so fantastically twisted and gnarled they sometimes rested their elbows on the ground. Here a nightly vigil, hoping to see a bear, or a deer, or maybe a wildcat in yonder thicket glaring at me with hate in his eyes. Now and then there was the mournful wail from a coyote lamenting because the lock had not been stolen from the hen house door. An energetic cricket chorus was gleefully singing the praises of the night, as well it should. A full moon was riding high over head, prodigal with its silver, generous with its light; moonbeams trickling through the tree branches, tracing fanciful designs on the grass-carpeted lawn-playgrounds for elves and wood nymphs. Over at the ripples in the stream the waters were playing with sapphires, diamonds and pearls, chattering delightedly at the beauty of its find.

The leader of the cricket chorus called for another number and in the witchery of that hour the lawn transformed into a sylvan glade and those tiny creatures skipping and dancing about were... I rubbed my eyes and moved forward for a better view, but it broke the spell. The lawn was empty, the oaks silent and inscrutable. From a nearby grove came the derisive hoot from that septic the owl, coldly realistic, scornful of those who dream dreams. Then my host called me to a breakfast of sizzling ham and eggs, with hot coffee whose fragrance has no rival at that time of day.

Mountain pass

While at this home there was a thrilling and nerve-shattering ride over a mountain pass, famous because it twists, turns, writhes and coils. This was a terrific ordeal for new and inexperienced eyes. As the car glided smoothly upward, dashing through holes in the wall, slipping in and out of crevices, rushing under overhanging rocks, I suddenly braced myself for the impact — a head-on collision with a rocky cliff. But the cliff skillfully dodged and my sigh of relief changed to a gasp of horror — the car was speeding directly over a precipice. But the precipice shrugged its shoulder and strangely enough we were still on the road. It was here and there, and round and round, and our car seemed to enter into the spirit of the occasion as it began a rhythmic swing and sway, gracefully exaggerating the movements on the narrowest parts of the trail. Here the highway tightened its coils and the car quickened its tempo and enthusiastically started into a Grand Right and Left with the mountain, terminating with a flourishing Do Si Do on the very outside of a hairpin turn. Up over the summit, out along a lofty shelf of projecting cliff, and we look down on everything earthly. The scene below is one of surpassing beauty and grandeur, a panoramic masterpiece of the Almighty's handiwork.

The trip down the trail was marked with the same thrills and uncertainties. As we moved out along an overhanging shelf, the car clung affectionately to the mountain side one moment and the next executed the "Dance of Death" on the brink of a precipice, just to amuse a solitary eagle spectator. As we descended into the valley, the highway, after all its contortions, stretched in relief into a straight line, bordered by oaks, pines and sycamore trees and substantial farm houses and green fields. Considering the circumstances, it is doubtful if anyone ever experienced more seeing in such a brief space of time.

Airfield

My curiosity led me to an airfield at the first opportunity, not only to hear but actually to see a plane fly. I wanted to see those places where man puts on seven league boots in order to play that child's game of "Tick, Tack, Toe, Round I Go," on the earth's surface.

A famous interceptor and pursuit plane was strutting its stuff. It flashed across the sky like a meteor, so great its speed. So tremendously is it powered, in maneuvers its roaring could be likened to that of the Bulls of Bashaam; while in its rocket like skyward climb, its wailing is like a band of banshees, purgatory bound. In that plane a man, supposedly earth-bound, disdainful of gravity's law, up in the blue, showing the swallow how to fly. Where are man's limitations? Certainly away beyond present horizons.

Stars

During the years of darkness my mind had ever tried to recapture childhood memories of the heavens at night: the star spangled canopy above, the diadem of stars, and other poetic terms as told in prose, verse and song. So, on the first starlit night, and many later ones, too, away from the city lights, it was to gaze at that starry firmament with seeing and wondering eyes. Yes, the stars do twinkle, some friendly and even roguishly. Others glitter with a cold and menacing intensity. All mysterious and remote, symbols of the unknowable, except from observation and the distances learned from geometric facts. A star was pointed out — a near neighbor — only eight and one half light years away. Now for some calculations. Light travels 186,000 miles a second, 60 seconds in a minute, 60 minutes in an hour, 24 hours in a day. Good night! The mental machinery falters, the mind cannot conceive of such stupendous distances. It is beyond the range of our comprehension. It can be calculated but not appreciated.

While viewing that everlasting parade of celestial bodies through the stellar spaces, came the realization that our earth is only a small part of this universe and this universe is only as a grain of sand among countless universes in that awe-inspiring display of supreme creation. In this contemplation the ego shrinks and shrivels as one tries to catalogue himself on those measureless pages of time and space. He searches his vocabulary for a word meaning almost nothing — infinitesimal, insignificant — and these are a million times lacking in descriptive power in measuring man's consequence in the mighty plan. And yet man is important for are we not assured that even the sparrow's fall is marked and recorded.

It was with reverence, humility and awe that I gazed into that fearful immensity, for there is law, order and precision transcendent.

General

The first few weeks after my sight was restored there were times at night when I would arise and turn on the light just to reassure myself that it was not a dream. Then awakening in the morning with the light streaming in the windows, I welcomed it with the eager and joyous anticipation of a small boy on circus day. My curiosity was as keen as his, while my interest, recovering from its arrested development, was turning to all things.

There were man's creations to be seen such as: substantial business blocks, magnificent school structures, palatial hotels, ornate and highly decorated theaters, great hospitals, graceful ocean liners, automobiles, stream-lined trains streaking it across the western plains, beautiful parks and countless other things which excited my curiosity.

Reading has been slow and difficult for me. The untrained eye does not encompass whole words at a glance. It takes time to acquire such sight skills. No sooner had I begun to scan the papers and magazines, than the advertising pages of the latter excited my admiration. Some of these pages are masterpieces of the printing art. That's my appraisal. There is such a skillful portrayal of salient facts, such a sharp delineation of the main characteristics, such a clever and conspicuous display of the outstanding features of the article advertised, that it should arouse the interest of a wooden Indian.

Few people ever give a second thought to how skillfully the eyes differentiate in facial lineament, how accurately the distinction is made in human countenances, even up to thousands, recognizing each at a single glance. But this was not so with my untrained and inexperienced eyes. I could not make this distinction at first. Tom, Dick and Harry looked just alike. I could say to a matron of forty years or more that she did not look a day over twenty-five, with no intent of prevarication. However, there is one feature in which there is a striking dissimilarity. White, even teeth attract my attention at once. The smile of people possessing such dental perfection dazzles and fascinates me. Conversely, discolored and uneven teeth, with absentees conspicuous in the foreground are equally repelling. There is a sort of a broken down picket fence appearance. In such instances, somehow, my eyes exaggerate and distort a smile into a leering grin; the mouth seems large and cavernous and the picture is something which resembles a cartoonist's nightmare.

Although fully aware of the style of women's dress, I was amazed and startled at the spectacle when I first beheld it. There it was, the greatest "leg show" of all time: mother, daughter and sweetheart, all in the parade; grandma, too, was there, as well she should be, and, it can be truthfully said, most of them had two good reasons for wearing abbreviated skirts. Truly it is a great exhibition of nature's finest handiwork in symmetrical contours.

The beach, too, was rather trying to unsophisticated eyes. There was a remarkable exhibition of economy in the use of cloth. True, most of the bathers wore a heavy coat of tan underneath the veil of the afternoon haze, and a little bit more, but there must have been a real forest of "hickory limbs" near by.

And now since my liberation from the bondage most dreaded by the human family, and there is no more groping, faltering or hesitating; no cane antennae; no consultation with echoes; less menace in the sound of the auto horn — but free and fearless movement directed and supervised by the eye, there is ever a feeling of thankfulness for my great good fortune, luck, kindness of fate, or whatever it may be termed. However, in my lexicon it has only one definition, a blessing of which I am profoundly conscious and for which I am deeply grateful.

I now know how to estimate and appreciate the eye and the work it does: the effortless ease with which it performs its task, automatically doing its duty even though it is constantly employed in the waking hours; its instantaneous and accurate interpretation to the brain of form, color, substance and pattern, of everything within range of vision, its immediate adjustment to distance, and likewise its accommodation to lights and shadows. Sensitive and responsive, it is the first to register the feelings. In its depths are mirrored all the emotions that stir the human heart. It is the camera supreme.

In the miracle of sight we find the richest portion of our living. It is the crown jewel of the five senses. Its beauty and perfection are an inspiration to painters and to writers of prose, verse and song, and a challenge to the world of science.

— C.M. Bartlett

After surgery, my father visited his brother Frank Bartlett and wife Jennie and my two cousins, Mary and Frances.

The following news story appeared in the June 2, 1942 SANTA BARBARA NEWS PRESS

"How County Scenery Looks to 'New' Eyes"

> *Suppose you had seen nothing for nearly 25 years and, now well advanced into middle life, found your eyes opened on a Santa Barbara landscape you had never seen before, even as a youth? This was the glorious experience of C. M. Bartlett of Story City, Iowa, who is now visiting his brother, Frank S. Bartlett of 1108 Santa Barbara Street.*

> *"I can't describe what it meant to me," C. M. Bartlett says with real emotion in his voice, "to come to Santa Barbara, after a successful operation on my eyes in Los Angeles, and to see this gorgeous color and flowers, this panorama of mountains and the ocean."*

> *Bartlett, an Iowa grain buyer, conducted his business even after he had lost his sight, and plans to go back to it shortly.*

A few weeks ago he took a ride over the San Marcos pass with his brother. He wrote his impressions in a letter to his wife in Story City, and she passed them on to the local newspaper, the Story City Herald. The article was published in the Herald last week:

San Marcos Trail

When a Californian comes into possession of a sack of cement he undergoes some sort of a change in his make-up; he thinks he is a Caesar, the builder of roads, If he does not find a level space he builds over, around, or through the mountains.

And right well he has done, too. A trip over the San Marcos pass, the highway over the mountain out of Santa Barbara, will convince the most skeptical. It turns, twists, writhes and coils. It has more curves than a collection of rams' horns and a dozen of front row chorus girls, and all the features that make a mountain road thrilling and interesting. It is avoided by snakes, as crawling here results in a lame back. Motorists on this road riding in the front seat grow weary of looking at the back of the heads of those in the back seat.

Sun Prankish

The sun does a cunning solar trick, too, glaring at you through the windshield and the next instant, slyly peeping through the back window.

I did not know of these things when starting out with my brother over this trail. I found out, though. We had not been traveling long, and I was just commenting on what a triumph of engineering skill was this road, adding also how I appreciated California's salubrious climate, when I braced myself for the impact — a head-on collision with a rocky cliff. But the mountain skillfully dodged and my sigh of relief ended in ghastly dismay — we were speeding directly over a precipice! But the precipice shrugged its shoulder and we glided on to the road straight, for nearly 30 yards.

Gravity Flouted

The car dodged through holes in the wall; slipped in and out of crevices; one minute clinging affectionately to the mountainside and the next instant doing the "Dance of Death" on the brink of a precipice, with a disdainful disregard of the physical law, which says "What goes up must come down."

We glided between sheer walls of rock, hundreds of feet up, and I thought of that old childish game, "Heavy, heavy hangs over thy head." Out into the open again and the car starts doing the "Grand right and left" with the mountain, culminating in a hectic Do, Si, Do on a hairpin turn.

View Awesome

Far up to our right I could see a white ribbon draped over the mountain, and I was assured we would soon be there. It was the highway and the top of the pass. We reached it soon; how, I don't know. Our car, silhouetted against the clear sky, must have appeared as a fly on the ridgepole of a barn to eyes in thevalley below. From here the grandeur of the view is inspiring and awesome, a scenic wonder, a thing of beauty one would never forget.

On the descent and the car doing the same tricks with mountain and precipices again and again, dashing into what appeared as a tunnel caused by the interlacing of tree branches overhead, we glided thorough leafy glens, basky dells and sylvan glades, down around sweeping curves in what seemed a Peaceful Valley guarded by tall pines, eucalyptus, live oak, where the birds were holding a concert.

Anyhow, that's the way it appears to new eyes.

— C. M. Bartlett

Index

Bibliography...

Armel, Anne Lobel. "Can a Woman Make It in This Town?"
Jacksonville Monthly, August 1982, pp. 24-32.

Chiaramonte, Al. "Two Music Educators Receive Honorary Degrees,"
The Florida Music Director Magazine, August 1982, p. 27.

Foley, Bill. "Colt Fever's Legacy," pp. 22-23, in Portraits of Our Past
(Jacksonville Times Union Printing Co., February 21, 1999).

Hickerson, J. Mel. HOW I MADE THE SALE THAT DID THE MOST FOR ME:
Fifty Great Sales Stories Told by Fifty Great Salespeople (John Wiley & Sons, 1981).

Kinne, Frances Bartlett, B.M.E., M.M.E., PH.D. A Comparative
Study of British Traditional Ballads and American Indigenous Ballads
(Johann-Wolfgang-Goethe University, Frankfurt/Main, Germany, 1957).

Munsen, Katherine Jacobson and Steve Corneliussen.
Lake Comar, Story City Historical Society, 1996.

Munsen, Richard and Katherine. BAIL OUT OVER THE BALKANS:
Escape Through Nazi-Occupied Yugoslavia (Sigler Publishing, Inc., Ames, 1994).

Olson, Paul A. PANORAMA OF FORTY-THREE YEARS AS A COUNTRY EDITOR
(Story City Herald Printing, 1948).

Simpson, Deborah. THE MIRACLE YEARS: A Biography of Alexander
Brest as Related to Deborah Simpson (Jacksonville University Press, 1991).

"SOUTHERNERS: In Pursuit of Excellence,"
Southern Living, September 1977, pp. 90-92.

Stanton, Susan. "The Bottom Rung: Local Celebrities Reminisce
About Their First Step Up the Ladder of Success,"
Jacksonville Today Magazine, July/August 1989, pp. 50-53.

Suggs, Clarence J. (Council President). Resolution 83-1214-384:
A Resolution Honoring Dr. Frances B. Kinne and Recognizing Her
Distinguished Career as an Educator, University President and Citizen of Florida
and the City of Jacksonville, City Council of Jacksonville, Florida, November 22, 1983.